Writing
Qualitative
Inquiry

WRITING LIVES

Ethnographic Narratives
Series Editors:
Arthur P. Bochner & Carolyn Ellis
University of South Florida

Writing Lives: Ethnographic Narratives publishes narrative representations of qualitative research projects. The series editors seek manuscripts that blur the boundaries between humanities and social sciences. We encourage novel and evocative forms of expressing concrete lived experience, including autoethnographic, literary, poetic, artistic, visual, performative, critical, multi-voiced, conversational, and co-constructed representations. We are interested in ethnographic narratives that depict local stories; employ literary modes of scene setting, dialogue, character development, and unfolding action; and include the author's critical reflections on the research and writing process, such as research ethics, alternative modes of inquiry and representation, reflexivity, and evocative storytelling. Proposals and manuscripts should be directed to abochner@cas.usf.edu

Volumes in this series:

Erotic Mentoring: Women's Transformations in the University,
Janice Hocker Rushing

Intimate Colonialism: Head, Heart, and Body in West African Development Work,
    Laurie L. Charlés

Last Writes: A Daybook for a Dying Friend,
Laurel Richardson

A Trickster in Tweed: The Quest for Quality in a Faculty Life,
Thomas F. Frentz

Guyana Diaries: Women's Lives across Difference,
Kimberly D. Nettles

Writing Qualitative Inquiry: Self, Stories, and Academic Life,
H. L. Goodall, Jr.

Writing Qualitative Inquiry

Self, Stories, and Academic Life

H. L. Goodall, Jr.

Left Coast
Press Inc.

Walnut Creek, California

LEFT COAST PRESS, INC.
1630 North Main Street, #400
Left Coast Walnut Creek, CA 94596
PressInc. http://www.LCoastPress.com

ISBN 978-1-59874-323-4 hardcover
ISBN 978-1-59874-324-1 paperback

Library of Congress Cataloging-in-Publication Data

Goodall, H. Lloyd.
Writing qualitative inquiry : selves, stories, and the new politics of academic success/ H.L. Goodall, Jr. p. cm. -- (Writing lives.) Includes bibliographical references and index.
ISBN 978-1-59874-323-4 (hardback : alk. paper) -- ISBN
978-1-59874-324-1 (pbk. : alk. paper)
1. English language--Rhetoric--Study and teaching (Higher) 2. Academic writing--Study and teaching (Higher) 3. Narration (Rhetoric)--Study and teaching (Higher) I. Title.
  PE1404.G6444 2007
  808'.066--dc22
2007050625

Printed in the United States of America

♾™ The paper used in this publication meets the minimum requirements of American National Standard for Information Sciences—Permanence of Paper for Printed Library Materials, ANSI/NISO Z39.48–1992.

08 09 10 11   5 4 3 2

For articles drawn from scholarly journals, all permissions were granted by the Copyright Clearance Center. These articles are: Robin Boylorn, "E Pluribus Unum," Chapter 1, p. 25; Sarah J. Tracy, "The Construction of Correctional Officers," Chapter 1, p. 35; Tony A. Adams, "Seeking Father," Chapter 2, p. 72; Harvey Lemelin, "Running to Stand Still," Chapter 2, p. 85. Permission to reprint excerpts from material originally published by *Qualitative Inquiry* has been granted by the Copyright Clearance Center.

Excerpt in Chapter 2, pp. 71–72: From *Love My Rifle More than You: Young and Female in the U.S. Army* by Kayla Williams with Michael E. Staub. Copyright © 2005 by Kayla Williams and Michael E. Staub. Used by permission of W. W. Norton & Company, Inc. For excerpts by author: Chapter 2, pp. 65–66: From Part One, "Destinations and Arrival," by H. L. Goodall, Jr. pp. 27–28. Originally published in *Divine Signs: Connecting Spirit to Community* by H. L. Goodall, Jr.; © 1996 by the Board of Trustees, Southern Illinois University, reproduced by permission of the publisher.

Chapter 2, pp. 63–64: From Part Four, "Knowing Your Audience, Knowing Yourself: What Is This Thing Called Rock n Roll, Huh," by H. L. Goodall, Jr., pp. 227–29. Originally published in *Living in the Rock n Roll Mystery: Reading Context, Self, and Others as Clues* by H. L. Goodall, Jr.; © 1991 by the Board of Trustees, Southern Illinois University reproduced by permission of the publisher.

Excerpt in Chapter 2, pp. 73–74: Reprinted with the permission of Simon & Shuster Adult Publishing Group from *A Staggering Work of Heartbreaking Genius* by Dave Eggers. Copyright © 2001 Dave Eggers.

From *Devil in the White City* by Erik Larson, copyright c 2003 by Erik Larson. Used by permission of Crown Publishers, a division of Random House.

CONTENTS

This book is for you . . .

For without you, dear reader

I wouldn't have had the chance to be a writer,

Which is to say

I wouldn't have had the chance to be me.

To be a convincing "I-witness," one must,
so it seems, first become a convincing "I."

—Clifford Geertz

Those authors who would find many readers
must endeavor to please while they instruct.

—Samuel Johnson

Preface

So You Want to Be a Qualitative Researcher Who Tells Interesting Stories?

Qualitative research done via narrative nonfiction writing in the academy goes by a number of names—narrative ethnography, personal ethnography, performative writing, autoethnography, creative analytical practice, lyrical sociology, autobiography, narrative heuristics, etc.—and is very much a global academic movement among the human sciences. Qualitative inquiry that makes use of narrative writing and performance is currently practiced in over fifty-five countries and forty disciplines.[1] Research done in the various styles or reporting associated with narratives are regularly featured in leading journals and appear as chapters in scholarly volumes or as books that contribute in important ways to our understanding of research subjects as well as to our overall storehouse of knowledge about how we "do" the work of being human and try to make sense of it.

Once considered too soft, too personal, or too journalistic to count as a rigorous form of inquiry (and, yes, those debates still do go on, albeit less frequently and with less attendant rancor), qualitative inquiry written in narrative formats now enjoys a heightened popularity among researchers, particularly ethnographers. Why?

Why indeed. What is it about narrative writing that appeals to theoretically and applied-minded scholars trained in ethnographic fieldwork, interviewing, survey research, the use of focus groups, critical methods, and various forms of coding data and textual analysis?

What is it about writing and performing narratives that adds valuable new dimensions to our work and to our lives?

Over the years, I've asked narrative practitioners about their turn to stories, to ways of writing qualitative inquiry that rely—in part or in whole—on the construction of narratives.

The storyline I receive in reply is remarkably similar. It usually features a scholarly apprenticeship rich in theoretical materials and research methods in graduate school increasingly experienced with a sense of frustration, even disenchantment, with forms of scholarly writing and reporting. That frustration was or is caused by reading and writing work—often very good work—that either did not seem to capture the fullness or complexity of lived experiences and/or do not allow for creative methods of expression about those experiences.

Into this mix are also accounts of people torn between social science and humanistic inquiry who want to find a way of creatively combining insights from both worlds, as well as of individuals who simply love to write and perform. I would be remiss if I didn't say that there are even some folks—and I do mean some and not all—drawn to narrative writing because they don't find the meaning of life (or much joy) in math.

Not that they have to. There are excellent examples of scholarship done as narratives by some of the best scientists in every field. Consider Stephen Jay Gould, Steven Hawking, Paul Davies, Don Johanson, Barbara Kingsolver, Lewis Thomas, Carl Sagan, Loren Eisley, Juliet Schorr, and many others who have used the power of storytelling to compel academic and public interest in their academic work.

But whatever the combination of contributing causes, into this long dark night of the graduate student soul, there always appears in this narrative a *teacher* whose work (and, in some cases, whose fieldwork-driven lifestyle), inspires what inventors describe as the "ah-HAH!" moment. Suddenly, the path out of the darkness is brilliantly illuminated.

"I want to do what *you* do" is the experiential exigency that becomes an excellent reason to stay in school, to redouble efforts at mastering theory and methods, to learn to write better, to complete the degree, and to get on with the often less well-illuminated academic and/or professional life.

Let's assume that you are reading this book because what I have just described fits your experiences. You may be at the beginning of your qualitative journey, or well into it. Either way, you identify with what you've just read.

Perhaps it even made you smile.

Welcome!

The Power of Story

What was it that made your path suddenly become illuminated? My guess is that you read a story. Nothing more or less than that. The power of the story is its ability to change your life. And not just yours, but other people's lives as well. Perhaps you identify with a character, or share a similar challenge. Perhaps you learned how to imagine your life differently, and *better*. Maybe it set you on a path of discovery that led to a realization of what you wanted to do, or become, or whom you wanted to be with or give your life for.

Most of us enter the scholarly world because we think we can do something important in the world. We are motivated to want to change things for the better. We want to be inspiring teachers and writers. And we want our work to have impact beyond the academy among persons who may find in what we have to say the same life-changing moment that we had reading that story so many years ago.

Unfortunately, most forms of academic writing fail to accomplish those goals. Think about it. When was the last time you read a study that truly moved you? This is not to say that traditional academic studies are worthless; it is to say that they seldom satisfy our needs as readers beyond providing useful information that we can draw on for our own work. That is no small thing, but neither should it become the *only* thing valued about academic prose.

We can choose to live larger than that. We can find new ways to use our research to reach a wider public audience and to have real impact in the world. And that choice has everything to do with the *way we choose to write.*

Narrative provides us with a range of forms and styles for discovering meaning and communicating it to readers through stories. It is also an epistemology, or a "way of knowing." Let's explore the idea of narratives as a way of knowing in relation to writing qualitative research.

Narrative Ways of Knowing: Writing and Epistemology

Sara Worth is a philosopher interested in aesthetics and literature. In an intriguing paper prepared for an MIT conference in 2005, she developed the idea of "narrative knowledge" as a special form of reasoning. Drawing on work by literary theorist Noel Caroll, psychologists Donald Polkinghorne and Jerome Bruner, and philosopher Martha Nussbaum,

Worth points out that "traditional forms of knowledge (knowing *how* and knowing *that*) are not sufficient to cover a third kind of knowledge (knowing *what it is like*) in the way that storytelling can."[2] Moreover, she argues, what is learned from reading and writing stories produces a distinctive form of knowledge that is rooted in empathy for other human beings and an enhanced capacity for both imagination and moral reasoning.

She concludes:

[W]e gain narrative reasoning skills from reading literature. In turn, these reasoning skills add not to our storehouse of propositional knowledge necessarily, but to our storehouse of skills that make us more interesting and more empathetic human beings—the kinds of human beings who need narrative arts and good conversation, who are interested in other human beings, and who have knowledge that is more than just propositional.[3]

Worth's insights about narrative epistemology as a distinct way of understanding and being the world parallel thinking over the past four decades about writing/rhetoric as a way of knowing.[4] Although much of this work has been accomplished in rhetorical theory or in the cognitive sciences, a good deal of its practical application has been in college programs that feature "writing across the curriculum" or "communication across the curriculum" as well as in K–12 writing workshops designed to improve children's abilities to express themselves.

The basic idea is that when we engage in writing or telling a story, we create alternative pathways to meaning that are imaginative *and* analytical; that are guided by a narrative (rather than propositional) rationality; and that are relational—in the production of meaning, they connect the teller of the tale to the listener or reader of the story.[5] The very act of writing a story, or telling a tale in public or just to a friend, changes not so much how or what we know (although telling a good story well can certainly do that), *it alters the way we think about* what we know and how we know it. We identify (or not) with the characters; we "see" scenes develop and deploy language to represent them; we imagine possibilities for actions and then find words to do the work of those actions for us; we provide perspectives on the unfolding events in ways that create empathy (or not) with the plight of those persons we depict as persons; we historicize and contextualize meanings; and we determine the ending and whether justice is done. To be drawn to stories as a researcher is to be drawn into a way of life that gives meaning and value to those sources of knowledge that can be gotten at in no other discursive way.

Narratives *are* our way of knowing.

Allow me to give a personal example. Although I have been writing narratives for over thirty years, it wasn't clear to me exactly how powerful the narrative way of knowing was until I composed *A Need to Know: The Clandestine History of a CIA Family*.[6] The research that went into that book—in archives and interviews, reading scholarly and popular literature on the era and the organization, learning about theories of the family and secrecy, and so on—was crucial to my propositional understanding, but it wasn't until I actually put words on paper in the form of a *story* that I truly grasped the historical scope and healing power of the material. More importantly, it wasn't until I positioned myself within the story, first as a child and later as an adolescent and adult, that I learned to fully appreciate the complexities that I was blind to at the time and that I had obscured from my own view. Nor did I understand until I wrote it how the unfolding secrecy narrative itself became a dominant theme in my family's shared reality, a secret so corrosive that it contributed significantly to our deeply individualized pain and ultimately to our dysfunction.

What I gained from this very up-close and personal narrative epistemic was more than a family story to pass along to my son and to my readers; what I gained was the freedom to move out of the depths of my own darkness and into a way of living within my own story that liberated me from half truths, suspicions, and fear. But really, in the end, what I gained personally was less important than what writing my story has done for my family and the many readers who have written to me about how my story echoed their own stories and how my writing it empowered them to come to grips with their own family secrets, that, like mine, were nurtured in the culture of fear that pervaded the cold war and that, unfortunately, once again has our world in its evil embrace.

That is *my* story, but it is also a story that does good work for other people elsewhere in the world. Until I learned how to tell it, and actually gained the narrative courage to tell it, I had a "need to know" that could not be satisfied in any other method of writing or reporting. Textual criticism of archival data didn't do it, nor did historical reconstruction of the era based on investigations of documents and artifacts. Neither my interviews nor deep reading in the history and practice of espionage slaked my thirst. Telling the story *as a story*, as a quest for knowing that became the act of knowing itself, *that* was what I needed, and that *story* is what I found. And although I have more questions than answers as a result of that narrative journey, my original desire for knowing has been largely sated. I know I've done the best work I can do.

And isn't that what it is all about?

From My Story to Your Stories and Your Academic Lives

The idea for this book grew out of two concerns for the future of narrative as a method of qualitative inquiry that have been expressed to me over the past few years.

The first concern was a personal one. Given that I was fortunate enough to author a popular book on "writing the new ethnography" but had no plan to revise it, colleagues asked me to reconsider my decision. I thought what was needed was not the same book, updated, but rather a new book.

It would be a book that provided practical advice about writing, publishing, and promoting personal narratives for scholarly and public audiences, personal narratives that seem to have matured into "creative nonfiction"; but it would also address some emergent political issues in higher education that currently surround, inform, and often complicate this style of inquiry.

We live now amid a radically changing academic culture. Colleges and universities worldwide are redefining and reorganizing themselves, using entrepreneurial and business models. As a teacher-scholar with over thirty years of experience in American higher education—more than twenty of which was spent in administration—I am intimately acquainted with these business models and the powerful influences they have on all aspects of university life. But most importantly, I know how these business models have informed the new values and metrics applied to tenure and promotion processes. Increasingly, the politics of success in the academy means reframing the scholarly worth and public value of this style of writing and performing within these entrepreneurial and business models, yet there is precious little advice available about how to accomplish it.

Furthermore, because these new business models place a high value on using scholarship to reach wider public audiences—to have "impact" beyond the status accorded to appearances in traditional academic publication outlets—the time could not be more right for encouraging the next generation of narrative/performance ethnographers to fashion their scholarship to appeal to intelligent audiences *outside* the academy. How new scholars accomplish that reframing of their writing for public audiences will have a direct bearing on not only the quality of life for them, but on the future of this style of qualitative inquiry *as* meaningful scholarship that is taken seriously both inside and outside the academy.

We have worked too hard, for too long, to settle for less.

Narrative writing as a method of inquiry among qualitative researchers has contributed to a global expansion of interest in new forms of scholarly expression. Since its appearance in the mid-1980s, the power, grace, passion, and appeal of personal narratives has spawned two identifiable generations of authors. It has also created a substantial body of work published in academic journals, two major book series, and the formation of an international organization. Viewed one way, this is a story of well-earned success for a relatively new method of inquiry.

And thus my second concern.

Despite the success and widening acceptance of alternative forms of scholarly expression, there are also continuing (and often heated) controversies about the scholarly worth of personal stories and persistent questions about the scholarly contributions made by them. For new scholars, or even for those of us who have been at it for awhile, the stakes are high. Questions about what makes for a "good" and *scholarly* story; how to frame a tenure and/or promotion portfolio based on qualitative work that features prominently narrative accounts; concerns about how to present arguments about the scholarly contributions of stories to academics in the social sciences either not familiar with narrative inquiry or not friendly to it; and how one's deeply personal (and often very political) narratives may be viewed outside the academy by disgruntled members of the public or right-wing advocacy groups are part and parcel of concerned conversations at every convention.

I address both of these broad concerns and provide practical solutions to issues of authoring, evaluating, and promoting success through narrative scholarship within and outside the academy. I say "I," but this book is very much the product of a collaborative process involving others whose imprint is evident to me throughout this manuscript. First and foremost, I thank Mitch Allen, my publisher and editor, who not only encouraged me to write this book but also took the time to provide a detailed critique of the first draft and so much in-depth editing of the chapter dealing with publishers that I ought to make him its coauthor. And as far as unacknowledged coauthors go, I also want to thank my "left tackle," Angela Trethewey, who not only read, edited, and significantly improved the chapters, but, in her role as associate director of the Hugh Downs School, intervened to prevent my administrative duties from consuming me so I could finish the book.

Getting a book on writing narratives reviewed by great writers of memorable narratives can be daunting. However, I am happy to say that my reviewers on this project provided sympathetic and insightful comments that significantly improved the book, and all of them did so with great style, wit, and grace. Norman Denzin and Jane Hare—thank you for all you are and all you do to make the world of qualitative inquiry such a rich conversational environment!

Before the manuscript that became this book was written I taught a graduate course in "Creative Nonfiction as a Method of Inquiry." I want to thank my students in that class for their questions, their observations, and their stories, the success of which convinced me to write this book. In particular I want to thank Annagret Hannawa, Aaron Hess, Zachary Justus, Yvonne Montoya, Sarah Riforgiate, Kendra Rivera, Desiree Rowe, Karen Stewart, and Jian Yang. Karen Stewart gets a double thanks for designing the cover that graces this book.

I am fortunate to have excellent colleagues in the Hugh Downs School at Arizona State University, including a vastly talented group of academics who have contributed to this book in their own unique ways. My sincere thanks to Jess Alberts, Steve Corman, Pauline Davies, Belle Edson, Linda Lederman, Sarah Tracy, and (again) Angela Trethewey, with whom I have enjoyed many conversations about research processes, writing practices, and new media. Let me also offer a very special thanks to a very special man whom I have been privileged to know— Hugh Downs—whose intellectual curiosity, passion for ideas, and years of communication excellence serve as a daily inspiration and reminder of the power of public communication and storytelling to add to our storehouse of knowledge and indeed to forever change our world.

I also want to thank Carole Bernard, my production editor and long-suffering locator of my obvious errors, less obvious ones, and the oddity with which I often compose notes. To her, I owe far more than I can repay, because she makes me appear far more literate and aware of style manuals than I really am. Thanks also to Hannah Jennings of Hannah Jennings Design, for her superior design work on this project.

Finally, and with great humility for the simple fact that they put up with my weirdness when I am writing, I want to thank my wonderful loving family, Sandra and Nic Goodall, who make sure I don't veer into the self-absorbed abyss while absorbed in a writing project and who otherwise provide both love and good suggestions for my continuous improvement as a person and a scholar.

H. L. (Bud) Goodall, Jr.
Tempe, Arizona

Notes

1. Report by Norman Denzin to the 3rd Congress on Qualitative Inquiry, May 2007.

2. Worth (2005). For a complete listing of papers from that conference, please point your browser to: http://web.mit.edu/comm-forum/mit4/subs/mit4_agenda.html

3. Worth (2005, p. 19).

4. See Scott (1967) and (1976). See also Gregg (1984).

5. For a complete assessment of writing as a method of inquiry, please see Richardson (2000b). For a complete account of narrative rationality, please see Fisher (1987). For an account of the relational nature of this style of writing, please see Goodall (2000).

6. Goodall (2006a).

Chapter 1

The 5 Rs of Narrative Writing

How should we think about writing narratives? In this chapter, I use Lee Gutkind's notion of the five key ideas central to the practice of creative nonfiction to discuss the basic thought processes associated with this style of writing for qualitative inquiry.[1] For beginning writers, this chapter provides an orientation to practical issues fundamental to crafting nonfiction narratives. For more experienced writers, it offers a refresher course in the rudiments of narrative representation and evocation, framing, reflexivity, and "thick description."[2]

How I Came to the Narrative Epistemic

I, like so many others, developed my narrative roots by reading outside of the academy. I read novels and poetry, drama and investigative journalism. I, too, was frustrated by the lack of compelling stories coming out of my discipline (at the time) as well as by the general lack of respect for narratives within my scholarly community. There seemed to be a need for a bridge between what I was reading outside the academy—compelling stories—and what I was reading in my scholarly journals and books.

I was strongly attracted to academic literature—great ideas, interesting theories, inspired applications—and the ongoing conversations about them. I was also dismayed by the tough going that characterized much of the prose that was used to write theory and report on practice. Why couldn't a research-based form of inquiry also be a compelling narrative?

That was when I decided to supplement my academic training in rhetoric and communication studies with work in creative and biographical writing. My first exploration into that parallel world was in a nonfiction-writing graduate class, where I was introduced to the idea of "new journalism" under the heading "creative nonfiction."

Lee Gutkind, founder of the Foundation for Creative Nonfiction, defines creative nonfiction as:

> Dramatic, true stories using scenes, dialogue, close, detailed descriptions and other techniques usually employed by poets and fiction writers about important subjects—from politics, to economics, to sports, to the arts and sciences, to racial relations, and family relations. Creative nonfiction heightens the whole concept and idea of essay writing. It allows a writer to employ the diligence of a reporter, the shifting voices and viewpoints of a novelist, the refined wordplay of a poet and the analytical modes of the essayist.[3]

He explains that creative nonfiction emerged in the 1960s and 1970s under the banner of "new journalism," which was an experiment in genre that infused investigative reporting with structural and stylistic techniques borrowed from fiction, drama, and poetry. Gutkind calls creative nonfiction "the literature of reality,"[4] and credits Gay Talese[5] as one of the earliest and best practitioners. Talese described his writing as an attempt to get at "the larger truth," which is, Gutkind observes:

> What the creative nonfiction writer is always seeking, both the literal journalistic fact-oriented truth and the three dimensional truth or the meaning of what it is they have observed and experienced. The meaning is what we are working for and the meaning is the way we are able to render the objectives, the reason we have become writers. We have become writers to help make a change in the world and by capturing the meaning of what it is we see and hear, what it is we observe, we can help change, a very little bit of how a reader perceives an idea, a human being or a situation.[6]

The above definition and description of creative nonfiction has everything in common with what I call "new ethnography"[7]: By new ethnography, I mean "creative narratives shaped out of a writer's personal experiences within a culture and addressed to academic and public audiences" (Goodall, 2000, p. 9).

Later, in *Writing the New Ethnography*, I hit on the same themes that Gutkind stresses: a focus on meaning; the skills of an investigative reporter; the importance of attention to language; the use of techniques for storytelling borrowed from fiction, poetry, and drama; and, finally, the centrality of analysis based on careful research, reading, and reflective thought.

So why am I advocating that qualitative writers take as a model "creative nonfiction" for crafting narratives?

There are five very good reasons. Read on.

Real Life Stories: Representation, Evocation, and Framing

The focus of any good narrative is its accurate rhetorical *representation* and rich *evocation* of what happened (or what is happening) in a particular time and place. To make both of these work as good stories and good scholarship requires *framing*. We'll begin our exploration with an examination of these three key concepts that shape and inform writing about real life stories.

Representation

Representation is *never* a simple matter of transferring "truth, the whole truth, and nothing but the truth" from lived experiences to the page. Of course, the people named (or given pseudonyms) *are* those of real people,[8] and the events depicted *are* events that really happened, but beyond those fundamental elements of reporting are important questions of *language* and *perspective*.

Language Is a Partial Representation of Reality

Finding the "right" words is difficult because words—symbols—do not have a one-to-one relationship to reality, nor are our choices of word usage ever neutral. When we use symbols to represent our lived experiences, descriptions of persons and events, and evaluations of meaning attributed to them, we select from an array of language possibilities those words, images, and sounds that best capture our perspective on the whole of it. We construct *a* truth, but not the only truth. We *represent* reality; we don't reproduce it.

This is an important consideration for writers, because it encourages us to become reflective about issues of representation as well as sensitive to nuances of word choices and images. One way to demonstrate awareness of the representational problematic is to include your thoughts about those language challenges in the story. Another option is to include the views and voices of those others who are represented in the text, either as dialogic partners to the construction of meaning or as commentators on what you have written. Of course, neither of these methods fully resolves the constant challenge of representation, because whatever method you select will itself be made in language. There is no "Archimedean language" capable of fully revealing truth. The best we can do is, first, accept that our representations—however richly imagined and imaginatively rendered—are always *partial* and never complete. Second, armed with that knowledge, we must continue to question our choices and search for better ways to make known those concerns in the body of the text.

Perspective Always Reflects a Partisan Point of View

How do we learn to see things in one way, and not another? Where does our capacity for critical interpretation of experience come from? Why is it that we can be profoundly struck by the insights of writers whose stories open up worlds we never knew existed?

The answer to all of these questions turns on issues of representation that center on *perspective*. We learn to see things in one way and not another because we are born, reared, and acculturated in a particular way and not in another. How we learn to see and interpret the world is therefore a product of where we come from and who we are. As a Western white heterosexual male of a certain age, child of relative privilege, and product of an elite education, I have a perspective shaped and informed by those accumulated facts of my life. I am, as my cultural studies colleagues put it, "raced, classed, aged, gendered, and abled," and where I "stand" in relation to all that I see, feel, know, and experience is shot through with those markers of cultural and biological identity.[9]

Perspective, therefore, is never neutral and always partisan.

Why is this important? It is important because there is no such thing as an "omniscient narrator," any more than there is an "immaculate perception."[10] I see and interpret meaning with full membership in all of those biological and cultural groups and am rendered *partisan* because of them.

So are you. So is everyone.

Well, then, how should an understanding of partisanship in perspective inform narrative nonfiction? There are a variety of textual strategies used to identify one's standpoint, from outright statements such as: "I write as an Asian-American feminist," to working one's personal details into the storyline. The point here is less about whether it is preferable to state or envelope the biological and cultural elements of one's representational perspective into the account and more about *what you do with them.* Perspectives are like opinions: Because everyone has one, what distinguishes them is their *quality.* What do they enable? What do they constrain (and is the writer aware of it)? How do these details make the story more credible as well as more interesting?

These reflexive moves help the reader evaluate the interpretations of the author more fully. If we know "who" is writing an account and fully understand her or his position in the world in relation to the subject matter, we are better able to judge the plausibility, utility, and accountability of that interpretation

Robin M. Boylorn provides another writing method for introducing race and gender as an embodied perspective on race and gender *in the academy.*[11] She begins her evocative account with what she calls "A Poetic Beginning":

Colorblind

Midnight falls into morning
Daylight drifts into day
And it is there
Where now meets eternity
Where Black fades to white
Where every color under the sun touches the sun
That color is insignificant
That you can't tell where one ends
And the other begins
> Here, though
> Where I stand
> Where I sit
> Where I breathe
> Where I enter

Here,
Color is everything
It determines worth
Accountability
Fate
me
It labels me
Black
Female
Soul-child
Mysterious
Dark eyed
Beautiful
Brown skinned, girl
In the eyes of the beholder
powerless
vulnerable
helpless
In the eyes of me
"If I know my name,
I know that in the academy,
like in America,
the sister is caught between the rock of racism and the hard place of sexism."

(pp. 651–652)

Boylorn then provides a transition to her multivoiced account about "institutional racism" that also explains her writing strategy:

Poetry acts as an embodied translation of lived experience. More than poetic prose, poetic ethnography allows for the voices of participants to accurately represent their experience evocatively. While utilizing the sensuousness of poetry, poetic ethnography honors the voices that contribute to the project while allowing the voice of the author to contribute to the discussion without disrupting it.

As the methodology of this text, poetic ethnography proves to be a useful tool for discussing controversial topics such as race because it allows the author and the speaker to be authentic, without alienation. ... What follows is an exploration of Self and Other, as I discovered alternative ways of transcribing an interview and an experience. (pp. 652–653)

Robin Boylorn's novel approach to interpreting interview data allows her to create interest via alternative forms of written expression—poetry, prose, an imagined interview between herself and the published remarks of a black scholar in 1969, her personal experience as a doctoral teaching assistant entering a predominately white classroom, the experiences of other black graduate students, and reflexive passages in which she searches for both unity and difference through the lived experiences of race and gender. By blurring the genres through evocative writing, she maintains reader curiosity and participation in the narrative throughout the story, culminating in a surprising conclusion that I won't spoil for you here.

Boylorn uses her standpoint to overtly construct perspectives and critique them. Her framing device is the poem that begins the narrative and her explanation of her writing method establishes a "set-up" for readers that must be "paid off" by the conclusion for the experience of reading to be interesting, informative, and satisfying. Which brings me to question of what makes a narrative interesting.

Evocative Storytelling

Beyond issues of representation, there are two keys to writing a successful real-life story. One key is to *have an interesting story to tell.* What makes a story "interesting" is the grist of many long seminar discussions and the stuff also of many Internet chatrooms, but in my experience as a reader/evaluator of narrative scholarship, what truly makes a story interesting is *evocative storytelling.*

The 4 Cs of Evocative Storytelling

Evocative storytelling is dependent on four interlocking criteria:

1. Conflict: Conflict is the basis for most good stories, whether the conflict begins in a mystery or a problem to be solved.
2. Connection: The writer *creates reader identification* with the subject matter, standpoint, and style of telling the story
3. Continuing Curiosity: The writer uses the *novelty or uniqueness* in the events depicted, the characters described, the form of the story, and the truth/discovery/conclusion that is ultimately revealed to maintain reader curiosity and page-turning interest throughout the narrative.

4. *Climactic Satisfaction:* The ending delivers on the promise of the beginning. It's *unforgettable.* After reading the story, it stays with you.

For example, when I wrote *A Need to Know: The Clandestine History of a CIA Family*, I began my story with the following narrative:

> Harold Lloyd Goodall, Sr. died, either in Virginia or Maryland, at the age of 53 on the night of March 12, 1976. My mother told me that he died at home in his bed in Hagerstown, Maryland, but the Social Security Death Index indicates that he died in Virginia, although it doesn't say where in Virginia.
>
> I have my doubts he died at home.
>
> My mother also said that she requested an autopsy because just three days before he died he had been told that he had a bad cold and just needed some bed rest. A doctor he saw at the Veteran's Administration Hospital supposedly gave him this advice, but my mother couldn't recall the name of the doctor and hospital records do not show that he had any appointments in March.
>
> Nor did I ever see a report of an autopsy. One year later, close to the anniversary of his death, my mother told me that she had been told—by "the government"—that he had died of "multiple bleeding abscesses on both lungs." This was about the time of a news report that Legionnaire's Disease was responsible for the deaths of several men, all veterans, in Philadelphia, all of whom had also died of multiple bleeding abscesses on their lungs. My mother claimed that "the government" now believed that my father, too, had died of Legionnaire's Disease.
>
> That may or may not be true.
>
> My mother never showed me the letter "from the government" that supposedly provided her with this information. She told me she had "thrown it away." I have no doubt that she had done precisely that, if, in fact, there had ever been a letter in the first place. But by then, by March of 1977, I was so disillusioned with the idea of truth in relation to my father's life, much less his death, that I didn't pursue it.
>
> He had led a secret life. And even in death, she kept his secrets.

In the above excerpt, I try to focus the reader on a conflict between my mother and me over the "truth" concerning my father's life and death. I use the universal "begin at the death" trope to create a sense of connection between my story and those of readers who have, or will have, found themselves in similar circumstances due to the death of a loved one. And, because I invoke the form of a mystery story, I seek to pull the reader into the account via a sense of curiosity. How will the story turn out? What is the truth concerning my father? Why did my mother deceive me?

The next 400 pages of the book work through the mystery of my father's clandestine career, the effect it had on my mother and me, and how his death will never be fully resolved because, probably, he was a spy. Using recovered documents, interviews, historical research that provides the cultural surround for the account, as well as my father's codebook (F. Scott Fitzgerald's novel, *The Great Gatsby*), I tell a personal story of the early history of the Central Intelligence Agency and the cold war. The larger story, at least for me, is one of historical parallels between the culture of secrecy during the cold war and the ongoing culture of secrecy in the current global war on terror.

How do I satisfy the reader's desire for a climactic conclusion? One challenge for me when I wrote it was that I still don't know for sure how or why my father died. What he left me was what I call a "narrative inheritance." That inheritance has led me to make a critical connection between the cold war and our present circumstances, both on international and familial levels. Like this:

> My father and my mother both earned a better narrative ending than the one I had previously given to them. When I thought I had finally put away their lives, when I thought I had freed myself from their story, I did not acknowledge the great gift they left me, a gift of understanding history in a very human way. ...
>
> If nothing else, I have no brought their story here, where this story of love, country, secrecy, and family should have come long ago. ...
>
> We must as a nation lead by example rather than by force. We must show the world's mediated citizens that living in a free and open society with a democratic form of government yields a culture of happiness and prosperity, not a culture of fear and unparalleled national debt. If we cannot fold these values into our campaign for public diplomacy, we will fail to win the hearts and minds of those still open to persuasion.
>
> My father told me that Gatsby turns out all right in the end.
>
> That is hopeful. But I think that ending has yet to be written.
>
> Rest in peace my father. Rest in peace my mother.
>
> What I have inherited from your narrative tells me there is still a lot of work to do.

Evocative Language

Evocative language is a writer's capital, but it is a major source of return on the investment a reader gives to the finished story. The principles of evocative language usage are straightforward:

- *Show, don't tell:* Don't lecture the reader. Develop scenes, describe details, give voice to characters and let actions speak instead of making arguments about them.
- *Describe before you evaluate or analyze,* otherwise known as "show me the data." Readers like to reach their own conclusions rather than have the meaning summed for them. Rich descriptions of scenes, details about characters and events—all of these are data in a story.

I elaborate on the above elements of evocative storytelling below in "Riting in Scenes."

Framing

The third key to a successful real life story is its *framing.* Framing is a literary device that establishes a unique perspective on the storyline that follows from it. It also provides a way to wrap up the account, which is why most writers think of beginnings and endings as inherently connected. There are at least four types of framing devices useful for narratives: the single word, an image that works as a metaphor, the literary allusion, and a personal experience that parallels the account about to be given. Let's examine these in greater detail.

A Single Word

Check out William Safire's column "On Language" in any Sunday issue of the *The New York Times Magazine.* His technique is to use an unusual word or phrase in current usage as a point of entry into (usually) a political discussion done as a history of the use of the term.

In a recent column called "Hotting Up," he begins with the lines[12]:

And the hotties are cool.
The headline on the front page of *The Financial Times* was a stunner: "Murdoch denies Beijing kowtow as Dow Jones rhetoric hots up."

Safire then tells the story of tracking down the first usage of "hots up" (P. G. Wodehouse in 1923), which becomes more intriguing as he meanders through its recorded political uses and usage evolutions (from "hots up" to "hottie") up to the present time. He explains, "hottie" used to refer to "a hot water bottle, a foot-warming device of red rubber filled with leaking hot water that went out with kowtow." Notice the nuanced metaphorical allusion to Rupert Murdoch captured almost as an excuse to once again use the term "kowtow"? Safire then speculates that "hottie" is perhaps the only term about physical attractiveness that is gender equal, which seems an odd turn for the storyline until he connects it to hip-hop artist Kool Moe Dee, who links the term to "old skool black slang" and opines that when white people use it, because as slang it's pretty tired, "it's all good." Safire ends his discourse by tipping his rhetorical cap to the "slangy Brits" in what appears to be a tribute to Wodehouse, but when understood as the completion of a framing device, is actually a sly political reference to Rupert Murdoch's thwarted attempt at a takeover of the Dow Jones, which, in Safire's world, means "it's all good."

An Image Used as a Metaphor

In a piece I wrote for *QI* about life in post-9/11 America,[13] I began my story with where I happened to be when I learned of the first plane hitting the World Trade Center. I was (literally) in an optometrist's shop operated by two Middle Eastern gentlemen getting my eyeglasses adjusted. The account begins with these lines:

> When the first news flash about an airplane hitting the World Trade Center broke over the airwaves, I had just handed over my only pair of progressive lenses to an unknown eyeglass technician at a local optical shop.
>
> Without my glasses on, I am nearly blind. My unassisted vision has dipped below 20-800, and I have severe astigmatism, which renders the empirical world past the tip of my nose largely incoherent.
>
> There are also psychological dimensions to being without my glasses, even for the few minutes it usually takes to adjust the frames.
>
> I become aware of my own vulnerability in ways that border on the paranoid. Cannot see anything or anyone clearly, and because what I do see is little more than areas of fuzzy color punctuated aurally by voices attached to structures of various sizes and shapes that with my glasses I know as human beings but without them appear more as geometric possibilities, I tend to close in on myself, pulling my six-foot-two-inch frame into the smallest space possible, as if bracing for an imminent attack. (p. 74)

I return to that sense of vulnerability at the end of the story with a gentle reminder that the images from that tragic day did indeed adjust our vision about how we see and understand the world.

A Literary Allusion

A literary allusion can be simply a quotation from a work of literature that provides the reader with a sense of connection between that quotation and the piece that follows from it. Or it can be an allusion via genre style.

One genre that often serves as the stylistic basis for an allusion is the hardboiled detective story, a la Raymond Chandler.[14] Henry Louis Gates, Jr., who grew up admiring detective stories, used the form to construct the personal narrative "Canon Confidential: A Sam Slade Caper," that opens his fine treatise on the culture wars, *Loose Canons*[15]:

> Her name was Estelle. I should have known the broad spelled trouble when she came into my office and started talking about the canon. The literary canon.
>
> I stubbed out my Lucky Strike and glanced up at her, taking in her brass-blond hair, all curled and stiff with spray. Like she had a still of Betty Grable taped to the corner of her mirror.
>
> Turned out she'd been peddling her story for the past couple of years. Nobody would take it on; I shouldn't have either. But when I was a kid I used to write doggerel. Maybe that's why I didn't throw the babe out of my office.
>
> "Tell me what I need to know, sugar." I splashed some bourbon in my coffee mug, put my feet on my desk, and listened.
>
> Seemed there was some kind of a setup that determined which authors get on this A list of great literature. (p. 3)

Gates returns to this stylized form in chapter 9, aptly titled "The Big Picture" (Raymond Chandler's best novel was *The Big Sleep*).

A Personal Experience

The use of personal experience to frame a larger question is a time-tested technique for writers of narratives. Although there is friendly dispute about who used it first, I chart the trajectory from Ernest Hemingway's war reporting in Spain during the Spanish Civil War.[16] Hemingway found himself under siege in the first use of bombers on a civilian population, a horrible foreshadowing of the carnage in WWII. But, by his own account, he had no way to write about it as a traditional journalist, so he borrowed from his fiction writing and created a dramatic *story* about the event by focusing on a single wounded volunteer soldier. Fact may be stranger than fiction, but this story provides evidence of the usefulness of fiction-writing techniques in the reporting of facts, particularly those borne of a personal, emotional truth.

Ethnographers have also long appreciated the value of placing themselves into scenes from the outset of a study of others. Clifford Geertz, in his famous discipline-changing account of Balinese culture as seen and interpreted through witnessing an illegal cockfight, begins with these lines:

> Early in April of 1958, my wife and I arrived, malarial and diffident, in a Balinese village we intended, as anthropologists, to study. A small place, about five hundred people, and relatively remote, it was its own world. We were intruders, professional ones, and the villagers dealt with us as Balinese seem always to deal with people not part of their life who yet press themselves upon them: as though we were not there. For them, and to a degree for ourselves, we were nonpersons, specters, invisible men.[17]

Geertz uses this "outsider" frame as a lead into a story about how his movement from naive observer to knowing interpreter of their culture turned on a moment of luck and an afternoon of illegality watching how men acquired status during a cockfight. This brilliant narrative marks the beginning of the "interpretive turn" in symbolic anthropology, yet it still generates considerable debate among critics who maintain that the story is so well written that its literary quality deflects attention away from questions about its veracity. I mention this critique because it is still used by detractors of particular styles of personal narrative scholarship.

Autoethnographers, for example, typically use the construction of personal experience as more than a framing device, as the whole of the story is most often drawn *entirely* from personal experiences. No surprises here: Unless you are writing about a car, that is what makes it *auto*-ethnography.[18]

Pardon me.

But Art Bochner has used a personal experience—the death of his father—as a framing device to set up a longer reflection on how academic institutions (the professional source of authority over our lives and the institutional counterpart to biological fathers) and the pace of academic culture set up a "gulf" that works against our emotional best interests.[19] Here is the abstract of that account:

When I learned that my father had died while I was attending a national communication conference, two worlds within me—the academic and the personal—collided, and I was forced to confront the large gulf that divided them. In this article, I weave the story of that experience into the wider fabric of disconnections that promotes isolation and inhibits risk taking and change within universities and academic disciplines. In the process, I question whether the structures of power constitutive of academic socialization are not as difficult to resist as those of one's family, and the consequences as constraining. I use personal narrative to show how storytelling works to build a continuous life of experience, linking the past to the future from the standpoint of the present; to problematize the process of assigning meanings to memories via language; to draw attention to the significance of institutional depression in universities; and to blur the line between theory and story.

The above description of framing devices is not intended to be exhaustive. How could it be? Language is the tool of symbolic invention and of rhetorical and narrative craft. Writers are always about the business of breaking new ground. But these four techniques illustrate four ways of thinking about abstracts, beginnings, and endings as framing devices designed to create interest in a story.

Choosing a Framing Device

How should a writer choose a frame for a narrative? Is there a "best practice" for making this decision?

Think of choosing a frame for a story as you would think of a choosing a frame for a work of art. For artwork and for a narrative, not just any frame will do. What is crafted must attract attention without taking away from the content of the work, and yet it must also be understood as *part* of the work. As I've explained in the previous section, framing can be accomplished in a number of intriguing ways, most of which center on a central decision point: *how to place the real life story within a larger social, political, or institutional issue or research question.*[20] For this reason, I recommend beginning your quest for a framing device by thinking about the *abstract for an academic article* as a resource for articulating the connection between your personal experiences and the larger research issue or question. Art Bochner's abstract above is an excellent example.

Here is another one.

This "layered account," based on qualitative research gathered at a county jail and state women's prison, illustrates the ways in which organizational discourses and micro-practices encourage emotional constructions such as withdrawal, paranoia, detachment, and an "us-them" mentality among correctional officers. Using philosophies from Michel Foucault, the analysis extends theoretical notions of emotion labor, illustrates the harnessed yet pervasive nature of sexuality in a total institution, and sheds light on the emotional challenges faced by a troubled, hidden, and stigmatized employee group. The text jumps among theoretical arguments, notes about methodology and writing, and creative nonfiction vignettes and in doing so, attempts to embody the emotional and jarring nature of the correctional environment.[21]

This abstract is taken from one of the most-cited examples of creative nonfiction in the communication field. It is Sarah Tracy's award-winning piece "The Construction of Correctional Officers: Layers of Emotionality behind Bars." Below is an excerpt from the story, just to give you a sense of her writing style and subject matter:

I'm shadowing a young female officer at Women's Minimum. Her post, today, is to sit in the transport area and search work vans as they enter the facility. It's tedious work. Both she and I are bored. Finally, she has a break and I attempt to rupture the routine, asking if "anything interesting" has been going on lately. She sits down, swings her black-booted feet on to a desk in front of her and says, "You want to hear something that is truly disgusting? I swear this might just epitomize my career." I am eager for a juicy story. And that is what I get.

Me and Gretchen [another officer] had to go down to inmate Potters's cell [in the minimum area of facility] because she was destroying state property—ruining the shades, banging on the wall. Earlier in the day, I went by the room and she was sitting on her bed leaning against the wall, naked from the waste down, legs open with a bunch of paper or tissue between. Anyway, we go together and bring her to segregation. As we're cuffing her in general population, we start to smell this really awful smell.

Well, we have to strip her out in the segregation intake room and she's not doing the squat and cough thing [as per normal strip search procedure], and I can tell that she has something up in her. Every time I ask her to do it, she doesn't really squat. Meanwhile, she has this yellowish-whitish liquid running from her crotch down her legs and it is smelling awful. Poor Gretchen is just sitting there looking green. Well, eventually I call Captain Frank and tell her Potters's not doing the squat thing. Frank comes up and comes in and tells her, "OK, what do you have in you? Pull it out!" At this point, Potters [who is about 23 years old] is sitting in the corner buck-ass naked, laughing her head off. She proceeds to pull out this seven-inch maxi-pad and starts flinging it around. It's covered in blood and shit and it's getting all over and she's laughing like a maniac. You'd think she'd be embarrassed, but no, she's just sitting there laughing hysterically. At this point, the smell is so bad that Gretchen is green and about to throw up, and I leave the room looking for a sink to throw up in. The captain is right behind me … and you know, Frank, she's pretty gross and everything. …She'll fart in front of you and laugh. So you know if she's grossed out that it's got to be pretty awful. So, we're sitting there trying not to throw up, and then the captain tells me that I've got to take Potters to the shower. Well, I've got to make sure that she doesn't do anything weird, so I have to watch her. The whole time she's calling me a fag and saying I'm enjoying watching her shower. I'm like, "Yeah, this is the greatest sexual thrill of my life. "This is the last thing I'd ever want to see. Well, she thinks she's done and I say, "No, you're not, keep washing." I make her wash herself like five times. (p. 515)

The above excerpt demonstrates why the story is *interesting*. It is evocative, highly descriptive, and dramatic and it shows rather than tells. It also demonstrates that the account presented is clearly drawn from a research interview, which adds to the credibility and representational power of the scene. Yet it might not have attracted the scholarly attention it generated without the strategic deployment of a framing device that links the ethnographic story she tells *to ongoing conversations in the research literature* on the idea of emotional labor. Some authors use the opening paragraphs to frame their accounts; some choose to do it, or to reinforce it, in reflexive passages throughout the story, but in this case, Tracy frames her account within the *abstract*.

Her use of the abstract as a framing device allows Tracy to accomplish three important writing goals: (1) she provides a relationship between the story she is about to tell and the scholarly literature it uses and addresses; (2) she alerts the reader to the novel structure she will use to emotionally and stylistically evoke the "jarring" nature of the prison environment; and (3) she can return to evoke the theoretical themes outlined in the abstract throughout the narrative. By using that strategic space to open up the theoretical idea in a language and style that mirrors the usual academic tone used to discuss the topic, Tracy is freer in the story to "play within the frame," to be creative as a scholar and storyteller, without once again having to articulate it.

So, bottom line, begin your decision making about a framing device with a little writing experiment: *compose the abstract*. For some readers, this advice may seem counterintuitive because it presumes foreknowledge of how the story works out. But the point of the experiment is not to carve into symbolic stone what the eventual abstract will become (or whether you will use one); instead, it is designed to help you think through key decision points vital to selecting a framing device:

- *What is your story really about?* What makes it unique? Can that source of uniqueness be used to frame the story?
- *What is the point of telling/revealing it?* What makes it interesting? Can what makes it interesting be used as a framing device?
- *Who is the intended audience and what are the resources for creating identification with them?* Can the source of identification be used as a framing device?
- *How does the story connect to an ongoing scholarly conversation* (Tracy's example), *or the absence of one* (Bochner's example)? Can you use the presence or absence of a scholarly conversation on the topic as a framing device?

Once you have answered these questions, you should have articulated one or more good ideas to explore. But your work is not yet complete. The next question is: What *method of language deployment* best fits your idea(s)? To review, is it:

- a single word;
- an image that serves as a metaphor;
- a literary allusion; or
- a personal experience?

To find your answer, work the idea(s) through all four possibilities. And *voila*!

Or not. (Sometimes that happens. When it does, it may be a sign that what you planned to write about isn't as interesting or unique as you once thought.)

It may mean that you need to think of ways to come at the idea differently: what Kenneth Burke calls "perspective by incongruity."[22] Take a comic perspective on something tragic; see the event you envisioned as part of a heavenly ordained universe instead as one ruled by Darwinian evolution or chaos theory; try seeing the story from someone else's point of view (i.e., instead of telling it as a hero's narrative, frame it from the villain's experiences, or a bystander's). If you thought it was all about gender, think of it instead as all about class, or race, or sexuality, or ethnicity. Work your story against other theoretical postures—better if they are oppositional or seemingly crazy—that you haven't previously considered. Move from Foucault to Weick. Or from Butler to Rorty.

Resolving the "or not" dilemma just may take a while longer. No one said thinking, or writing, was easy.

Reflection: Reflexivity in the Storyline

Reflection is a term with multiple meanings. In this section, I will consider two of them that currently inform narrative writing in general and autoethnographic writing in particular.

Mirror, Mirror on the Wall, Who Is the Most Vulnerable Academic of All?

Walking by a mirror, you notice your reflection. What you see is an image of yourself, *but* what you think about that image depends not only on how well you see but also on how you feel about yourself in relation to that image. Perhaps you dwell on that thought, perhaps not. Either way, reflection can refer to a mirror image and to what seeing it causes to happen inside of you.[23]

"Narcissist" is the pejorative name we give to people who stare too long, and too admiringly, at the image of themselves. In the world of autoethnography, academic detractors often make the charge that an overt and sustained meditation on oneself is at best cleverly disguised narcissism, or fantasy, or not "real" scholarship.[24] Me-search, not re-search. From the academic detractor's perspective, it is the equivalent of *nontheory-driven navel-gazing.* But what is "navel-gazing"?

According to my handy *Encarta World Dictionary*, "navel-gazing" means "pointless self-analysis, instead of considering broader issues." Hmmmmm. This definition, with its emphasis on "self" married to the pejorative "pointless" seems to reinforce criticism of some autoethnographic practice. But, as we discussed earlier in this chapter, all representations of reality are partial and partisan. This definition is no exception.

Whether a narrative is pointless depends on the perspective of the reader, but, as we learned earlier, perspectives are like opinions, and not all opinions are of equal value. What is perceived as "pointless" by a traditional academic unfamiliar with narrative approaches to constructing knowledge, or worse, opposed to them, may count to the author of the story far less than the perspective of a narrativist intimately familiar with these approaches.

What I have described is a relatively common dispute.[25] The point is that although there is risk of rebuke and ridicule associated with any approach to performing research and constructing knowledge, there is, at present, greater risk associated with autoethnography than with traditional scholarly writing. Does this mean that autoethnographers should cease writing personal stories? Not at all! But it does mean that we may need to become more savvy about how we incorporate theory and research findings into them.

Which brings me to a second meaning of "reflection."

From Mirror to Method: Getting off Our Glass, Or, Finding a Better Reflective Surface

Encarta World Dictionary: Reflection: "Careful thought, especially the process of reconsidering past actions, events, or decisions." Now that is more like it!

In my humble opinion, too much of the criticism directed at autoethnographic writing (mis)understands "reflection" as "pointless self-analysis" rather than "careful thought." I am not suggesting that *all* autoethnographic work should be free of that criticism, but neither do I believe that all autoethnographic researchers should be tarred with the same pre-blackened brush.

What I will say is that autoethnographers do themselves no professional favors when they play into the hands of their detractors. Reflection—which in our academic community is usually called "reflexivity"—implies that there is some careful thought that is informed by existing scholarly thinking *in addition to* whatever personal (or "*self*-reflexive") passages are folded into the reflective passage.

Description and Typology of "Better Reflective Surfaces"

As Nightingale and Cromby describe it:

> Reflexivity requires an awareness of the researcher's contribution to the construction of meanings throughout the research process, and an acknowledgment of the impossibility of remaining outside of one's subject matter while conducting research. Reflexivity then, urges us "to explore the ways in which a researcher's involvement with a particular study influences, acts upon and informs such research."[26]

For me, this definition of reflection offers a finer reflexive surface.

Think of a reflective passage as a meditation on a theme ("the awareness of the researcher's contribution to the construction of meanings") that is *driven by lived experience and informed by scholarly resources.* Again, according to Nightingale and Cromby:

> There are two types of reflexivity: personal reflexivity and epistemological reflexivity.
>
> Personal reflexivity involves reflecting upon the ways in which our own values, experiences, interests, beliefs, political commitments, wider aims in life and social identities have shaped the research. It also involves thinking about how the research may have affected and possibly changed us, as people and as researchers.
>
> Epistemological reflexivity requires us to engage with questions such as: How has the research question defined and limited what can be "found"? Thus, epistemological reflexivity encourages us to reflect upon the assumptions (about the world, about knowledge) that we have made in the course of the research, and it helps us to think about the implications of such assumptions for the research and its findings. How has the design of the study and the method of analysis "constructed" the data and the findings? How could the research question have been investigated differently? To what extent would this have given rise to a different understanding of the phenomenon under investigation? (p. 228)

Although the above typology and discussion may seem more in line with research done as formal social science, I would argue that the same questions apply to research done for a story. For example, Martin Parker's cleverly titled "Becoming Manager: Or, the Werewolf Looks Anxiously in the Mirror Checking for Unusual Facial Hair," is, as he frames it in the abstract, "an autobiographical reflection [he uses a mirror as well as "careful thought"] on becoming the head of a management department in a small English university."

If that was *all* the piece was about, it would be a mildly amusing take on how Parker's life changed when he assumed the job. *Yawn.* But instead, Parker couches his self-reflexive passages within a larger story about identity that is not fixed or ever finished (thus the phrasing of the title "Becoming Manager" rather than "Becoming *a* Manager"). He uses both types of reflexivity—personal and epistemological—to develop his story. Using a framing abstract, he explains it this way:

> There is little or no published writing by practicing managers that takes reflexivity particularly seriously as a method. This is what I intend to do here, and the article hence takes the form of a series of rather staccato fragments that rotate around the ways in which I think I have changed, and the

ways that other people's attitudes towards me seems to have changed. ...
So this is an article that attempts to be reflexive about the kinds of claims
that I make about myself and the sort of language I am using to describe
others. The key question for me is whether I can be said now to have
become a manager, and to ask what this might mean. Or, opening the
same question in a different way, to consider whether management can
be fruitfully thought of as a becoming, or learning, that can be endlessly
questioned and reflected on. If the latter is the case, then perhaps notions
of the unity and hegemony of a managerial occupational identity can be
undone too.[27]

Reflexivity is a powerful authoring tool that, when used to question the construction of a personal point of view, may be used to draw a reader into the thoughts of the writer. When used to explore the epistemic foundations of that point of view, the reflection affords a way of appreciating the intellectual awareness and care used to develop her or his unique point of view.

But where should an author "put it" in the account?

Pragmatic Considerations

There is no "one right place" in any universal sense, but there always will be a "right place(s)" within the telling of your story. I have learned to think about the placement of reflexive passages in two ways: as a "break" from the narrative and as an integral aspect of it.

When used as an integral part of the storytelling, as in the above example from Parker, reflexivity is thoroughly woven into the whole of the storyline. It serves as the *method for writing through a particular set of experiences* while commenting on the experiencing of them.

By contrast, when used as a "break" in the storyline, the reflexive passage serves as a *pause for reflection that transitions the reader* to the next episode or sequence of events. When used this way, reflexive passages can be as brief as a single sentence or two—fleeting thoughts, important questions, profound insights, punctuated moments—or they can be as long as they need to be to get the job done.

Finally, once you have determined where to place the reflective passages in your story, it is important to think about how you will alert the reader to them. It may be helpful to the reader to "signal your intention" by setting the reflexive passage off from the main body of the text *visually* by either separating the section from the main text by blank spaces or by "marking" the departure through centered asterisks or some other symbol before and after the passage or by *italicizing* the passage.

In sum: reflexive passages accomplish two interrelated writing goals: (1) comment thoughtfully on some aspect of how and why the experience is being constructed; and (2) bring into the text epistemological positions (which may include literary/historical analogies as well as theories and research findings) to enrich and inform the reader of your thought processes as they are reflected in the narrative.[28]

'Riting in Scenes: Thick Description

As I mentioned earlier, the key to 'riting in scenes can be summed up in two concise Writing Commandments:

- Show, don't tell (Thou Shalt Be Descriptive!)
- Describe before you evaluate or analyze (Thou Shalt Show Me Your Data!)

Commandment language aside, why is the best narrative writing *descriptive*, and *why should you show readers your data prior to reaching conclusions*? And why do both of these commandments lead to the same conclusion about good narrative writing: *Write in scenes!*

Why do those of us who teach narrative approaches to knowledge construction encourage students to develop dramatic scenes; include conversations; and provide detailed accounts of how people look, dress, talk, walk, and otherwise engage in the business of everyday life? Why not limit our writing, like the pair of old fictional detectives on black and white television used to do, to "just the facts, ma'am."

These are good questions. For writers trained in English departments, the answer may seem obvious: That is how good narrative prose is crafted. The tradition of "'riting in scenes" has been a hallmark of fiction, drama, and narrative nonfiction. However, for those of us trained outside of English departments and particularly in the social sciences, the question of what makes good prose has, until lately, had far less to do with descriptive narrative techniques and plotlines than with accepted traditions of scientific scholarship. The question was not "to story, or not to story" or even *how to tell* a good story, because good science was not about good storytelling. At least it wasn't "storytelling" in the sense we know today of highly descriptive, contextually detailed, narrative ways that we now associate with personal ethnography and performative prose. To get from traditional science writing to innovative scientific narratives required a major shift in our thinking as well as in our writing practices.

42

How and when did that shift occur? To answer that question requires a brief historical detour via the epistemic turn that marked a move away from "realism" to "impressionism" in ethnographic accounts of culture.[29] The icon of that "interpretive turn" was an essay called "Thick Description: Toward an Interpretive Theory of Culture," written by a well-respected but rebellious anthropologist, Clifford Geertz.[30]

Thick or Thin?

Clifford Geetz described his narrative method of doing ethnography as "thick description." At the epistemic center of his discussion is a key question about how anyone interprets the meaning of anything.

For Geertz, meaning is always *contextual*, which means that no one (in this case, the reader) can make sense of behavior until and unless that behavior is *situated within a scene*. The example Geertz famously uses is how to interpret the meaning of a wink.[31] If all we get from the writer is the bare fact of the wink reported on the page, it's a "thin description." We don't have a clue as to what it means, either to the person doing the winking or to the receiver of the wink. It could be a flirtation, or a sign of shared secret, or an involuntary eye-twitch, or any one of a hundred other possibilities including that it might be totally random and mean nothing at all. *Unless the writer provides context details, we are left without the narrative resources to make sense of the behavior.*

What are "context details?" They are the descriptive details of how meaning is/was constructed within a particular time and place and within the "codes of signification"—what already exists as cultural rules guiding interpretive practices—indigenous to a culture. In the following passage from Nick Trujillo and Leah Vande Berg's joint account of her death, see if you can locate them:

> Two nurses came in around 6:30 in the morning and said they needed to turn Leah to prevent bedsores, as they had done the previous night. When they started to move her, Leah became very distressed. She opened her eyes widely and craned her neck. In her withered condition and with bulging eyes and a stretched neck, she did not appear to be human. As ghastly and surreal as this might sound, she looked like E.T. from the Steven Spielberg movie.
>
> I held her hand and told her it was okay, but she remained agitated even after the nurses left the room. Her breathing changed dramatically, shifting to what sounded like a higher octave but in a minor chord.
>
> "Something is different," I said.

Our friend Sylvia, who had arrived an hour earlier, backed off and let me have privacy with Leah as I stroked her hair and coached her to die. I told her that it wasn't her fault, that I was so proud of her, and that she could do this. Her breathing slowed and her gasps shortened, until I could see only faint reflexes in her mouth and throat.

A few minutes past seven o'clock, Leah took one last micro-gasp, and then became completely still.

Sylvia approached and asked, "Is she gone?"

"I don't know," I said. "I've never done this before."

I put my finger on Leah's neck to feel for a pulse, and her throat quivered ever so slightly. We let her lie in peace for several additional minutes. She probably was dead for five minutes before I went to get a nurse.

I walked to the nurses' station and asked for help.

"Be right with you, honey," the nurse said as she continued to fill out paperwork.

"Take your time," I said calmly. "My wife just died and she's not going anywhere."

The nurse dropped her pen, stood up, and gave me her full attention.

"Are you okay?" she asked.

I told her I was fine and that I had been expecting Leah to die at any time for the last week. The nurse checked on Leah and called for a doctor.[32]

If we were writing a "just the facts, ma'am" behavioral account of Leah's death and Nick's response to it, it would read something like this: "Two nurses turned Leah over in the hospital bed. Leah was agitated. Nick and Sylvia noticed something different. Sylvia left. Leah died. Then Nick told the nurse." Pretty thin, right? Not very interesting or informative, either.

But more importantly, without the inclusion of contextual details—a hospital setting, the actual words spoken, the bedsores and the agitation when the body is moved, the hand holding and reassurance, the description of her cancer-ridden body, the reference to the image of E.T., the "micro-gasp," the coaching Nick provided her, the ambiguity of knowing the exact moment of death, the reference to time as a marker, albeit an incomplete one, the nurse busy with her paperwork, the ironic humor in Nick's response to the nurse's concern—the scene would be devoid of clues to the codes of cultural signification that give deeper meaning to the death experience as well as to the reading experience.

If your scholarly goal is to create cultural understanding through an exploration of the meaning of lived experiences, then "'riting in the scene"—providing readers with those evocative contextual clues to coding them—is the essential semiotic method by which you accomplish your goal. If your goal is to create a rich literary text, the method is the same. In both cases, the inclusion of these details of hospitalized, Western death and the experience of a husband who coaches his wife to die allow for a connection between our culturally based expectations of "how death happens" (including questions about what, in the same circumstances, we might do) and the description of Leah Vande Berg's particular death.

Nick's account may challenge what you know or believe, or it may reinforce it or alter it or contribute new information to what you think about the death experience. Or it may contest it. But without the writing of the death scene in such rich descriptive detail, our reading experience—as well as our understanding—would be less precise, less full, and less contestable. In short, your participation in the account, your invitation to the ongoing conversation, would be severely limited.

Thick Scenes, Rich Stories

Geertz's use of thick description to demonstrate an interpretive approach to cultural analysis through evocative literary writing was a major turning point not just for anthropology but for post-structural theory and research done throughout the social sciences. In a profound epistemological reflection, Geertz asserts:

> Cultural analysis is intrinsically incomplete. And, worse than that, the more deeply it goes the less complete it is. ... There are a number of ways of escaping this—turning culture into folklore and collecting it, turning it into traits and counting it, turning it into institutions and classifying it, turning it into structures and toying with it. But they are escapes. The fact is that to commit oneself to a semiotic concept of culture and an interpretive approach to the study of it is to commit oneself to a view of ethnographic assertion as ... "essentially contestable." Anthropology, or at least interpretive anthropology, is a science whose progress is marked less by a perfection of the consensus than by a refinement of debate. What gets better is the precision with which we vex each other. (p. 29)

Nick Trujillo's story—powerful as it is—may well be "vexing" to readers who expect a smoother, less ambiguous tale of death for a loved one. It may raise anxieties, or even cause alarm. Yet its contribution to ongoing debates about the meaning of death in our culture, or how we should die, or how we should endorse the death choices of others, is precisely what Geertz anticipated. Thick description affords us the luxury of reading, writing, and interpreting symbolic action; it provides us with the context and coding of a wink, or, in Trujillo's case, a death. And those interpretations open up the text for new questions, alternative readings, affirming and resistance narratives.

For writers of all varieties of narrative nonfiction, thick description enhances 'riting in scenes, and the result is a richer text and (usually) a better story. It establishes an always perspectival "you are there" view of the setting and privileged access to events that make up the storyline. It also encourages careful thought about the language choices that constitute the description of the scene, because individual words or phrases must accurately represent the events as well as carry the emotional weight and feeling-tone of the narrative.

The Final Two "Rs": Research and Reading

Writing a compelling narrative requires more than the ability to tell a good tale. The ability to tell a good tale is largely a matter of *form*: introductions, bodies, and conclusions in essays; dramatic structure in narratives that move the characters and the account from initial conflict to its eventual resolution; the three-part nature of most jokes; the "who, what, when where, why, and how" of journalism; etc.[33] Form may be the appeal that draws readers in and provides them with expectations for what they might find in your story, but it's the *content within the form that makes the story credible, worthwhile, and memorable.*

As in all explorations of cultural knowledge via personal experience, the in-depth research includes immersing oneself in the scene; interviewing others; reflecting on how existing scholarly explanations might shed light on the experience; and reading widely in general as well as deeply in the subject matter. Let's briefly examine each of these content resources.

Immersion

Bronislaw Malinowski, the father of modern anthropology, believed that good ethnography required a three-part research process: *immersion* (for at least a year, sometimes longer), *detachment* (relocation back to one's home terrain), and *re-immersion* (after a sufficient length of time, to check on the accuracy of the original observations and any changes that have taken place).[34]

It's an understatement to say that his method and fieldwork became the initiation ritual for modern anthropologists and is still the widely accepted standard today. But serious questions have been raised about the supposed length of time required to "know" a culture (these days thought to be dependent on the individual qualities of the observer rather than on the length of a grant); what kind of "knowing" (physical, emotional, intellectual, spiritual, informant, friend, lover, etc.) leads to intimate knowledge of a culture; the challenges of "detachment" (both in the field and afterward); and the value of re-immersion in relation to the original observations.[35]

Malinowski was a gifted ethnographer and one of the finest prose stylists of his generation, despite the fact that English was his second language. He was also a diarist who kept detailed personal reflections on his fieldwork, including his deeply conflicted relationship to his subjects, his feelings of loneliness and frustration, his sexual desires, accounts of novels he read to escape the boredom of fieldwork, and his regular use of drugs.[36] He wrote the diary for himself, in his original Polish language, and it was not until after his death that his second wife published it. The publication caused quite a stir, not simply because it revealed the inner turmoil of his fieldwork with the Melanesian people, but because Malinowski, who literally invented observational science in anthropology and was universally heralded as a major figure, was suddenly revealed to have been politically incorrect.[37]

Immersion in a culture provides the basis for knowledge constructed out of reflexive personal experience and detailed interviews and observations of others. As Malinowski's example teaches us, there may be no reliable field guide to the emotional and embodied challenges of immersion, although there are well-established research methods to guide formal and informal data collection. Today, of course, many of the conflicts that were "scandalous" when his diary was published have become the basis for provocative scholarly articles, intense personal examinations, and open forums in many disciplines. As a group of what Michael Agar calls "professional strangers," we no longer avoid discussions of how our gender, sexuality, race, age, politics, or personal vulnerabilities inform our fieldwork and our writing.[38] We write *through* the conflict; we *engage* the struggles on the page; and often we simply raise questions that we know have no answers. In this sense, we have more in common in Malinowski's diary, as well as his fieldwork, than we may know.

Interviewing

Interviews are excellent qualitative research tools. They afford the interviewer an opportunity to ask questions, probe answers, gain access to patterns of thinking, and acquire an appreciation for the interviewee's perspective. Interviews may be *highly structured* (exact questions in a predetermined order), *semi-structured* (exact questions in a predetermined order, but some flexibility in probing answers), or *informal* (think of a conversation with a friend).

Recent advances in interviewing include attention to the conceptual frameworks of the interviewer and how those frameworks shape semi-structured and heavily structured depth interviews,[39] a new focus on the person behind the interview, also known as the "interviewee,"[40] the interview as a "conversational partnership,"[41] interactive interviewing,[42] and how interviews are represented in life story narratives and in qualitative research generally.[43]

Our interest here is not in types of interviews or interviewing techniques—there are plenty of books and articles on that subject—but instead in the use of interviews as research resources for varieties of performative, narrative, and poetic accounts based on qualitative research.

For academic markets, life story interviews afford researchers rich opportunities to acquire individual perspectives on any number of topics, from historical accounts of communities to survivor stories to unique personal experiences.[44] For mass markets, informational interviews and radio/television documentaries (as well as podcasts) are attractive formats for combining creative nonfiction stories with in-depth interviews. For example, *Rolling Stone* magazine has a long history of featured interviews, some of which have obtained status as "literary" interviews.[45] Similarly, the Chicago Public Radio broadcast of "This American Life" affords listeners and viewers the opportunity to create and enjoy original narratives that combine interviews with introspection, cultural commentary that often comes with a political edge.[46]

The research literature provides a variety of examples of how interviews were *turned into* performances, narratives, and poems.[47] However, there is precious little advice about how the authors of these works accomplished their objectives. What seems clear is that it is not a question about method so much as it is a question about *writing*—what makes good dialogue, how to make use of creative forms of expression, and what may strike readers as interesting, relevant, and new.

For a piece I wrote about the *Ferraristi* of Long Island,[48] one fine summer's day my wife, son, and I participated in a elite "poker" rally. Our host, who was then president of the Ferrari Club sponsoring the event, lent me a 328 for the day, so even though I was "undercover" as an ethnographer among the elite, I fit right in. My wife, Sandra, also participated by "working the registration desk" with Paula, our co-host. In that capacity, she interviewed the participants for personal background information. My job, in my capacity as a participant/observer was to overhear these interviews. Here is a brief excerpt of one of them that I used in the story, derived from my scrawled field notes:

> Sandra: Address?
> Giovanni ??????: Yeah, got one.
> S: City?
> G: Yeah, city. (winks)
> S: Okay. (elongated, curious) : Will you be driving alone, etc.?
> G: Yeah. (upbeat, enjoying himself)
> Paula: We need to know how many people to seat at the rest./$50/$100
> G: (Pulls out fat wad of $100 bills and gives P one). Nods, smiles. Indicates a staple for the form. Winks. Leaves.
> Details: G is short, stocky, perfect moustache, works out, probably mid 50s. Manicured nails. Looks like a wise guy and this may be an act, or not.

Not intrinsically interesting, right? Yet there was an aura of mystery in the encounter that made me want to write it in more detail. Here is the story that emerged from the field notes:

> Here in front of me stands a relatively short, obviously stocky, neatly mustached, muscled-but-with-a-mild-pasta gut mid-fifties man in a red Ferrari golf shirt named Giovanni Something I Can't Read on his form, who seems capable of giving only a singular monosyllabic response to each and every question posed by Paula and Sandra.
>
> "Address?" Sandra asks when he hands her his form, giving him the benefit of her best professional smile.
>
> "Yeah," he replies. When nothing happens, he adds, "Got one."
>
> He smiles at Sandra, then at Paula, in what I can describe only as a very professional manner.
>
> Sandra pauses and then decides that he isn't kidding. "City?" she says, a little less certain and with a whole lot more smile.
>
> "Yeah," he replies. He winks. "City."
>
> "Okaaaay," she intones. "Will you be driving alone today or do you have a navigator?"
>
> "Yeah," he says, upbeat. He is clearly enjoying this.

"We need to know how many people to seat at the restaurant," Paula adds, now a little more shyly than before but also holding on to her smile. "If it is just you, then it's fifty dollars; if there are going to be two of you, then it's one hundred dollars."

Giovanni pulls a wad of bills from his trousers. He peels off a hundred dollar bill and hands it to Paula. His hands are thick, his nails well manicured, and his movements are silent. He doesn't ask for change. He doesn't say how many people to expect at the restaurant. Sandra indicates nonverbally to him her intention to staple the bill to the form.

He nods. He smiles. He winks.

And then he quietly walks away. Here is a man who clearly doesn't want his name on any mailing list. (p. 738)

Reflecting

Reflection is a research and writing activity when it draws on deep personal knowledge of a subject that is enhanced by informed sources. I've discussed the concept of reflection/reflexivity at some length already, so I'll limit this discussion to one exemplar drawn from a narrative: "Federer as Religious Experience," by David Foster Wallace.[49]

I use this piece for two reasons. First, it is an interesting immersion story that does a remarkable job of combining a deep reflection on the aesthetics of tennis with deep personal knowledge and research on the subject.[50] Second, it offers a new way of thinking about how an intimately informed observation of a game can roughly equal the beauty of a "religious experience." In this way, Wallace offers us another way of thinking about the role of sports in our culture by sharing his love of the game, and by reflecting on his technical knowledge of tennis to improve how we understand it. I use this narrative also because it achieves a curious cultural symmetry with Clifford Geertz's "Deep Play: Notes on a Balinese Cockfight."[51]

This present article is more about a spectator's experience of Federer, and its context. The specific thesis here is that if you've never seen the young man play live, and then do, in person, on the sacred grass of Wimbledon, through the literally withering heat and then wind and rain of the '06 fortnight, then you are apt to have what one of the tournament's press bus drivers describes as a "bloody near-religious experience." It may be tempting, at first, to hear a phrase like this as just one more of the overheated tropes that people resort to describe the feeling of Federer Moments. But the driver's phrase turns out to be true—literally, for an instant ecstatically—though it takes some time and serious watching to see this truth emerge.

Beauty is not the goal of competitive sports, but high-level sports are a prime venue for the expression of human beauty. The relation is roughly that of courage to war.

The human beauty we're talking about here is beauty of a particular type; it might be called kinetic beauty. Its power and appeal are universal. It has nothing to do with sex or cultural norms. What it seems to have to do with, really, is human beings' reconciliation with the fact of having a body.

"Sacred grass of Wimbledon?" "Near-bloody religious experience?" Beauty, courage, war. "Having a body"? Are you curious how all of these terms will be resolved?

I should mention that another reason I read Wallace is because of his footnotes. He is famous for them.[52] In one footnote in the present narrative he writes:

(9) We're doing the math here with the ball traveling as the crow flies, for simplicity. Please do not write in with corrections. If you want to factor in the serve's bounce and so compute the total distance traveled by the ball as the sum of an oblique triangle's two shorter legs, then by all means go ahead—you'll end up with between two and five additional hundredths of a second, which is not significant.

Back to the main body of the narrative. As you read more about this specific match-up between Federer and Agassi, Wallace drops in a short history of composite rackets, topspin, and their new relationship to power baseline tennis.

Back to the game just in time for the grand finale of the narrative, wherein all textual tensions are resolved:

Roger Federer is showing that the speed and strength of today's pro game are merely its skeleton, not its flesh. He has, figuratively and literally, re-embodied men's tennis, and for the first time in years the game's future is unpredictable. You should have seen, on the grounds' outside courts, the variegated ballet that was this year's Junior Wimbledon. Drop volleys and mixed spins, off-speed serves, gambits planned three shots ahead—all as well as the standard-issue grunts and booming balls. Whether anything like a nascent Federer was here among these juniors can't be known, of course. Genius is not replicable. Inspiration, though, is contagious, and multiform—and even just to see, close up, power and aggression made vulnerable to beauty is to feel inspired and (in a fleeting, mortal way) reconciled.

The test of reflection is its intellectual contribution to the narrative, its ability to provide what Kenneth Burke calls "equipment for living."[53] Wallace's summary sentiment: "power and aggression made vulnerable to beauty" provides us with just such equipment.[54] Reading this narrative means never seeing tennis the same way again.

No matter what *your* subject, your goal should be to create that self-same feeling in your readers.

Reading Widely and Deeply

If it is true that a scholar's life is a writing life (and I believe it is), then it is even truer that a writer's life is a reading life.[55] Notice I didn't limit that definition of "writer" to those of us who have chosen a scholarly path. In fact, all writers benefit from *reading widely* across subject fields and disciplines, from academic and popular sources, in fiction and nonfiction genres.

Why?

William Safire once put it this way: "By elevating your reading, you will improve your writing or at least tickle your thinking."[56] I find that reading widely[57] provides fresh ideas and perspectives that often turn into resources for what I am working on. I also find that being knowledgeable about ongoing conversations in politics, culture, literature, and business provides avenues for analogical thought that inform my everyday conversations, scholarship, and teaching.

We also benefit from *reading deeply.* Just as a scholar spends a lifetime acquiring knowledge that when forged with her or his own experiences and fired by the imagination becomes valued expertise, so, too, do narrative authors rely on acquiring a deep knowledge that lends authority to our voices and credibility to our stories. In my field, as in yours, there are always new articles, book chapters, and scholarly volumes to read, and, as most cutting-edge research is interdisciplinary or transdisciplinary, that list keeps growing.

The scholar's life is a writing life, and a writer's life is a reading life. Indeed!

Activities and Questions

1. Choose one of your favorite essays or pieces of scholarship. Read the text with an eye toward locating the points at which the author(s) make evident personal and epistemological reflexivity. How do these moves enhance the text? If those forms of reflexivity are absent, what is lost as a result?

2. In *Bird by Bird*, Annie Lamott encourages budding writers to begin by writing a "one-inch frame" as a way to encourage the development of rich descriptions. Imagine that you are looking at a scene in your life through a one-inch square lens. Describe that scene in as much detail as you can. Include not only the sights, but the sounds, the textures, the smells, and the emotions contained within that frame. Getting close to the scene in this way may provide you with building blocks for your story.

3. Record (using field notes or an audio recorder) a conversation in the context of an interview or in your daily life. Choose a snippet of that conversation to represent as a story. Play with several different ways of narrating the encounter by adding context, nonverbal and emotive details, and other inflections. Which version is most interesting to read? Why?

4. In my earlier book, *Writing the New Ethnography*, I asked my readers to account for their own reading practices. I think those questions are still important. Why do you read? What is it about a piece that keeps you reading? What do you want from a text? What was the most important thing you've learned from your reading of late? Answers to these questions should inform your own writing practices.

Notes

1. Please see Lee Gutkind's discussion at: http://www.creativenonfiction.org/thejournal/articles/issue06/06editor.htm

2. This term is borrowed from Geertz (1973).

3. From: http://www.leegutkind.com/Genre.aspx

4. Talese and Lounsberry (1995). Two other volumes worthy of your time are Sims (1984) and Wolfe (1998).

5. When *Esquire* determined the best nonfiction they published, they selected Talese (April 1966), a piece of new journalism that defined creative nonfiction; for a wider sampling of his work, see Talese and Lounsberry (2003).

6. From http://www.leegutkind.com/AboutMe.aspx

7. Goodall (2000).

8. Composite characters are sometimes used, but Gutkind discourages that practice and so do I. A composite is by definition a fictional

construction, even if everything that is used to build a composite character is true.

9. There are many excellent examples of journal articles and books written from a clearly articulated standpoint. Consider, for example, these articles: Shope (2006); Richardson (2005; Alexander (2004); Jackson (2004); and Fox (2007). Consider also these books: De la Garza (2004); Trujillo (2004); Pelias (1999); Tillman-Healy (2001); Lockford (2004); and Holman Jones (2007). The best study I have read about a disability standpoint is Lindemann (2005).

10. John Van Maanen uses these terms to describe "realist tales," or ethnography done during the middle of the 20th century by (mostly) anthropologists and sociologists who were less than critical of their own position in relation to their subjects. See his classic work, Van Maanen (1988).

11. Boylorn (2006).

12. Safire (2007).

13. Goodall (2002a).

14. Raymond Chandler was my inspiration as well. My first narrative ethnography was an homage to his stylistic influence as well as to the idea that "mystery" was an appropriate perspective for an interpretive researcher. For details, see Goodall (1989a).

15. Gates (1992).

16. The other usual nominee is Jack London for a piece he did for *Collier's* about the 1906 San Francisco Earthquake. See London (1906). However, it is the bombing of Madrid that sets the stage for Hemingway's experience of waking up in a hotel under fire; this frame is used to create the background for a "surprise and sense-making" episode in what he calls "a new kind of war." See Hemingway (1937).

17. From Geertz (1973). You can access the article via the free articles site from *Daedalus*: (http://findarticles.com/p/articles/mi_qa3671/is_200510/ai_n15745138) or from (http://webhome.idirect.com/~boweevil/BaliCockGeertz.html).

18. This is a pun, of course, and not at all original. But the first time I heard it, the pun inspired me to use Geertz's "Deep Play" idea and apply it to Ferrari enthusiasts on Long Island. The result really is an "auto-ethnography"; if you are interested, see Goodall (2004).

19. Bochner (1997).

20. Framing the issue within a larger research context is also an excellent way to avoid the charge that you are "only" telling a story and that your work does not connect in any meaningful way to the literature on the subject. More on this idea in Part III.

21. Tracy (2004).

22. See discussion of this idea, see Burke (1989).

23. For an excellent example of self-reflection based on (literally) a mirror image, see Pelias, "Mirror, Mirror" (2004, pp. 39–45).

24. See, for example, Coffey (1999); Shields (2000); and Buzard (2003).

25. Arthur P. Bochner and Carolyn Ellis have written extensively on this topic. See Bochner (2001, pp. 131–157) and Ellis (2004).

26. Nightingale and Cromby (1999).

27. Parker (2004).

28. Admittedly, this second goal is controversial among narrativists. Followers of Art Bochner's "story as theory" perspective often point out that narratives contain rich perspectives on social/professional life and therefore need no further enhancement. The usual exemplar is Charles Dickens, who clearly had a well-developed "theory" of the social world about which he wrote without once using scholarly sources. Others have voiced the opinion that the textual authority and power of the story is diminished if it can only be made legitimate with the inclusion of scholarly sources. Although I respect these differing perspectives, I think there are very few Charles Dickenses among us, and I disagree wholeheartedly with the idea that scholarly resources diminish the power of the story. But there is an additional consideration that I feel should be taken into account: When creative nonfiction stories are used to support a scholarly profile, scholarly resources—however they are written into the text or used as footnotes—make the case for tenure, promotion, and merit much easier because they explicitly locate the author in an ongoing scholarly conversation.

29. See Van Maanen (1988).

30. Geertz (1973, pp. 3–30).

31. Geertz took his example from a lecture "The Thinking of Thoughts: What Is 'Le Penseur' Doing?" presented at the University of Saskatchewan by the philosopher Gilbert Ryle. The lecture is available online through http://lucy.ukc.ac.uk/CSACSIA/Vol14/Papers/ryle_1.html

32. From Trujillo and Van de Berg (2008).

33. For detailed treatment, see Burke (1974).

34. Malinowski (1961). See also Nilan (2002), who uses the original formulation to discuss shifting subject positions and the problems of detachment that ensue from it.

35. For a general discussion, see Fine (1994). For examinations of the role of "embodied knowledge," sexuality, taboo, and erotic subjectivity in fieldwork, see Kulick and Willson (1995); Markowitz and Ashkenazi (1999); Newton (1996), and Wolcott (2002). For a discussion of friendship as method, see Tillmann-Healy (2001). For a germinal account of a feminist "friendship" model applied to interviewing, see Oakley (1981).

36. Malinowski (1989).

37. For a sample of the criticism and defense of the man, see Powdermaker's response to Geertz (1967). (http://www.nybooks.com/articles/11916). In one revealing passage from Powdermaker's review, Geertz makes this observation about Malinowski: "He emphasized knowing one's self as a way of understanding others—their emotional as well as rational life." This statement suggests that the self-criticism and incredible detail in analyzing his attitudes toward the natives, his dreams, and his hypochondria were necessary to attain the self-knowledge that could fairly serve as a comparative basis for observations and analyses of others.

38. See Agar (1996). See also Behar (1997) and Behar and Gordon (1996). And for a "novel" treatment of these issues as they arise in a fictional classroom, see Ellis (2006).

39. Wengraf (2001).

40. Holstein and Gubrium (2004); see also Evans (2007).

41. Rubin and Rubin (2005).

42. Ellis, Kiesinger, and Tillmann-Healy (1997); Ellis and Berger (2002).

43. McCormack (2004); Shostak (2005).

44. There are a variety of scholarly outlets for these forms of creative nonfiction. There are also new media outlets. For example, Professor Daniel Makagon of the Department of Communication at DePaul University hosts "Soundscapes," a bimonthly "audio documentaries" broadcast. See the website at: http://wmtu.mtu.edu/soundscapes/Soundscapes1.htm; Professor Mark Neumann, director of the School

of Communication at Northern Arizona University hosts DocumentaryWorks; see the website at: http://documentaryworks.org/contact.htm

45. For a listing, see http://en.wikipedia.org/wiki/The_Rolling_Stone_Interview; for an example of an interesting interview with Steve Jobs about the impact of iTunes and the parallels of getting into the music business with how he got into the computer business, see http://www.rollingstone.com/news/story/5939600/steve_jobs_the_rolling_stone_interview

46. Please visit: http://www.thislife.org/

47. See Denzin (2001) and Kiesinger (1998). For an application that shows interview data crafted into poetic representation, please see Sparkes and Douglas (2007).

48. Goodall (2002).

49. Wallace (2006).

50. At one time, David Foster Wallace was ranked 79th among junior tennis players. He has written previously about tennis in both his novel, *Infinite Jest*, and in an exceptionally fine piece about the Canadian Open, "Tennis Player Michael Joyce's Professional Artistry as a Paradigm for Certain Stuff about Choice, Freedom, Discipline, Joy, Grotesquerie, and Human Completeness." You can read that account in his collection *A Supposedly Fun Thing I'll Never Do Again* (1997). I also agree with reviewers that even if you don't like tennis, reading Wallace's performative writing about tennis will gain your attention and interest anyway.

51. Geertz (1973). Available online at: http://www-personal.si.umich.edu/~rfrost/courses/MatCult/content/Geertz.pdf

The "curious symmetry" between this ethnographic classic and Wallace's account of the Federer Moment is in how both observers learn to read the action in a game as a sign of cultural organizing.

52. Read what Robert McCrum, reviewing Wallace's newest collection of creative nonfiction essays, *Consider the Lobster*, says about them: "Footnotes! Wallace was pioneering this territory long before Dave Eggers. He loves nothing better than a vertiginous plunge to the foot of the page. He is the self-appointed president-for-life of the American Subscript Society. To Wallace, a footnote is the equivalent of the concert pianist's cadenza, the moment he can depart from the score and dazzle us with his virtuoso gifts."

53. The concept of literature (and theory) providing "equipment for liv-ing" is found in Hyman's (1964) essay, "Literature as Equipment for Living." Burke's (1959) classic example is: "proverbs (discourse) are strategies for dealing with situations. Insofar as situations are typical and recurrent in a given social structure, people develop names for them and strategies for dealing with them" (p. 103). Proverbs provide descriptions of typical events and the attitude that we ought to adopt in relation to those events.

54. Although not a proverb, Wallace's sense of being inspired by, and reconciled to the idea of power and aggression being rendered vul-nerable through beauty provides us with both a description of a ten-nis event and the attitude we ought to have toward it. By seeing a Federer Moment in this way, we learn how to approach other mo-ments in life, when the seemingly impossible is made possible or when genius is revealed.

55. For an extended discussion of "readerly practices," please see Chapter 6, "The Future of New Ethnographic Writing" in Goodall (2000).

56. Source: http://www.richmond.k12.va.us/readamillion/readingquotes.htm

57. One excellent resource for writers is a clearinghouse of global news, books, and opinion found at Arts and Letters Daily (http://www.aldaily.com/)

Chapter 2

Fingers on the Keyboard ...
Developing Narrative Structures

The question I hear most often from students in my writing classes is: "Where do I begin?"

In response, I have learned to break into song. Usually it's the Andy Williams classic "Where do I begin, to tell the story of how great a love can be. ..." I sound more like a bluesy Johnny Mathis than suave Andy Williams when I sing it, but I also must live with the fact that even on my best vocal days I'll never reach the pinnacle of that pop song performance, which was, of course, by the immortal Shirley Bassey.

I'm not being irreverent. I respect the question. I am, as a writer myself, only too aware of its intimate pragmatism, its various interrogative subtexts (e.g., How do *you* begin? Where do we go for inspiration? Is there a secret?), its essential innocence and optimism. For surely if there is anything to keep us returning to the keyboard, it is the optimism that arrives when we begin a story.

Unless nothing happens. Which happens, too.

But I also recall a character from Albert Camus's novel *The Plague*,[1] a would-be writer named Joseph Grand who never gets past his first sentence—because he is trying so hard to make every word perfect. He knew where to begin, but that is all he knew. Then the plague (a metaphor for terrorism and war) comes to his sleepy town of Oran, and, close to death, it appears that sentence may be all he wrote. Sad, isn't it?[2]

Don't think about it. Instead, be inspired by Anne Lamott's wisdom:

> I know some great writers, writers you love who write beautifully and have made a great deal of money, and not one of them sits down routinely feeling wildly enthusiastic and confident. Not one of them writes elegant first drafts. All right, one of them does, but we do not like her very much. … Very few writers know what they're doing until they've done it.[3] (pp. 21–22)

Lamott goes on to say that one strategy for dealing with the blank page is to stop thinking about the whole of the story and instead to concentrate on smaller blocks of it. I like that advice.

She also advises writers to expect "shitty first drafts." The point is that you should not be dissuaded from writing by a blank page; nor should you try to make your first draft perfect.

So what *should* you do?

The Writing Process: Two Rules and Four Steps

You are not going to let the blank screen intimidate you, right?

Say it. Say: Right.

And you are not going to do a Joseph Grand, are you?

Say it. Say: Of course not.

But what are you going to do? What are you *supposed* to do? What is the secret known only to veteran authors that has thus far escaped you?

The secret is that there is no secret.[4]

Don't be disappointed. Knowing there is no secret should liberate you from the fear that you don't know what the secret *is*. Thus liberated, the next question should be: So what should I do?

You are probably thinking: If it's not a secret, then just tell me.

Okay. First rule of writing: *Write every day*. Writing is a skill before it becomes a craft or an art. As is true with any other skill, it requires regular disciplined practice. As with any other skill set that you want to be good at, you'll get better at it *faster* if you practice it every day. Don't whine that you don't have the time (nobody has the time); don't complain (nobody cares about your "issues"); and *never* make excuses for not writing every day. Like the famous Nike ad succinctly says: *Just Do It*!

Rule of writing, the second: When practicing your skills, *follow a process*. Here, in four easy steps, is exactly what you should do when you write:

1. Place your posterior in the chair, turn on the computer, place your fingers on the keyboard, and begin writing. Keep writing until the initial small unit (see above) is complete. Don't edit it.
2. Go shopping, or watch a movie, read, make love, or go out for dinner. Engage in a lively conversation about the future of the planet. Whatever. Don't look at what you've composed again until tomorrow. Why? Because you are *too close to it*.
3. When tomorrow comes, place your posterior in the chair, turn on the computer, and before you do anything else, read what you wrote the previous day and edit it. Don't dwell too long on any part of it, as you will continue to edit it *from the beginning every day until you are finished*. Read it, edit what you can today, and then move on to the next small new writing unit.
4. Repeat the process until you either (a) are pretty satisfied with it, or (b) reach your deadline. Please note that you will *never be totally satisfied with it*.

Now that you understand the basic writing/editing process, let's examine methods of constructing narrative beginnings.

The Set-Up: Narrative Beginnings

There are many ways to tell a story. For authors of narratives working out of academic contexts, I imagine a continuum of possible narrative structures based on the many accounts I've read and reviewed. At one end is the "pure" narrative, a story told without explicit references to theories or research findings[5]; at the other end is the "pure" academic essay, a research report, or explication of theory without narrative devices. Between these ends of my imagined continuum are ethnographic short stories and fictions,[6] personal (autoethnographic) narratives,[7] autoethnographic poems and performances,[8] layered accounts,[9] layered accounts with poetry,[10] layered accounts with poetry and art,[11] narratives about stories,[12] and essays about narratives.[13]

My focus in this volume is on those forms of writing that range from ethnographic short stories and fictions through varieties of layered accounts. Central to all of these forms is the idea of a "set-up." The set-up can be anything that creates expectations—a gun left on a table, a bit of conversation that gets interrupted, a character that is introduced, an impending storm, a glance that lingers a little too long, a situation that is, as an inverse of Kenneth Burke's famous phrase has it, "a shorthand term for motive."[14] A set-up must then be "paid off" somewhere in the resulting storyline for the story to be satisfying for readers.[15]

For example, W. Benjamin Myers's performance script, "Straight and White: Talking with My Mouth Full"[16] offers a unique set-up in the following passage:

> As a writer, I have a problem with foreshadowing. I do not understand how to make it effective? I am not sure how to use it. What I don't like about foreshadowing is that you have to tow a fine line for it to be considered successful. If I use foreshadowing that is too excessive, it will do its job too well and give away how this story ends. If my foreshadowing is too subtle, it does no good unless you the reader have already heard this story. Subtle foreshadowing only seems to works for people who will bother to hear the story again. Since I doubt that anyone will take the time or put in the effort to hear this all too common story again, I am opting for that excessive fore-shadowing with the intent of giving away the end of this story. This overly successful foreshadowing can free me from attempting to tow a fine line and it frees you from the hard work of figuring out where this story is go-ing. This next line is my foreshadowing: I end up straight and white. If this is your first time hearing this story, I hope that bit of blunt foreshadowing does its job. Now that you (the presumably straight and white reader) know that I end up straight and white like you, you can read my piece knowing that I have sufficiently done my job by letting you know that you need not at any point worry that I will stop being straight and white (much like yourself, presumably).

One reason Myers's opening paragraph works so well is because it begs so many questions on the part of audience members/readers. What does he mean by "I end up straight and white"? Is this a refer-ence to sexual orientation and ethnicity or something else? Ask that question and the set-up is already in place. But that isn't the only one in this passage. What can he possibly mean by his presumption that audience members/readers will themselves be all straight and white, or that he will end up as straight and white as the reader/audience? This confusion heightens the appeal of the intro as well as provides exactly the right level of foreshadowing that he openly worries about in the first sentence. Is his worry itself ironic?[17] The set-up is key to engaging read-ers and audience members.

There are three temporal "places" from which authors of these nar-ratives construct "beginnings" and make use of set-ups. They are:

- entry into the *initial* setting or situation;
- entry into the *middle* of the story (*in medias res*); and
- entry from the *end* of the action (flashback/reverse chronology).

Where do *I* begin? Usually I begin with my entry into the scene that opens the culture I want to explore. Below are two examples of how I accomplish writing those smaller units. The first orients readers to a *setting*; the second orients readers to a political *situation*; both orienting scenes feature a set-up:

From *Living in the Rock n Roll Mystery*[18]:

Willie Moffat's is a Cajun fern bar and restaurant on University Drive, just down the hill from the BMW-and-Buick dealer and across from the chain Italian place that serves soft garlic loafs free at lunchtime and has the audacity to call them breadsticks.

That's okay, nobody complains but me. Everybody else just walks in there with their thirty-dollar haircuts and suited for success, stuff their mouths with faux breadsticks, and don't notice that the food that comes after is genuine pre-pak, and served lukewarm at that. The parking lot glows with money. It's the shine of the times.

Over at Moffat's, where I am, there are fewer cars in the parking lot, less overall shine, but the food and the company is much better. This is the noon hour, and in here the only guy with a thirty-dollar coif is the chef, Black Maxie, which ought to tell you something. Besides, there is a brand-new set of neon on the marquee outside that tells another part of the story:

APPEARING TONITE!

LIVE!

HUNTSVILLE'S HOTTEST ROCK N ROLL BAND!

WHITEDOG

On the way here—just after the weather forecast predicting heavy thunderstorms and lightning to begin later this afternoon—I heard the radio spot on WTAK. It began with a few scorching bars of one of our Led Zeppelin covers, then the announcer's voice cut in: "You've heard about them all over town, now come and hear them, live tonight at Willie Moffat's WHITEDOG!" Then the background music changed to something cooler and the announcer cut back in: "Willie Moffat's is proud to feature WHITEDOG tonight, and if you come early you can hear them perform the new WHITEDOG hit "I'm Gonna Run to You." Mike Fairbanks's sweet vocal track lifted out of Drew Thompson's lead ride with the song's beginning words: "Do you remember, the times we shared. ..." Then the announcer came back in with the tag, "Be there for live WHITEDOG tonight at Willie Moffat's."

Not bad, not bad at all. I'd go. I'd pay to go.

Then it hit me. This has been happening a lot lately and I'm not sure I like it. I'm driving along and hear something about WHITEDOG on the radio and I start tapping my hand, maybe singing, liking very much what I hear, and then BAM! It slams into me, just like that, that what I am liking is me.

I'm in WHITEDOG. That's my rhythm guitar on the radio.

It's like some kind of queer amnesia. It's like looking at an old photograph and suddenly realizing that the guy in the middle with the chicken and the grin is you. No, actually it's more dramatic than that. It's experiencing yourself as the other, an estranged version of seeing yourself as others see you, and then, just when you are feeling it, the whole social construction collapses, and when the dust clears that one magical window on the self disappears.

I am back inside myself, in the singular I of multiple me's, turning off of University Drive, pulling into the parking lot at Willie Moffat's, preparing myself to prepare for tonight, something I could not have ever prepared myself for, as it turns out.

Once out of the car I am feeling like just a regular guy in ordinary blue jeans standing next to his car, in this case a white Mustang GT, feeling the hint of fun and madness that is everywhere at this moment in the air. Maybe it's the weather, the news of the impending storm against which is the here and now of this breezy but otherwise perfect day.

I don't know what it is. I just know something is.

Something. There is something in the air, something heavy on the way here. Something I'll have to deal with out there near the horizon, sweeping up from the south and west, moving this way fast.

Maybe a tornado.

I take a deep breath, inhale the close surround of life. In the middle of it I smell the garlic from the chain place across the street. Garlic is an alluring scent, its pungent sweetness belying the ugly undercurrent of its nature, almost human when looked at this way, the bulb of it like a world unto itself and it's clove looking all too much like an exploded heart (pp. 227–229).

From *Divine Signs: Connecting Spirit to Community*[19]:

Take South Carolina #15 exit off I-85 heading up from Atlanta at the legal speed limit, pause at the stop sign at the end of the exit ramp, and—if you are prone to consider the meaning of such things—you see that you are now at a complex intersection of American culture. This place—this intersection—displays local histories, regional politics, and deep, danger-ous—ultimately spiritual—conflicts. What are these stories? What is this place all about?

Intersections, like political elections, force you to look left and right, to make choices based almost entirely on what you imagine you see in the light of what you believe. To the right, toward Anderson, are familiar signs of God-fearing, gun-toting interstate existence. Here are the popular corporate icons to fast self-service gas to which are now attached square two-color convenience stores specializing in the open sale of sugar-coat-ed, high-calorie nothings displayed seductively in brightly colored plastic wrap; cold no-deposit, no-return soft drinks and primary American beers in cans; multiple extra-strength pain relievers, caffeine tablets, and gas alleviators; NASCAR models, caps, and memorabilia, Confederate flag T-shirts and pro-gun, anti-Clinton, kiss-my-ass bumper stickers; and public displays of criminal nicotine sold here at discount prices. Next door are the blessedly close reassurances of personal decay; faster, greasier, deadlier foods—friend antibiotic cow slathered with melted fat on bleached bread—slopped with special sauces or dressings, topped with chemically treated vegetables, served in cartoon-coordinated paper cups and bags. These are sources only of instant gut gratification for obvious needs that fast gratifying and plastic never fully satisfies, but that interstate travel or just the everyday velocity of life induces. And yessir, there are the never-clean locked restrooms "For Customers Only" sweetly stinking in the rear, and a quarters-only pay phone stripped of local directories that has long served as a public astray and vomitorium outside by the loud highway, down at the inconvenient but legal edge of the property, where hearing and safety is severely, maybe purposefully impaired.

To the left—toward Clemson—is an authentic, perfect white southern mansion fronted by a small private pond and surrounded by a highly ornate iron fence and naturally intoxicating magnolia and oak trees. You can use it to momentarily imagine a gone world that probably never was, fill in the imaginary blanks with movie scenes and heavily accented dialogue, just as you always have. Across the highway from this white elegant elephant are two competing gas station/convenience stores, a new Wendy's, and behind them an unnecessarily long, somewhat ironic, curving drive up a man-made hill that leads not to another perfect white mansion but to an Outback Steakhouse, a Cracker Barrel restaurant/mini Southern country theme park, and an overnight inn of interstate proportions.

You have been here, we all have. If not this road, then some other one. If not this dream, then one you imagine as purely your own.

On the highway now—a four-lane blacktop upon which are painted huge orange tiger paws—continuous, fast, competitive traffic from else-where seems always to be going somewhere and doesn't pause at all for this admirable, astonishing view, as if this conflicted place, this intersection and all it suggests, only exists if you want it to.

You want it to. (pp. 27–28)

Before I move into criteria useful for evaluating a beginning, allow me this brief philosophical reflection: Beginnings are a matter of choice. You, as the author, have to decide when something "began." For some stories, there are natural beginnings (where and when two people met; where and how the narrator pulled into town; etc.); for others, beginnings must be crafted out of the whole of the experience and a call must be made about where the story started, even if at the time of the experiencing, there was no "story" yet and things didn't necessarily seem that way.

For example, performance artist Scott Gust provides the following "beginning" for his powerful account of cyber-grieving, one that explicitly acknowledges the problematic of where a story actually begins[20]:

> In three more weeks I will know the answer, or maybe not. The answer may come or not come, but there is nothing I can do either way. In fact, there is every possibility that I have not even properly identified the question. Lately, it seems like it is harder to ask questions than it is to give answers. In three more weeks, he will have been dead for one year. In three more weeks I will find out whether or not his gay dot com profile will remain in cyberspace even if no one has signed in under that user name for more than one year.
>
> One way or another, in three more weeks I will have to start figuring out how and why it came to be that I would be a person who would make an electronic webpage, a cyber personal ad, the place I would go to mourn and heal. How did I get to be like this? Where and when did my personal life become so entangled in digital webs? This is a story that seems to have many beginnings, but most recently it began on New Year's Eve. As I turn my critical gaze to the threads of experience that wrap my fingers like a cats-cradle, I wonder how I can write and theorize these narratives without pathologizing myself into some kind of pathetic, computer-dependent loser. Furthermore, I wonder why I care.[21]

As Gust rightly acknowledges, stories often have multiple beginnings, and one task for an author is to select from among them the beginning that best fits the narrative she or he wants to write. In Gust's case, this selected beginning also allows him to return to this theme at the end of his performance (I'll return to it at the end of this chapter), thus wrapping the narrative in a circular pattern that further reflects the continuing and circular nature of his remembrance.

What should a "beginning" accomplish? Beginnings work well when they *bring the reader into the head of the writer, into the tone and feeling of the story, into the uniqueness of the setting or context,*[22] and—this is key—*when they create a sense of mystery or end on a question.* A beginning, regardless of point of entry, should also *set up the theme* of the piece, and its *language* should serve as a vehicle for that theme, moving from the individual words to larger ideas.

An entry story to begin the story is also a small unit of writing that can be accomplished in a (relatively) short period of time. Here is another example of the same technique, this time from Duncan Murrell, a fine creative nonfiction writer and editor. Note how, in this beginning, he meets all of the criteria above:

> I came to town in the bristling dark of a hundred highway signs ruined and powerless. The wind had twisted their posts until they bent over as if genuflecting. I wasn't use to it being so dark along I-10, the flat four-laner from Mobile through Mississippi to New Orleans. In the daylight it was green and deep and thick and mysterious, but also beautiful. Now it was just wild. I knew what was out there, the humps of canebrakes, the miles of lowland and bayou, the acres of grass and hillocks of pine. No mercy. I punched the station wagon up to eighty and hit Elysian Fields Boulevard at around ten P.M.
>
> There was some light in the city at least. A few stoplights worked, and few houses along Elysian Fields had light. The rest were empty that first week of January 2006. Down by the river there was plenty of light, and it was easy to pick out my turn onto North Rampart, a left past The Phoenix, where the hustlers and the leather boys and the bears were already out, and down almost all the way to the tracks, to the old shotgun where I'd decided to live. There weren't many people around, but I knew where I could get a drink just as soon as I got the car unloaded. I got on the gas a little too much.
>
> In the street a woman stood watching my headlights run up on her. She had light eyes and skin that could have been black or white. She'd pulled her hair back and tucked it under a fedora. She was carrying an old seabag, and after I'd slammed the brakes we made eye contact. She was tall and stood only slightly stooped. God knows how old she was. I couldn't tell. But I thought she looked like she wanted to tell me something, which normally I wouldn't have thought, but this was New Orleans, where the women were wise and keen and walked the streets bearing their lives in sacks, always ready with an introduction to the beyond. So I waited, wondering what she would say and whether she intended to get out of the street. She mouthed these words:
>
> "Why don't you slow the fuck down, bitch?" Then she continued on down St. Roch. When I passed through the intersection, I thought about

stopping to talk to her. Surely that wasn't all she had to say. But I also wanted to get to my house and get my drink at Smitty's, and so I resolved to go find her some other day. I had time to get the story. I knew what that story would be. Chaos would resolve itself through conflict into redemption and inspiration, the people of New Orleans would endure their trials, their resilience would be known in their success. I would find that place full of tough and contrary people in love with their city, headsuckers and rosary prayers and maskers all. Such a place, never overcome in three hundred years of disease and high water, would only—could only—make good. This had always been the story. I would simply observe, and in the end I would walk away happy, my story in hand. Resilience in their success. It would be easy to see.

I talked to the woman with the bag many times after that. Month after month I ran across her walking here and there, all over the city. I think she lived everywhere. She told me her stories, she bitched at me, she hit me up for money. She was drunk one day and in church the next. I saw her shouting at the mayor once. After many months in the ruined city, she heard my confession. Now I wish I had never gone to New Orleans. I had no business there. I have nothing but penance to do now. (pp. 35–36.)[23]

Before we move on to middles and endings, I want to discuss one form of narrative structure that is popular in academic forays into narratives: the "layered account."[24] This style of writing is particularly well suited as a way of introducing personal narratives into academic journals with an explicit articulation of the connections among personal experience, theory, and research practices.

These accounts either begin with a narrative vignette (set-up), or they begin with a theoretical introduction to a research issue or question followed by a narrative vignette. From either set-up, the pay-off moves back and forth between narratives and reflections on those narratives or their content.

Since its introduction, many academic authors have used the layered account to explore a wide variety of topics. You will recall that earlier I made use of Sarah Tracy's work on correctional officers and emotional labor, which is also a layered account.

In the following two examples, I juxtapose an academic layered account about identity/relationship with a narrative account about identity/relationship generated for the mass market. Notice the use of a set-up in both cases as well as the language resources brought into frame and to create interest in the accounts.

> My mom always told me that I'd either be gay or that I'd marry a Black woman. From 16 on, I heard this every time I found myself in a duel with my father, every time I informed her of my hatred toward that man, every time I wished him dead.
>
> My mom always told me that I'd either be gay or that I'd marry a Black woman. Not that I had articulated my desire for one or the other, but rather she knew of my father's two main fears—having a fag in the family or a cross-raced relationship. And she realized I'd do everything in my power to spite him.
>
> My mom always told me that I'd either be gay or that or that I'd marry a Black woman, a statement that became actualized when I "came out" to her at 22. Her response: "I told you so."
>
> I'm often asked how long I've known that I have been gay. Well, that depends. I've known that I've been attracted toward men since an early age, but I didn't know that I fit into the category of gay until the latter part of my teens. And although I do not believe that my gayness was ever a choice, this framing by my mother and my constant desire to spite my father make it appear as such. My story's not just about being gay, though. It's a story about the troubling relationship that separates my father from me and me from him. It's a story of sexuality and sport, of gayness and hegemonic masculinity, of a fag and his golf clubs. It's a story of love and hate.

****

Frank (1995) encourages us to live with stories, to engage them emotionally and viscerally rather than to just think about them. This idea guides my project. However, in the spirit of Krippendorff (1995), I wish to re-language Frank's notion. I seek to find what the opposite side of the coin looks and feels like: living with theory. I argue that such a move may further collapse the theory-story binary that haunts the halls of many university settings.

For example, my life feels like the tension between showing and telling: I live through moments of my past that appear without emotional engagement and dialogue; I also live with moments loaded with feeling and conversation. Furthermore, I experience my connection to my dad via a relational paradigm (Bochner, 2004; Yerby, 1995). I am a victim; so is my father. I am an oppressor; so is he. We victimize and oppress together, simultaneously hurting and being hurt while never deciding to quit. We're both seeking love. Maybe we're both in love. Somehow.

****

Characters

Father: "middle-age man who wants to say, 'Son, come here.'"
Son: "mid-twenties man who wants to say, 'Father, why?'"
Son: mid-twenties man who wants to say, "Father, come here."
Father: middle-age man who wants to say, "Son, why?"
Mothers, sisters, aunts, grandparents, friends: "various ages, who constantly say, 'I don't know what to say'" (Pelias, 2002, p. 37).

Extras

Hegemonic masculinity: culturally dominant, stylized sets of repeated acts (Butler, 1990); a condition never physically or psychically actualized (Butler, 1999); the "ephemeral, contextual, and complicated" nuances of being a man (Hopkins, 1998, p. 54); a never-ending journey toward ever-changing ideals (Gelber, 1997).

Homophobia: The "hatred or fear of homosexuals" (Oxford American, 2001, p. 387); a socially produced, insidious force that infiltrates the most mundane of affairs; an embodied insecurity that waits for the most opportune moments to strike; often affiliated with hegemonic masculinity.

Love: A feeling that transcends all categories; reciprocal; an action that puts both hegemonic masculinity and homophobia to shame; shared; an emotion that binds regardless of circumstance; mutual; a social construct (Jaggar, 1989).[25]

The above example highlights the features of a layered account written for an academic audience: the use of a narrative beginning told in reverse chronology/flashback style; the "break" in the storyline marked by **** to indicate a transition; the inclusion of academic theory that invites knowing readers to share in the interpretation of the account; and the use of dramatic *personae* complete with culturally loaded terms as extras—all of which will play important roles in the evolution of the story.

The hook is contained in the performative first line: "My mom always told me that I'd either be gay or that I'd marry a Black woman." The author repeats the line performance three times in the opening scene, and only in the third usage—the one about choice—does he verbally/visually italicize the "or" in it. The end of the initial scene conveys a sense of mystery and questions about how the author will work out the terms of something he calls a "troubled love story" with terms such as "sexuality and sport … gayness and hegemonic masculinity … a fag and his golf clubs."

Kayla Williams's "Prologue" to her creative nonfiction debut, *Love My Rifle More than You: Young and Female in the U. S. Army*, offers a similar set-up (reverse chronological/flashback beginning), without the academic trimmings. It is not a layered account in the strict sense of the term, but the book is a layering of action with reflection done in a personal narrative. Here is how it begins:

Sometimes, even now, I wake up before dawn and forget I am not a slut. The air is not quite dark, not quite light, and I lie absolutely still, trying to will myself to remember that that is not what I am. Sometimes, on better mornings, it comes to me right away. And then there are all those other times.
Slut.
The only other choice is bitch. If you're a woman and a soldier, those are the choices you get.
I'm twenty-eight years old. Military intelligence, five years, here and in Iraq. One of the 15 percent of the U. S. military that's female. And that whole 15 percent trying to get past an old joke. "What's the difference between a bitch and a slut? A slut will fuck anyone, a bitch will fuck anyone but you." So if she's nice or friendly, outgoing or chatty—she's a slut. If she's distant or reserved or professional—she's a bitch.
A woman soldier has to toughen herself up. Not just for the enemy, for battle, or for death. I mean toughen herself to spend months awash in a sea of nervy, hyped-up guys who, when they're not thinking about getting killed, are thinking about getting laid. Their eyes on you all the time, your breasts, your ass—like there is nothing else to watch, no sun, no river, no desert, no mortars at night.
Still, it's more complicated than that. Because at the same time you soften yourself up. Their eyes, their hunger: yes, it's shaming—but they also make you special. I don't like to say it—it cuts you inside—but the attention, the admiration, the need: they make you powerful. If you're a woman in the Army, it doesn't matter so much about your looks. What counts is that you are female.
Wartime makes it worse. There's the killing on the streets, the bombs at the checkpoints—and the combat in the tents. Some women sleep around: lots of sex with lots of guys, in sleeping bags, in trucks, in sand, in America, in Iraq. Some women hold themselves back; they avoid sex like it's some weapon of mass destruction. I know about both.
And I know about something else. How these same guys you want to piss on become your guys. Another girl enters your tent, and they look at her the way they looked at you, and what drove you crazy with anger suddenly drives you crazy with jealousy. They're yours. Fuck, you left your husband to be with them, you walked out on him for them. These guys, they're your husband, they're your father, your brother, you lover—your life. ...
I don't forget. I can't forget any of it. From basic training all the way to Iraq and back home again.[26]

71

Williams's beginning narrative gets our attention with the initial tension created by the "choice" of being a bitch or a slut. The joke is the set-up on two levels. First, it sets up the masculine framing of army life with a young, attractive female in the line of fire as the object of everyman's gaze. But the joke also complicates that masculine framing by adding her overt complicity in it, her admission of desire in a war zone, and her competitiveness against other women who interfere with her anger at the gaze and her need to satisfy herself.

As in Adams's story of the love/hate relationship with his father, Williams, too, tells us a troubled love story in her relationship to the U.S. Army and its men and women, and once again hegemonic masculinity, homophobia, and love play their parts as "extras." Unlike Adams, Williams doesn't bring in academic resources to make her case or to help readers share an interpretation based on specialized knowledge. Yet I am still able to read her account with those resources because I'm an academic and know something about the cultural theories that are constituted within that discursive space.

This last point is important because in the present era, *it is a mistake for any author to assume that intelligent lay readers are not similarly equipped with theoretical resources*. Although there is no doubt that academic journals typically expect most work they publish to contribute to the scholarly conversation in overt ways, it is also true that writers of ethnographic short stories, fictions, poems, autoethnographies, and performance scripts make those contributions in ways that take full advantage of what they assume readers *already know*. In Adams's case, simply referencing work by Judith Butler (without detailed discussions of them) plays to the academic audience he intends to reach with this story: If you are a fan of stories about gendered identities, you probably read Butler. You are familiar enough to understand what Adams is reflecting about her work in those definitions.

Similarly, a lot of readers of trade nonfiction have university educations and advanced degrees. They read widely and deeply. If they are interested in reading stories about gendered identities, they bring that interest and that background with them to the reading experience. My guess is that although Kayla Williams doesn't reference Judith Butler in her book, many of her readers are familiar enough with her work to do it anyway.

My last point about beginnings, and in particular about layered accounts, is based on a question you are probably asking: Why did I use Kayla Williams's account? It isn't a layered account, is it?

72

The answer is that her book (more so than the Prologue to it) provides a different way of thinking about layered accounts. Instead of moving from vignette to reflection and back again, Williams moves from action/event to reflection and back again. So the account is, in fact, "layered," just not in the typical academic style.

For those of you seeking trade markets, her book provides an example of how to take what you know about academic layered accounts and apply them to narratives intended for the mass market. The structure remains much the same; the difference is in the content of the reflective passages. And even as I say that, I know there are other writers of fiction and nonfiction who do make use of academic/research resources to enrich their layers.[27]

Regardless of the method you select to begin your narrative, you are essentially providing readers with good reasons to continue reading your story. You are offering narrative and rhetorical inducements to convince them to exchange their precious time for the pleasure of your company and conversation. Before moving on to narrative "middles," however, I want to offer one creative example of an *anti-inducement* that works as a beginning precisely because it provides readers with good reasons *not* to read most of the book:

RULES AND SUGGESTIONS
FOR THE ENJOYMENT OF THIS BOOK:

1. There is no overwhelming need to read the preface. Really. It exists mostly for the author, and those who, after finishing the rest of the book, have for some reason found themselves stuck with nothing else to read. If you have already read the preface and wish you had not, we apologize. We should have told you sooner.

2. There is also no overarching need to read the acknowledgments section. Many early readers of this book (see p. xxxix) suggested its curtailment or removal, but they were defied. Still, it is not necessary to the plot in any major way, so as with the preface, if you have already read the acknowledgments section, and wish you had not, again, we apologize. We should have said something.

3. You can also skip the table of contents, if you're short of time.

4. Actually, many of you might want to skip much of the middle, namely pages 209–301, which concern the lives of people in their early twenties,

and those lives are very difficult to make interesting, even when they seemed interesting to those living them at the time.

5. As a matter of fact, the first three or four chapters are all some of you might want to bother with. That gets you to page 109 or so, which is a nice length, a nice novella sort of length. Those first four chapters stick to one general subject, something manageable, which is more than what can be said for the book thereafter.

6. The book thereafter is kind of uneven.[28]

Bold move, wouldn't you say? But my guess is that it makes you want to read on. If you turn the page you encounter the Preface (which Eggers advises you not to read), where the first line announces that although this book is nonfiction, he made a lot of it up. Eggers then offers a reader's guide to his writerly choices about reconstructed dialogue, name changes for characters, switches of location, omissions, and some excerpts from the body of the book that he feels need to be clarified or elaborated. Of course, if you haven't read the book, much of what is written will make no sense, but then he advised you to skip it anyway, right?

And so on. There is not a page of the Preface, Table of Contents, or Acknowledgments that doesn't receive Eggers' creative, self-reflexive treatment. So, by the time a reader reaches the first page of the actual first chapter (on p. 40), she or he has already accumulated a lot of information about a lot of seemingly disconnected things that will only be connected through a thorough reading of the rest of the book. And that is the whole point. It is a bold, risky, and inventive beginning via anti-inducements to read on.

I end this section with Eggers in part because his beginning turns the usual advice upside-down and yet still manages to be a perfect set-up for his story, and in part because he disses the middle of his own book (#4). Personally, I think he is right (those pages are not his best, and mostly for the reason he gives), but I also believe that writing middles is hard work for all of us. Let's see why.

Middles

The second most-often-asked question in my writing classes is "How do you know what to do in the middle of a narrative?"

Of course, I break into song. This time it's Paul Simon's "50 Ways to Leave Your Lover," a classic piece of folk rock with a whole bunch of possible ways to resolve the basic impulse to flee a failed relationship and obtain your stated goal: "Just get yourself free." And once again, the lyrics to the song answer the question metaphorically, although the number 50 is entirely arbitrary.

Let's just say there are many ways to develop middles.

Let's begin with some parameters. First, middles are all about *plots*. A "middle" is where the action (and reflection) occurs. But it doesn't occur magically (except at Hogwarts); it occurs by *design*. And design is all about organizing structures. Although there has been some debate about the number and kind of organizing structures that exist for stories (somewhere between 1 and 69),[29] I find that four basic structures work best:

1. pure chronological progression
2. modified chronological progression
3. convergence narrative
4. nonlinear fragment narrative messy texts

Pure Chronological Progression

Chronology is probably the most favored style of nonfiction storytelling, probably because it allows the writer to show a step-by-step, scene-by-scene progression from the initial conflict to its resolution. It explains what happened to you (or your narrator or character), or because of you (or your narrator or character), in a linear sequence of events that fairly represents how you (or your narrator of character) experienced it.[30]

Think of it this way: In its most deconstructed form, the chronological progression is the account pattern we use when we give directions or provide instructions. I use this comparison because to develop a good chronology—like giving good directions or instructions—means thinking about your story from the *reader's point of view*: what must a reader see and understand is going on to connect the same dots you connected in the original experience? Thinking this way allows you to make choices about what to include that is essential to what later happened and to eliminate a lot of unnecessary extra-narrative clutter (unless you are aspiring to be like Dave Eggers, in which case the extra-narrative clutter is inherently part of your storytelling style).

The pure chronological progression is a good narrative choice if you have done a superior job with the framing and set-up. This is because by the time you reach the middle of the story most of the elements that you need to complete the account are already in place: the main characters, the context or setting, the conflict, the theme, and—with careful attention to language—the mood or attitude of the piece.

So how do you do it? I've used three methods:

- just write out what happened in the order it occurred, warts and all (then edit to remove warts and all);
- conceive of the progression as a math problem (what must be added, subtracted, multiplied, and divided to get the end sum); and
- develop a narrative storyboard to visual the events.

In more detail:

The "write what happened in the order it occurred, warts and all" method is typically my favorite method. In part this is because I am a compulsive field noter/diarist, so I usually have a fairly accurate representation of the events in my life stored in various files on my computer. I never know when the events need to be recalled for a story, so I keep files of my experiences and they are naturally organized in a linear fashion because I write them from day to day. When I create a narrative, I begin by using the Microsoft Word © "cut and paste" method, pulling material from several files together into a larger whole, then filling in additional reflexive passages that serve as transitions between the main events or scenes. I am also a compulsive editor of my own work, so I follow my own advice (given earlier) and begin each day's writing experiment by editing what I cut-and-pasted/wrote/edited the day before.[31]

A second method I have occasionally employed (either alone or in conjunction with the other three methods) is to think of the middle as a math problem. I know what the answer is, so I have to figure out how to get it, given the numbers and formulas I have already put into motion. Using this scenario, you may add or subtract characters and locations; add complications for the characters as well as knowledge about all kinds of things; subtract what you falsely believed as a result of the introduction of new characters and knowledge; multiply the complexities from what seemed so simple a thing at the beginning but has turned into a more complicated issue as a result of what you are learning along the way; and/or divide the larger story into smaller, more manageable units, resolving each of them until the final resolution is attained.[32]

This is an admittedly fanciful way to work, but sometimes seeing the story as a sum of all things considered means paying close attention to the *proof* of that sum. Asking what would the story look like as a math proof can be a delightful thought experiment as well as a way to make sure that what you think happened to cause this and that in the original experience actually *does* cause this and that in the narrative representation of it.

A third way to think about a chronological plotline is through the *events that have to occur* to construct a narrative bridge between the beginning and ending of the story. To enable this sort of progressive scene thinking, I recommend developing a *storyboard*.[33] Storyboards are widely used in the film, animation, gaming, software development, and commercial advertising industries to visually represent a script through key scenes. For writers, however, the concept of a storyboard serves as an analog to a narrative adaptation of it for the visual representation of a story. You won't yet have a script to translate into visual language, so instead think of the storyboard as a tool to help you *imagine the scenes* that move your story from beginning to ending.

Below (Figure 2.1) is an example of how I used a storyboard to develop photographs taken at the Ferrari event into a storyline that became the organizing device for the chronology used in the finished piece.[34]

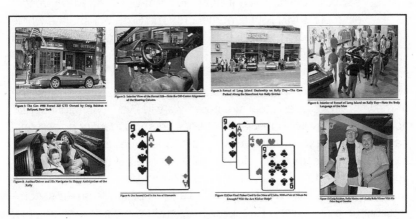

Fig 2.1   Storyboard for Ferrari Culture

Modified Chronological Progression

An alternative to a chronology is a modification of the purely linear sequence based on what will happen at the end of the story: a sudden *twist or reverse* of what readers expect to see happen. Agatha Christie is one mystery author closely associated with the development of plots leading to a surprise ending (e.g., *Who Killed Roger Ackroyd*), and Alfred

Hitchcock is the director associated with adapting the device for the big screen (e.g., *North by Northwest*). Since the mid-20th century, the plot structure has been featured in every genre.

There are two key elements to the narrative development of middles that lead to surprising endings:

- The *plot must be reliable on two levels*—the "normal" chronological progression of events that leads the reader to think that nothing unusual is likely to happen *and* the progression that will lead to the surprise ending; the sole exception to this rule is if the surprise ending turns out to be that the *narrator is unreliable*—in other words, the narrator has not been telling the truth all along. This element is the plotline is key for many stories about "deep cover" police investigators, secret agents, and ethnographers who disguise their status by pretending to be about business other than what they are really interested in.[35]

- *All of the clues for the surprise ending must be carefully placed into the story* so that when the surprise occurs, readers will say "Of course! I see it now." For film buffs, one fairly recent example is M. Night Shyamalan's "The Sixth Sense" (the whole plot and surprise ending is summed in one memorable line: "I see dead people").

I have often thought that although the genesis and widespread use of modified chronological progression is in films and novels, the framework provides an ideal structure for a wide variety of stories, particularly those involving *revelations about personal identity or personal narratives that feature a surprising death*. One excellent example is Julia Scheeres's *Jesus Land*, an incredible story about a white sixteen-year-old girl and her adopted sixteen-year-old black brother who are removed from their Midwestern roots to a religious fundamentalist community in the Dominican Republic. They endure a disciplinary regime, a detached missionary mother and violent father, and because of their love for each other, find their way through this nightmare and back into the world. Just when you reach a point in your reading when you think the conflict is finally resolved and there is a future for them, a sudden and seemingly senseless tragedy befalls one of them.[36]

Convergence Narrative

Erik Larson's best-selling book, *The Devil in the White City: Murder, Magic, and Madness at the Fair that Changed America* (2004) is an excellent example of a convergence narrative. Rich in historical details and archival research, Larson combines two seemingly opposite and simultaneously occurring stories into one powerful account of Chicago's 1893 World's Fair.

One story is of the brilliant architect of "the white city," Daniel H. Burnham, and the singular feat of creating a spectacular stage to showcase Chicago and the United States as the equal (if not the superior) of any capital and any world's exposition anywhere in Europe. Part of the narrative thread from Burham's story is woven through a supporting cast that forever changed American culture: Elias Disney, a designer of "the white city" and father of Walt, who may have used the stories of that place as inspiration for his own kingdom; Buffalo Bill, who earned in today's money the equivalent of $30 million from the fair; Frank Lloyd Wright, John Olmsted, and Elihu Root, all instrumental in the creation of "the white city"; and George Ferris, the inventor of the Ferris wheel (the featured attraction), who also made a small fortune from the fair but at a high personal cost.

The counter-narrative, named "the black city," focuses on one Dr. H. H. Holmes, an urban serial killer who came to Chicago for the purpose of taking advantage of that same stage setting, in his case, because it lured many single young women to the city. He was not the only purveyor of harm in this city, or within this story. Some were cutthroats, some thieves, and some suffered from varieties of mental illness. There is a murder toward the end of the account that is the result of madness, and the murderer is defended by the legendary lawyer, Clarence Darrow. All of these micro-narratives serve to counter the micro-narratives of the supporting cast of "the white city." In play, then, are large and small characters alive and about their business in the same place and time, a complexity of juxtaposed accounts that build a robust and thrilling storyline. It is a middle that readers do not soon forget.

It begins like this:

How easy it was to disappear:
    A thousand trains a day entered or left Chicago. Many of these trains brought single young women who had never even seen a city but now hoped to make one of the biggest and toughest their home. Jane Addams, the urban reformer who founded Chicago's Hull House, wrote,

"Never before in civilization have such numbers of young girls been sud-denly released from the protection of the home and permitted to walk un-attended upon the city streets and to work under alien roofs." The women sought work as typewriters, stenographers, seamstresses, and weavers. The men who hired them were for the most part moral citizens intent on efficiency and profit. But not always. On March 30, 1890, an officer of the First National Bank placed a warning in the help-wanted section of the Chicago Tribune, to inform female stenographers of "our growing conven-tion that no thoroughly honorable business-man who is this side of dotage ever advertises for a lady stenographer who is a blonde, is good-looking, is quite alone in the city, or will transmit her photograph. All such advertise-ments upon their face bear the marks of vulgarity, nor do we regard it safe for any lady to answer such unseemly utterances."

The women walked to work on streets that angled past bars, gam-bling houses, and bordellos. Vice thrived, with official indulgence. "The parlors and bedrooms in which honest folk lived were (as now) rather dull places," wrote Ben Hecht, late in his life, trying to explain this persistent trait of old Chicago. "It was pleasant, in a way, to know that outside their windows, the devil was still capering in a flare of brimstone." In an analogy that would prove all too apt, Max Weber likened the city to "a human being with his skin removed." (p. 11)[37]

Note the extensive use of quotations drawn from primary sources. The research is impeccable, and Larson's ability to find exactly the right passage for his purposes is truly remarkable. I am also struck by how contemporary he makes this "old" story by pressing readers to make comparisons between then and now: young women come to the big city to make their fortunes, mostly in the employ of good people, *but not always*. The use of want ads to troll for liaisons both moral and un-toward. The side-by-side interplay of vice and virtue. And somewhere, amid the sheer velocity of everyday life, there exists a "devil," a serial killer who does, in fact, remove women's skin.

We are then introduced to Burnham, only a name cited in a long preamble that brings readers up to speed on the enormity and purpose of the task of creating a world's fair in Chicago:

Even Burnham could not say for sure who had been first to propose the idea. It had seemed to rise in many minds at once, the initial intent simply to celebrate the four hundredth anniversary of Columbus's discovery of the New World by hosting a world's fair. At first the idea gained little momen-tum. Consumed by the great drive toward wealth and power that had be-gun after the end of the Civil War, America seemed to have scant interest in celebrating its distant past. In 1889, however, the French did something that startled everyone.

In Paris on the Champ de Mars, France opened the Exposition Universelle, a world's fair so big and glamorous and so exotic that visitors came away believing no exposition could surpass it. At the heart of the exposition stood a tower of iron that rose one thousand feet into the sky, higher by far than any man-made structure on earth. The tower not only assured the eternal fame of its designer, Alexandre Gustave Eiffel, but also offered graphic proof that France had edged out the United States for dominance in the realm of iron and steel, despite the Brooklyn Bridge, the Horseshoe Curve, and other undeniable accomplishments of American engineers. ...

At first, most Americans believed that if an exposition honoring the deepest roots of the nation were to be held anywhere, the site should be Washington, the capital. Initially even Chicago's editors agreed. As the notion of an exposition gained shape, however, other cities began to see it as a prize to be coveted, mainly for the stature it would confer, stature being a powerful lure in this age when pride of place ranked second only to pride of blood. Suddenly New York and St. Louis wanted the fair. Washington laid claim to the honor on grounds it was the center of government, New York because it was the center of everything. No one cared what St. Louis thought, although the city got a wink for pluck. (pp. 14–16)

Some pages later we learn that it required an act of Congress, but Chicago was ultimately selected. In the interim, we are informed of Burnham's history and his personal rise to prominence. Throughout this narrative, we are gently reminded of the presence of the macabre:

One telegraph boy (upon hearing Congress's decision) made his way through the dark to an unlit alley that smelled of rotten fruit and was silent save for the receding hiss of gaslights on the street he had left behind. He found a door, knocked, and entered a room full of men, some young, some old, all seeming to speak at once, a few quite drunk. A coffin at the center of the room served as a bar. The light was dim and came from gas jets hidden behind skulls mounted on the walls. Other skulls lay scattered about the room. A hangman's noose dangled from the wall, as did assorted weapons and a blanket caked with blood.

These artifacts marked the room as headquarters of the Whitechapel Club, named for the London slum in which two years earlier Jack the Ripper had done his killing. (p. 31)

The back-and-forth juxtaposition of Burnham's "white city" and the darkness that grew up alongside it set up a narrative framework that leads to an eventual convergence. As the white city is built and then opens to widespread acclaim, Dr. Holmes quickens his recruitment of victims and polishes his deadly skills. His triumph of unleashing evil in the city was an unqualified success.

And so it began. A waitress disappeared from Holmes's restaurant, where his guests ate their meals. One day she was at work, the next gone, with no clear explanation for her abrupt departure. Holmes seemed as stumped as anyone. A stenographer named Jennie Thompson disappeared, as did a woman named Evelyn Stewart, who either worked for Holmes or merely stayed in his hotel as a guest. A male physician who for a time had rented an office in the castle and who had befriended Holmes—they were seen together often—also had decamped, with no word to anyone. (p. 246)

Burnham's fair was also an unqualified success. The goal had been to be more spectacular and more popular than the Paris fair of 1889:

The true climax occurred after the grounds were closed, however. In the silence, with the air still scented with exploded gunpowder, collectors accompanied by armed guards went to each ticket booth and collected the accumulated silver, three tons of it. They counted the money under heavy guard. By one forty-five A.M., they had an exact total.

... In that single day 713,646 people had paid to enter Jackson Park. (Only 31,059—four percent—were children.) Another 37,380 visitors had entered using passes, bringing the total admission for the day to 751,026, more people than had attended any single day of any peaceable event in history. The Tribune argued that the only greater gather was the massing of Xerxes' army of over five million souls in the fifth century B.C. The Paris record of 397,000 had indeed been shattered. ...

Now Burnham and Millet made final arrangements for Burnham's own great day, the grand closing ceremony of October 30 that would recognize once and for all that Burnham really had done it and that his work was now complete—that for once there was nothing left to do. At this point, Burnham believed, nothing could tarnish the fair's triumph or his own place in architectural history.

Of course the "nothing" in that last line makes it almost inevitable that something would occur to do exactly that, much as Holmes's parallel success as an unprecedented serial murderer would lead—ironically—not to questions about his criminal behavior but instead about his finances. So, as the "white city" is closed and then dismantled, so, too, are all of the characters followed to their own unusual ends.

I use this example of a convergence narrative because the middle does so many things so well. It provides a parallel trajectory between the two major characters that is augmented with smaller stories of supporting characters all of which contribute to the eventual thematic convergence of good and evil. Historical research is not only extensive, but is integral to the rhetorical interest built in all aspects of the unfolding narrative. Research is drawn from a variety of sources: newspapers, memoirs, letters, and scholarly studies, but the research is woven into the account *seamlessly*. Facts and figures don't stand out so much as blend in naturally. We are presented with characters who mirror the complexities of our world, and of our concerns.[38]

Non-Linear Fragments Narratives: Messy Texts

My accidental introduction to this style of writing occurred when I read Jean Baudrillard's 200-page account of the United States, called, simply (and deceptively), *America*.[39] I had just moved to Salt Lake City, Utah, and was taken by his application of the ancient concept of the *simulacrum* to American cities, such as Salt Lake City, and to theme parks, such as Disney World, wherein they are transformed into "hyper-realities" ("the simulation of something which never really existed"). Here is an excerpt:

SALT LAKE CITY

Pompous Mormon symmetry. Everywhere marble: flawless, funereal (the Capitol, the organ in the Visitor Center). Yet a Los-Angeleic modernity, too—all the requisite gadgetry for a minimalist, extraterrestrial comfort. The Christ-topped dome (all the Christs here are copied from Thorwaldsen's and look like Bjorn Borg) straight out of Close Encounters: religion as special effects. In fact the whole city has the transparency and supernatural, otherworldly cleanness of a thing from outer space. A symmetrical, luminous, overpowering abstraction. At every intersection in the Tabernacle area—all marble and roses, and evangelical marketing—an electronic cuckoo-clock sings out: such Puritan obsessiveness is astonishing in this heat, in the heart of the desert, alongside this leaden lake, its waters also hyperreal from sheer density of salt. And, beyond the lake, the Great Salt Lake Desert, where they had to invent the speed of prototype cars to cope with the absolute horizontality. ... But the city itself is like a jewel, with its purity of air and its plunging urban vistas more breathtaking even than those of Los Angeles. What stunning brilliance, what modern ceracity these Mormons show, these rich banker, musicians, international genealogists, polygamists (the Empire State in New York has something of this same funereal Puritanism raised to the nth power). It is the capitalist, transexual pride of a people of mutants that gives the city its magic, equal opposite to that of Las Vegas, that great whore on the other side of the desert.

There was a curious "truthiness"[40] to what he was saying (at least in that passage, at least to *me*); moreover, the book was composed as what I understood to be a "surrealistic tale," which was then, to me, a relatively new form of ethnographic writing based on evocative collages done as nonlinear narratives.[41] Since that time, these nonlinear ethnographic narratives have been labeled "messy texts."[42]

What makes a text "messy"?

Whereas temporal sequences organize the previous three narrative structures, "fragments" narratives are not time bound. Nor are their plotlines organized by a rational search for solutions to problems or by an episodic working out of themes. Nor are they driven by characters. Like theories of postmodern fiction and/or philosophies that inform them, they may *appear* at first glance to be randomly organized, more closely resembling dreams or memories than coherent stories. But appearances can be deceptive (which is part of the quirky narrative allure and—when done well—philosophical purity of them). What may appear random is, on a second or third reading, often elegantly pieced together spatially by deeper emotional/semiotic logics.[43]

The point of a messy text format is to disrupt—or, in Jean Baudrillard's terms—to "hijack" reality. The point of the hijacking is to break the rhythms of taken-for-granted assumptions and perceptions of everyday life, the separation of facts and fictions, and to "interrogate" them.[44] The point is to rob the reader of the ordinary signs of meaning and of the comfort associated with a language and storyline that coalesce to offer a known and stable representation of what is "real." One might replace "reality markers" with non-sensical signs—such as radical or at least alternative referents for words; highlight poignant dissimilarities between what is given and how it is represented or given to mean; insert jumps or ruptures in the expected narrative flow; or include signs without explanation and left referentially alone, surrounded by white space on the page. What these disruptions accomplish is *foregrounding the writing of the text itself* by drawing attention to choices made in its creation and to the noticeable (some might say, artificial) deployment of language.

Why would a writer *want* to want to write this way?

One very good reason is that to pursue a "new idea" in a way that makes challenges existing theories or ways of thinking may require it. For example, education and health care researchers have used narrative fragments to provide alternative ways of understanding how children, patients, the mentally ill, and others "process reality." Below is an abstract introducing a fragments narrative done in a critical reflexivity style that incorporates an autoethnographic perspective, layered accounts, poetry, and therapeutic writing:

This article provides a sociological introspection pertaining to male sexual abuse from a wounded healer's (Etherington, 2000) perspective. Inspired from postmodern narrative and ethnographic works (Ellis & Bochner, 1992; Richardson, 1997), the author layers this account (Rambo-Ronai, 1995) with therapeutic writing (Etherington, 2000) and poetry and prose (Richardson, 1997). This style provides the narrator with the flexibility to move between various temporal and spatial settings and report various internal and external monologues. Also addressed are common misconceptions often associated with male survivors of sexual abuse. The final section highlights the evolution of the author from a victim to a survivor and then to a wounded healer.[45]

There are prose precedents for this style of reporting personal experience. Within the postmodern tradition (if that isn't a contradiction in terms!), Jean Baudrillard offers a way of thinking about jogging as an entry point into a much deeper cultural analysis of the relationship of affluence to varieties of eating disorders:

You stop a horse that is bolting. You do not stop a jogger who is jogging. Foaming at the mouth, his mind riveted on the inner countdown to the moment when he will achieve a higher plane of consciousness, he is not to be stopped. ...

Decidedly, joggers are the true Latter Day Saints and the protagonists of an easy-does-it Apocalypse. ... Primitives, when in despair, would commit suicide by swimming out to sea until they could swim no longer. The jogger commits suicide by running up and down the beach. ...

Anorexic culture: a culture of disgust, of expulsion, of anthropoemia, of rejection. Characteristic of a period of obesity, saturation, over abundance. The anorexic prefigures this culture in rather a poetic fashion by trying to keep it at bay. He refuses lack. He says: I lack nothing, therefore I shall not eat. ... The jogger has yet another solution. In a sense, he spews himself out; he doesn't merely expend his energy in his running, he vomits it. He has to attain the ecstasy of fatigue, the "high" of mechanical annihilation, just as the anorexic aims for the "high" of organic annihilation, the ecstasy of the empty body and the obese individual seeks the high of dimensional annihilation: the ecstasy of the full body. (pp. 38-39)

Within the autoethnographic literature, the use of messy texts to portray the lived experiences of bulimia are explored in Lisa Tillman-Healy's piece, "A Secret Life in a Culture of Thinness: Reflections on Body, Food, and Bulimia,"[46] and in Christine Kiesinger's "My Father's Shoes: The Therapeutic Value of Narrative Reframing."[47] Both of these stories provide powerful and evocative depictions of the cultural, emotional, psychological, and family discourses that contribute to the eating disorder and relational challenges that result from it. The texts are collages of prose, poetry, reflexive passages, and remembered scenes that reveal the lived experiences of these illnesses. They also underscore the value of narrative writing to, as Kiesinger puts it, "reframe" it.

The Pay Off: Endings

It would be fun to close the chapter with a section on narrative endings by evoking the same "when students ask this question I break into song" line that I used to open the previous sections on beginnings and middles. But that would be untrue. Instead, when we reach the place in the course where my students are about to share the endings of their accounts with the class, the question they most often ask is "How *does* it end?"

It is a different kind of question. Here's why:

Beginnings are focused on set-ups—framing devices, building interest in a situation and characters, asking questions, creating identification with readers, etc.—endings are about *pay-offs*. They are about answers. And whereas middles are about the craft of building tension, developing plotlines, structuring scenes, and complicating the original set-up, endings are *final.* They are about the sum of things, whether that sum is the one enduring meaning that emerged through the action and that defines the essence of the story, or the destruction of meanings thought to be eternal. One way or another, everything must work out. Endings are where the storylines *come to*, where all that has risen and all that is conflicted must finally converge: temporally, thematically, and spatially.

The craft of writing endings is less about the careful manipulation of plot or characters or scenes through narrative techniques than it is about recording what actually happened, what it meant, and what it all means. It is about satisfying the reader's desire to see how and why the story turned out the way it turned out, and, through that accomplishment, leaving those readers still wanting *more*.[48]

As I have suggested throughout this book, writing narrative nonfiction is best conceived as writing to develop a close, personal relationship with readers. And, as research about maintaining close, personal relationships has consistently shown, the dominant theme is *equity*.[49] Successful and satisfying relationships depend on perceived *fairness* in everyday exchanges of goods, services, sentiments, and time. In other words, relational partners expect a pay-off in relation to their investment of time and intellectual and emotional energy.

By analogy, if beginnings are all about creating positive or intriguing first impressions to *attract* a reader, and if middles are all about furthering and complicating those impressions by building closer identification with your characters, situations, and plot, then writing a successful ending is about accomplishing two relational tasks: satisfying the *investment* readers have thus far made in your story and doing so in a way that *increases the likelihood they will make additional investments* in your next release.

How *should* you end your story? That's up to you. But know that ending your story well means accomplishing those two relational tasks. Rather than providing exemplars, I ask instead that you think about the stories that have done the best job of satisfying your expectations. How were those pay-offs crafted? How did they make you feel? What were those authors able to do to make you believe that the time and energies you had invested in them were good investments? That's how you should endeavor to make your readers feel as well.

How *does* your story end?

That's the answer we all want to hear. But I can't answer it for you. It depends on how you've told your story. It depends on the content of your account as well as the way you've told the story.

That's true, but I fear the truth has disappointed you.

You were hoping for at least a few techniques, right? Just a couple of things to think about? You're probably thinking: This author has thus far provided techniques and things to think about in the previous two sections of this chapter, so how could he now not pay off your investment by at least giving some basic ways of ending a story?

Well, okay then. But I want you to understand that *you still need to know how your story ends* before you select one.

Got an ending?

Good. Remember, regardless of the technique chosen, you are writing *to that ending*, to accomplish that narrative goal. What follows are five possible ways to get there:

1. *Denouement:* After the "big scene" or climax that resolves or brings to fruition the original conflict, the author concludes with an account of each character by showing what happened to them after that. This technique "rounds out" the story by

providing readers/audience members with answers to questions they probably have about what happens to those characters. This technique is particularly effective if it includes sources of humor and surprise. The opposite of this technique is the "premature denouement," wherein the narrator sums up the fate of characters *before* the ultimate truth is revealed. Once that final truth is revealed, the premature nature of the denouement may be used to call into question the reliability of the narrator. Or, if it is made into a resource for the overall uncertainty in the storyline, it can serve as a powerful supporting *motif* to the general theme.[50]

2. *Deliverance:* Just when all hope is lost and the ending seems to spell death, dismemberment, divorce, the end of the world, or at the very least a jail sentence, someone steps into the story to save the beleaguered and redeem our hope in humanity. Of course, there is also the possibility of the *opposite* of deliverance, a scene in which the author has built up the reader's anticipation of rescue, only to see it never arrive.

3. *Détente:* This term is derived from the language of political diplomacy and refers to a lessening of major tensions between nations, usually because those nations have talked through their differences and therefore have a pretty good idea of what will happen in the future. Some endings based on the same relational logic: The ending is accomplished through talk that lessens the tensions between or among the characters but is *suggestive* more so than conclusive and the future, and leaves the impression that the future could turn out differently. The reader is left not completely satisfied, but—and this can be a good thing—with enough interpretive clues as well as interpretive space to work within.

4. *Relocation and Reflection:* Many stories feature final sections that are written in a time and place removed from the original action. Between the time of the action and this reflective time, the author has thought about what happened and come to some conclusions about its possible meanings.

5. *Return to the Beginning:* A favored method for signaling to the reader/audience that the ending has "arrived" is to return to the beginning paragraph or theme. For example, at the beginning of this chapter I used a performance by Scott Gust to illustrate

the choice about where to begin a story. In it, Gust muses on the "three weeks" theme, the gay dot com profile, and the anniversary of his friend's death—the three themes he used to frame the narrative about mourning in cyberspace. Here is Gust's ending:

> So many more than three weeks have passed since I began this essay, and I suppose I have some answers. His gay dot com profile remained in cyberspace beyond the first anniversary of his death, a year plus one day since the last time he signed in to that account.
>
> I still visit him there from time to time;
>
> I still avoid the more public memorial that occupies a less controversial piece of cyberspace;
>
> I still wonder what if his cyberpresence will last as long as I might need it.

Of course it is possible to craft an ending that combines elements from two or more of the above possible techniques. In Gust's example, he both returns to the beginning and reflects from a place of temporal relocation and considered reflection.

Finally, it is also possible to create an ending that "plays with" or renders ironic one of the above techniques, preferably in ways so obvious that the reader is tipped-off to what you are doing and still feels good about it. This technique is used most often as a vehicle for comedy, and if properly done, can provide what Kenneth Burke called "perspective by incongruity."[51]

Bottom line: By the time a reader reaches the period after the last word of the last line in the final paragraph of your story—no matter how moving or crazy or unusual the account has been—that *reader has to feel that it has been worth it.* If you can accomplish that goal, you will have written a good, maybe even a great story.

Period.

Activities and Questions

1. Compose an abstract for your current narrative project. How does the wording of your abstract frame the story? What might you do to make it better, more compelling?

2. Develop three alternative beginnings for your project using the possible ways to structure beginnings found in this chapter. Share them with your classmates and discuss the comparative advantages/disadvantages of each one.

3. Outline three middles for your project. Discuss how using different structural mechanisms create new opportunities to develop the storylines and how each of them also prevents or limits other opportunities.

4. What constitutes a good ending? What is the relationship between good endings and good beginnings? By your choice of a framing device?

5. This chapter focuses on structural devices for composing narratives, but there are also *content*-driven patterns that characterize particular genres of narrative. For example, Arthur Frank[52] writes about different types of illness narratives (*restitution* of the well body through medical intervention; *chaos*, when the patient is in an "eternal present" defined by constant pain; or *quest*, when the pain or illness is framed as being present to teach us something about ourselves). Similarly, Victor Turner offers four stages of ritual that may be used to describe and evoke the experience: breach, crisis, redress, and reintegration.[53] And Johnny Saldana offers a typology of performance trajectories for ethnodrama: monologue, dialogue, and ethnodramatic extension.[54] Discuss how these content-driven patterns (or others you may be familiar with) may be used to micro-manage your storyline within the overall structures discussed in this chapter.

Notes

1. Camus (1991).

2. Actually as it turns out, it is not so sad. Grand survives the plague and is said to be the "hero" of the story because he quietly endures and goes on. He may even go on to write the rest of his novel. Who knows? Notice I could have included this detail in the above

paragraph, but it would have diluted the impact of the story of a writer who only completes one sentence. Still, you owe your readers the truth, which is another good use of the note.

3. Lamott (1995).

4. This line is adapted from Earl Shorris's masterful study of midlevel managers, all of whom believe that the secret to their success, as well as to knowing the truth about the organization, is always located at the next level up in the bureaucracy. The secret, once they reach the corner office on the top floor, is that there is no secret. That is the one thing that all successful managers know. It is also the one thing that all writers know. See Shorris (1984).

5. See, for example, Ellis (2002) and Kiesinger (2003).

6. See, for example, Petersen (2007); Gilgun (2004); Ellis (1995); and Athens (forthcoming).

7. See, for example, Poulos (2006); see also Jago (2006).

8. Malagreca (2005); Goode (2006); Spry (2006).

9. See, for example, Rambo (2005); Miller (2002); Adams (2006); Communication Studies 298, California State University, Sacramento (1997); and Pinney (October 2005).

10. See, for example, Tillmann-Healy (1996); Hartnett (2002); Glesne (1997); Ohlen (2003); Carr (2003); Furman (2006); and Denzin (2006).

11. See, for example, Hall (2006) and Minge (2007).

12. Payne (2002).

13. See, for example, Langellier (1989); Bochner (1994); Ainsworth and Hardy (2004); and Taylor and Trujillo (2001).

14. The original line is "motives are shorthand terms for situation," and the discussion may be found in Burke (1989).

15. I don't know where the idea of a "set-up" and "pay-off" originated, but Phil Klass taught it to me years ago in a nonfiction course at Penn State. Since then I've heard them used in reference to films, digital media, writing of all kinds, and life in general.

16. The performance was presented at the 3rd International Congress of Qualitative Inquiry, Champaign-Urbana, IL, May 4, 2007.

17. I asked Ben to explain how he created this performance script. Here is his response:

I developed this piece for a show titled "My Body" at the Kleinau Theater directed by Ron Pelias. "Straight and White" came out of an exercise that had us talk about our relationship with a body part with a partner. Our partner would then narrate our experience back to us. I chose my teeth, and after talking about my experience with my braces and maintenance of my teeth, my partner used the phrase the "hegemony of straight and white teeth." Once I heard this phrase, I realized how a straight and white mouth parallels a straight and white identity in areas such as hygiene, class, religion and the medical community. I knew I had found my piece.

My goal was to expose the arrogance by highlighting how much work goes into maintaining a straight and white mouth (and identity). This parody has been one of the things that has sometimes been hard to balance. There have been a few people who thought I was advocating the very thing I was trying to parody and deconstruct, which I think is often the danger in parody.

To adjust, I have taken the parody to a bit more of an absurd level, which has meant I have had to let go of some of the nuance I like, but I also think it makes the piece more accessible.

18. Goodall (1991).

19. Goodall (1996).

20. I asked Scott Gust to explain how he decided to write this performance, one in a series he does seated on a stage in front of a laptop computer. He replied:

I created this performance as a way to study and express how my cyber-identity is both distinctive from and connected to other aspects of my lived experience. In particular, I reflect on how cyberspace has come to be an unexpected place of mourning the death of a beloved friend.

This performance is part of an ongoing series wherein I perform with my laptop computer. My choice to perform with my laptop is meant to be a Brechtian gesture that exposes the labor in which I must engage to craft this performance. I hope people who witness my use of a laptop in this intensely personal performance think about how much strategic effort I have put into creating an identity they will find appealing and/or authentic.

My laptop performances are also environmental. That is, whenever I perform with the laptop I change the performance to the technological capacity of the performance space.

21. Gust (2007).

22. You may be describing the most ordinary setting (as in my Clemson example of interstate eateries), but the uniqueness aspect should be part of how you choose to describe it (e.g., "fried antibiotic cow," etc.).

23. Murrell (2007).

24. The initial justification for this approach is found in Ronai (1995). The use of a layered account is also consistent with "the postmodern condition." As our lives become fragmented and separated from a master sensemaking narrative, so, too, do narratives display that fragmentation.

25. Adams (2006).

26. Williams (2005). Although novels tend to be the favored format for ex-soldiers' personal accounts of war, there is also a long tradition of war memoirs written as personal narratives. In recent times, some notable titles include Puller (1991) and Crawford (2006).

27. See, for example, Eggers (2000). For a fiction example, see Pessl (2007).

28. Eggers (2000, p. vii).

29. For a quick tour of available story plots, see Cecil Adams's instructive webpage: http://www.straightdope.com/columns/001124.html

30. This is a particularly favored format for memoirs. In recent years, some notable titles making use of it include Karr (2001, 2005); Wolffe (2000); Burroughs (2006); Kaysen (1993); and Nafisi (2003). I used this format for my own memoir; see (Goodall, 2006).

31. For a transparent example of this method in my own work, please see (Goodall, 1989b, pp. 42–54). This ethnographic short story begins with the line "Call me Ed," spoken by a corporate executive who, I believed at the time, was hiring me to do some communication consulting for his company. From those opening words and too-firm handshake over lunch, a basic masculine conflict between Ed and me frames the storyline. My field notes reflect a chronological progression of events and the evolution of my thinking when I found myself implicated in a much larger, darker, more mysterious plot by a powerful female community leader to use me, and the conflict she knew would ensue, to get rid of Ed. This story is written in the noir style of detective fiction because it fits the attitude of the narrator and sequence of events that led, finally and unhappily, to a resolution of the conflict, a newer and more enlightened understanding of "communication consulting," and, for me, a richer, if darker, understanding of power in a southern community.

32. Perhaps the best example of this method in my writing is found in Goodall (2006b, pp. 30–59). The "sum" in this case was the realization that my own initial deeply conflicted feelings about the global

war on terror could only be resolved by a personal acceptance of my own—and our own—complicity in it and by taking action myself. But to "get there," I had to add in cultural indicators that made complicity so easy for me (and for most Americans). This meant taking a hard look at a wide variety of signs of our fear-borne "(dis)-ease," and multiply the harm by a factor of SUVs, our increasing double extra-largeness, and the widespread increase in the use of anti-anxiety medications following 9/11 among our populace. I then subtracted much of the Bush administration clutter, such as the fact that there were no WMDs in Iraq or uranium deals between African nations and Middle East dictators; nor were there any "good reasons" to accept torture in our detention camps. I learned from doing the math that the only way to win a "war on terror" was to conquer our own fears, and because those fears had been manipulated by an effective propaganda campaign that relied on an old cold war narrative, I was perfectly positioned as a communication and cold war scholar to combat it.

33. See Tumminello (2005). This technique may be also useful for the other types of narrative structures in this section of the book.

34. See Goodall (2004).

35. This issue about revealing a "true identity" has raised many ethical questions among ethnographers as well as informed many classic works in the field. For example, the late Dwight Conquergood chose not to inform the local residents of Chicago's "Big Red" that he was an ethnographer doing fieldwork on local street gangs until after he had established trust and rapport with them. He believed that had he moved into the tenement and announced that he was a Northwestern University professor and wanted to study them, he would have not been able to complete his work. Dwight, a valued friend of mine, was well aware of the ethical questions involved in his decision; for him, the issue was not if he should reveal his true motive, only when and how he should do it.

36. Scheeres (2005).

37. Larson (2003).

38. Another excellent convergence narrative is Maraniss (2004). The two narratives contrast the ambush of the army battalion known as the Black Lions on October 17, and the student protest against Dow Chemical (manufacturer of napalm) at the University of Wisconsin on

October 18. You cannot help making comparisons between the terrible modern ordnance of war and complex emotions of those who fight and those who protest against them during the Vietnam era with certain historical parallels today.

39. Baudrillard (1989).

40. "Truthiness" is a word invented by the comedian Steven Colbert. See http://en.wikipedia.org/wiki/Truthiness

41. See Van Maanen (1988).

42. See Heaton (2002); for another discussion of "messy texts," see Denzin (1997) and Marcus (1994, pp. 563–574). For examples, see Pelias (1997); Heaton (1998); and Trujillo (1994).

43. For readers interested in the philosophical and literary foundations of postmodernism (which is beyond the scope of this volume), please see the comprehensive website devoted to the subject: http://carbon.cudenver.edu/~mryder/itc_data/postmodern.html

44. Interrogation is an interviewing technique employed to elicit hidden or secret information from criminals, terrorist suspects, and shady characters or informants. However, it is also a term that has been "hijacked" by postmodernists to represent critical reflexivity as a method of questioning a text or a practice, usually to undercover "hyperrealities," including hidden power relations or patterns of domination and repression.

45. Lemelin (2006).

46. Tillman-Healy (1996).

47. Kiesinger (2002).

48. More on this point later, in the third section of the book. But quickly: My point is that becoming a successful writer is also about cultivating and sustaining an enthusiastic audience for your work.

49. See Canary and Dainton (2003).

50. I use this technique in *A Need to Know* (Goodall, 2006a). I wanted to show how secrecy in my own family had led me to many conclusions about my mother and father that were later shown to be false.

51. Burke (1959).

52. Frank (2004, pp. 209–225) provides a synopsis of the three types of stories.

53. Turner (1988).

54. Saldana (2005).

Chapter 3

Submitting Narrative Work to Academic Journals and Academic Presses

Old School

For two years in the final quarter of the 20th century, 1978–80, I was in central Pennsylvania working diligently toward my doctorate in a department then called "speech communication."

There were still dinosaurs. Everyone smoked.

The eminent philosopher Henry Johnstone, whose office was carpeted with an ornate oriental rug and who poured exotic teas for his students, often padded around the halls of Sparks Building in silk slippers and occasionally lost his way, his mind otherwise occupied with Ideas. Gerald M. Phillips,[1] my beloved advisor and one of the finest minds I've known, chain-smoked cigars in his office with the door open and chewed small black volcanic mountains of imported espresso beans daily until his doctor told him he would have less than a month to live unless he quit both habits. So he quit. He had a couple of new articles to write and a book to complete. There was important work left to do. He hung a large handwritten sign on his office door proclaiming: "NO GODDAMN SMOKING!"

At the time, such a socially incorrect statement was unheard of in academic culture anywhere outside of weirdo California. No smoking in Phillips's office? *Really*? Some of us complained loudly on the grounds that we couldn't *think* if we couldn't *smoke*. I know of at least two of his advisees who switched to other faculty because of it.

Imagine that. Now imagine this:

Graduate students competed for little wooden desks called "study carrels" in grand old buildings called "libraries," where the truly virtuous among us[2] spent most of their time breathing the cool book-dust and ghostly air that accumulated in the stacks while perusing ancient rhetoric tomes personally retrieved from metal shelves scarred from heavy use, our carrels stacked high with the heft of them, and our handwritten notes scrawled on notebook paper left out for view, as if the words themselves—like their authors—were waiting there to be discovered and proclaimed a genius.[3] If not genius proclaimed, then at least status was attained by what we knew about the library and by the whispered accounts of how much time we dedicated to being there. For example, we were all so well versed in the card catalog that we could recite the nine general levels of the Dewey Decimal System as well as the sub-areas among those levels where "our" books and periodicals were recorded.

Can you do that? Would it matter if you could?

Not. But back then the idea that someday soon this, too, would pass was as yet unimaginable. Besides, beyond their value as repositories of knowledge, libraries were excellent places to browse the stacks in the hope of meeting people—potential dating partners—while so doing. Think of a primitive Barnes and Noble without the bright lights and handy Starbucks.

And this: Those of us fortunate enough to hold teaching assistantships mimeographed typewritten handouts onto fragrant blue-ink copies, mostly legible, that we then distributed to our students. Our students carried notebooks and pens to class; if they owned a phone, it was hanging on the wall in their dormitory or (for the truly affluent) resting on a table in their shared apartment. Cell phones and text messaging? No way. Unimaginable. If we required students to turn in *typewritten* term papers, it meant that an awful lot of otherwise intelligent young women would dutifully spend all night the night before it was due translating their lazy-ass boyfriends' scrawl onto the page. Only graduate students were **expected** to type, and men who admitted to typing were considered a "little funny" by the older faculty who still thought that was what secretaries were for.

I was thought a "little funny" myself.

But I had a reason for it. I was a little funny because I had long wanted to become a writer, and to become one I needed to type. I learned how to type in high school when I was one of a grand total of two males in the class. If I was considered a little funny in that setting (and I was), the other guy was frickin' hilarious. In college and later in graduate school, my having learned to type paid off. And when personal computers came into my life, I was way ahead.

Not all of us proficient in the use of a typewriter were equal, however.

Those many of us with old manual typewriters envied those fewer of us with the newer electronic models. When the first IBM self-correcting "Selectrics" were introduced, it was truly a sacred moment and, watching as the rotating ball moved backwards, lifting off typeface, we were as amazed as the wise men in the presence of the Christ child. No more "white-out!" No need to retype entire **pages** of text just to change a few words! That we could change fonts by purchasing another rotating ball for our self-correcting unit was beyond clever.

The advanced technologists among us—we didn't yet have a word for geeks—scoffed at our analog innocence. They alone had seen the future and that future was digital. Typewriters, they told us, would soon be obsolete, replaced by something called "personal" computers, and these so-called personal computers would revolutionize knowledge and the means by which scholarship was produced. They articulated their visions while manually entering data onto punch cards and stacking the cards in cues in what were then new computer centers where enormous mainframes hummed along with the cold steady precision of digital certainty.

I hated the computer center. I hated it not because I thought the geeks were wrong about the future—I believed they were right—but because a simple content analysis of a 500-word passage could take all night to validate what was already perfectly obvious to me after a careful reading. Had I come along later, I might have felt differently. Had I come along much earlier, I *would have* felt differently. But too much earlier and I would have likely joined ranks with the dinosaurs, asked secretaries to do my typing, and spent most days smoking in my office.

Faculty in those days mostly worked in their offices except on weekends.[4] On weekends they took work home. The idea of working from home on weekdays was yet to be widely practiced because it had yet to be enabled by personal computing technology and digitalized libraries.

Publication in those days of old was largely the protected province of regular faculty. Graduate students were only occasionally encouraged to submit a seminar paper to state or (at best) regional conferences, and then only with the thinnest hope of acceptance until they were in the final stages of their doctoral studies, when it became okay to reach a little higher. The idea that one of us would be bold enough to submit a paper to a journal *before* that time was relatively rare, and those few brave souls who did so were generally considered bumptious. "Don't rush to publication" was a common cautionary hush, as if worthy scholarship, like fine red wine or virginity, was improved the longer it remained corked.

Fortunately for me, Gerry Phillips didn't side with the corkers. He was a writer as well as a voracious reader, and he instilled in those of us who worked with him a love of language, storytelling, creativity, the lyrics of Gilbert and Sullivan, and a no-nonsense understanding of The Rules of Academic Publishing. Chief among those rules was that *disciplined writing practice produces published results.* He knew that writing improves *only* with continuous effort.[5] Early in my Penn State career, and shortly after Phillips had quit smoking, I ventured to ask him a question about academic publishing that so far none of my professors had directly addressed. To wit: How do you go about submitting work to journals?

He looked at me a little oddly and then smiled. He was big on drama so I wasn't surprised to see him rise solemnly from his desk and move deliberately to the office door, which he closed and locked before turning back to me. "Here's the secret," he began. "You write the paper and a cover letter. You put the paper and the cover letter into an envelope. You address it to the editor, you attach the appropriate postage, and you wait for a response. The response will probably be 'revise and resubmit,' unless what you have written is genius or doesn't fit the needs or readership of the journal." He shrugged. "You revise, you resubmit, and maybe it's published. If it is published, you repeat the process until they carry your dead ass out of the office feet first. If it isn't published, you should consider enrolling in some writing courses."

For years I had been trying hard to become a writer. I hadn't had any success submitting my work to magazines or to scholarly journals. I had been rejected by every major publisher in North America. I didn't admit any of this to Phillips, but I did take his advice. I enrolled in my first writing seminar: nonfiction writing, taught by Phil Klass. And then I enrolled in another one, biographical writing, taught by Stan Weintraub. Then a third. And a fourth. I convinced my doctoral committee to allow "creative and biographical writing" to substitute for statistics and computer science as a research tool. I reasoned that a scholar's life was a writing life, and therefore writing was at least as much of a research tool as running numbers.

My committee thought I was a bit of a maverick but allowed it. So I took the writing courses alongside the communication theory and research seminars, and from time to time I took chances with the prose style, titles, and framing devices used to compose term papers. For a seminar in early rhetorical history I wrote an Aristotelian analysis of the Meatloaf song "Paradise by the Dashboard Lights," complete with liner notes. For other seminars I applied techniques of creative nonfiction to topics as diverse as a criticism of measurements of interpersonal attraction ("In Praise of Medium Beauty"), theoretical bases of small group communication ("Dr. Strangelove's Bedfellow: Irving Janis's *Groupthink*"), and contemporary rhetorical criticism (*"Gravity's Rainbow*: Narrative as War Criticism, War Criticism as Narrative"). The titles now make me wince, but I was trying to find my voice. There was, emerging within me, a passion for finding ways to weave a story around research.

I wrote a narrative dissertation—a rhetorical biography of the interpersonal relationship of Scott and Zelda Fitzgerald—at a time when my friends and peers were churning out traditional rhetorical analyses of speeches and social movements or committing social science on sophomores. I went on the job market without so much as a convention paper on my *CV*, but with a publishing contract for a literary biography—courtesy of Stan Weintraub—in my hand.

I got two interviews and a lot of strange looks when I talked about my research. I was lucky to get a job.[6]

It was the summer of 1980. Vast academic culture and information technology changes were breaking out. To me, they were distractions. I wanted to be a writer who combined academic resources with creative nonfiction and whose narratives would be read by a wide public audience.

I wrote every day. I got my first article accepted and then a second.

The writing courses were clearly paying off.

But as I say, this old school stuff was a long time ago.

So why do I begin a chapter about the pragmatics of publishing in academic outlets with it? First, I want to underscore the idea that no matter when, where, or how you enter the academic life, you are entering a process of ongoing and continuous change. Not all changes are necessarily good, any more than they are always greeted with universal acclaim, but neither have we *ever* "gone back" to a simpler time.

Second, most of the radical changes that influence scholarly publishing and the creation and dissemination of knowledge are created by revolutions in technology. The stylus begat the pen that begat the typewriter that begat the personal computer that begat the Internet, which is where we are now but not where *you* will be in the near future. New forms of giving eye, mind, heart, and voice to ideas and new media for the dissemination of it—interactive, multi-mediated, hyperlinked, and Second Life—enrich and expand our scholarly and public intellectual information and entertainment environments. But the technological innovations of today—much like the innovation that was the self-correcting typewriter—will seem quaint within a few years.

My third point is perhaps most salient, at least for the content of this chapter: Despite the ongoing cultural changes that mark academic life, and no matter how revolutionary the new technologies, the process of submitting work to academic journals and presses still remains remarkably stable.[7] Gerry Phillips's dictum still holds: "You write the paper and a cover letter. You put the paper and the cover letter into an envelope. You address it to the editor, you attach the appropriate postage, and you wait for a response." These days the submission may be electronic, but the basic process remains the same.

For all of the wisdom Gerry Phillips imparted to me in that brief explanation of the process, there were for me—and are for you—questions that remain about it. This chapter addresses those questions.

I should also mention that Gerry recommended that I take my first writing course with Phil Klass.

Preamble: Do You Know the Importance of Format?

When I enrolled in Phil Klass's nonfiction writing seminar, I came into contact with a writer and editor who was already a legend in the science fiction community (his pen name is William Tenn).[8] Born in London in 1920 and raised by immigrant parents in New York, Mr. Klass told us he had entered the writing life after he was discharged from the army in 1945. He told us he wrote every day "to earn a living" and that he published in several genres, both fiction and nonfiction. To earn a living.

I got the immediate impression that his life as a writer who paid rent and raised a family with his writing, although by then quite successful, had not been easy. He had no formal training, no college degree, and yet here before us stood a man who was a full professor of English and Comparative Literature. I was impressed and a little nervous.

He began our class with a handout on format. By "format," I mean the accepted format for stories written by professional writers. It was a pretty straightforward format—manuscripts were to be typewritten, double-spaced, 12-point type, with 1½" margins on the left and 1' on the right, no spelling or grammar errors—but the "news" (at least for me) was that in the upper right-hand corner of the first page was the space for our name, address, phone number, and a word count.

I suddenly realized that all of the stories I had thus far submitted to *The New Yorker, The Atlantic Monthly,* and *Esquire* had lacked this formatted information. I had never considered a word count. My first question to Mr. Klass was whether this information, in this format, was an industry standard.

I thought "industry standard" made me sound smart and knowledgeable.

"Let me put it this way," he replied. "If a story comes across the transom without it, chances are it won't be read." He looked directly at my stricken face and immediately drew the obvious—and correct—conclusion. "A lot of aspiring authors fail not because their stories aren't any good, but because they don't follow standard formatting practice. Not following it is the mark of an amateur and writing, listen to me, *writing is a highly competitive business.*"

Mr. Klass often reemphasized the point he underscored on that first day. *Writing is a highly competitive business.* Everything you do counts. Any edge you can use, use. If you fail to catch a typo, you can bet your sweet ass that will be the reason the editor (or some underling) tosses your story in the circular file. There is no such thing as a good first draft. Editing is every bit as important as writing, and for newbies, even more so. What you turn in must be *as perfect as you can make it.* Failure to sell a story was still inevitable, but if you were lucky, that failure would be punctuated by an occasional success.

I begin with that reminiscence because I, too, want to emphasize the highly competitive nature of the writing game, including (and in some cases, especially) academic writing.[9] I don't use the term "game" lightly. Writing is a serious professional sport that, as any professional sport, requires more than raw talent. It requires knowledge of the sport and knowledge of the competition. It requires love of the game, where love is understood as the author of I Corinthians 13:4 understood love: "Love suffers long, and is kind." It also requires discipline, daily practice, informed passion, the ability to take and give criticism as well as to withstand rejection, and the tireless pursuit of improvement.

The writing life is not for weenies.

I also begin with Mr. Klass's opening gambit on formatting because one common error among new academic writers is the *failure to adhere to disciplinary formatting standards when submitting work for publication*. Just as I learned the hard way that *not* using the profession's accepted standards meant that editors seldom (if ever) even read my stories, so, too, does the same logic apply to academic submissions. It seems a small thing, but it is large. So, here it is upfront and personal— submission lesson one: *Adhere to the publication guidelines for the outlet you have selected.*[10] At minimum, those guidelines will include:

- acceptable *stylesheet* (e.g., APA, MLA, Chicago, etc.)
- preferred *length* (e.g., number of pages for conference papers and journal articles; word count for book publishers)
- *number of copies* to be submitted (e.g., three–five for most academic journals and conventions)
- submission *address* (e.g., name of the editor and address for the submitted materials)
- *other* requirements (e.g., most trade publishers, agents, and some academic presses require a self-addressed, stamped envelop (SASE) with return postage affixed to it if you expect to have your submission materials returned to you)

Electronic submissions are so common now that some of the above points are probably unnecessary. If electronic submissions are the preferred method of submission for your chosen outlet, follow the instructions found on the appropriate website.

First Submission Question: What Is Your Narrative about?

My guess is that you are currently working on an article for publication. Can you describe the contents of your article in a single paragraph?

You will need to do that to produce an abstract, but it is also a good exercise to use to explain to an editor or publisher what your narrative is about. The paragraph, oral or written, should provide a reliable map of the territory of the story and be delivered in a style that invites listeners/readers to want to know *more*. In the box below, write a paragraph that describes a current project:

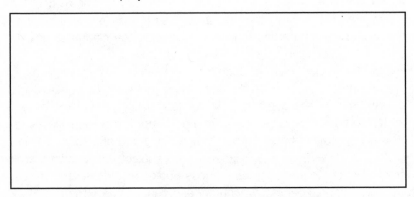

It's harder to do than you think. But it is absolutely necessary.

Second Submission Question: Who Is Your Audience?

Now that you have a handle on what your story is about, tell me who cares enough to want to read it? Your Mom and Dad don't count. Neither do your two best friends, your partner, and the professor who thinks you are doing good work in the program.

Nor is it likely to be the general public. "Everyone" is not a good answer, because it doesn't help you or your publisher identity a market for your work. Think about it this way: Do you read *every* article in your favorite academic journal or popular magazine?

Of course not. You read the articles you are most interested in. To answer this second submission question means thinking hard about who will be interested in what you have to say.

You've actually had quite a bit of experience doing this.

Our acculturation into narrative academic writing is the personal essay, which begins in high school (or perhaps earlier) with an exercise called "timed writing." Teachers prompt students to "write about yourself" in relation to some issue or assignment relevant to the class. The length of time allowed for the exercise varies, but usually ranges between forty minutes to one hour.

The narrative is "about" whatever the teacher says it's to be about, and the audience is the teacher. My guess is you got quite good at adapting what you wrote to the needs and expectations of your teachers.

By the time college-bound seniors are ready to apply to colleges, the practice and feedback they have received on "timed writing" is (sometimes) useful when they construct the personal essay about why they want to attend particular schools. The audience is admissions personnel; the topic is you.

But the stakes are much higher than the timed writing.

My guess is you wanted someone to tell you the "right way" to do it.

And my second guess is they did. That essay, considered by admissions counselors to be one of the most important elements in a successful application, has morphed into a mini-genre of its own. Books, articles, and websites are devoted to the subject. It has also, partly as a result of the advice given in those books, articles, and websites, become a source of great wry humor and general irony among admissions counselors who read thousands of them annually.[11]

When our son attended a session for prospective students at a fine Eastern Liberal Establishment college, the counselor performed a comedy routine based on the letters she had read that all adhered to what she called "the three themes of admissions success": *to have overcome great hardship* (usually emotional but also good if it is financial); *to have learned the value of diversity; and to respect the relationship between hard work and positive educational outcomes.*[12] "If I read those same three paragraphs one more time," she said, "I will want to kill myself, but, instead," she smiled wickedly, "I will probably kill your child's application."

What admissions counselors want to see, in addition to the ability to construct a proper sentence and develop a theme, is honesty, originality, passion, and uniqueness. They want to know who the *person* is behind the application and how that person *adds value* to the freshman class. They want to read a compelling narrative that gives them a little extraordinary colorful lift out of the gray workaday world they lead reading most ordinary college applications. In some cases, that colorful lift means the applicant will tell the story of having done something wonderful; in other personal narratives, it means that the applicant will find something wonderful in what otherwise seems ordinary. The quality of the experience will be reflected in the quality of the prose.

Do you sense a pattern emerging?

My point is that by the time you reach a graduate course in qualitative inquiry, or ethnographic methods, or autoethnography, etc., you have spent *years* cultivating answers to this question as well as strategies for deploying a personal narrative style and voice to obtain your goals. You may not have been encouraged to apply it *to* a research project or to use it to construct a personal narrative account *of* the project, but deep down inside you have at least *some* of the resources and some of the experiences you will need to draw on to become a good nonfiction narrative writer. You've already used what you know to get into college and grad school, to make yourself interesting to people you meet, to develop friendships, and, perhaps even to become, *a-hem, er,* "intimately" attractive to one or more persons.[13]

You have also become successful academically based on a unique human fingerprint: that combination of the way you talk about your personal history, deliver your heart, and show your intelligence. You need to learn how to use that voice, those experiences, that unique sense of the world you bring into the world to render the world more interesting and sensible, *to attract readers.*

Now that you are in a graduate class, or just a place in your life where you want to explore writing narratives, the second question about the submission process is one that I want you to understand you have been warming up to all of your life, only inflected a little differently given your status as a scholar: *What is your narrative about* (and how does it contribute to the ongoing scholarly conversation?) *and who is your* (scholarly) *audience*?

As a person who often is asked to evaluate personal narrative manuscripts, I can tell you that the same qualities of honesty, originality, passion, and uniqueness that guided evaluations of your work in the past will also be used to evaluate your scholarly narratives. Those qualities make what you write about interesting and evocative. But because you want to publish your work in a scholarly outlet, you also need to make what you write *contribute something new to our scholarly understanding* of whatever it is you are writing about. And that means thinking very carefully about the scholarly needs and critical expectations of your *audience.*

If you are new to the sport of academic publishing (and assuming you are already in a qualitative class), the best three ways to find out what scholars in the field are talking about and more about your intended readers are:

1. attend *conferences and conventions* that feature significant gatherings of qualitative enthusiasts, particularly those who read and write work done in a narrative style[14];

2. join *listservs* dedicated to qualitative methods and/or autoethnography; and

3. read the *journal archives* that feature qualitative work in your area.

In the end, who you are writing *for* will determine who to send your article *to*. I'd suggest using what I usually tell scholars: You are your audience. What journals do you read? Which publishers' catalogs do you keep? Which websites and listservs do you scan? Which conferences do you attend? Your audience is those people who do the same things as you do and read the same journals and books as you do.

When you think you have a good general idea of where your work fits into the scholarly airspace and who might be interested in reading it, you are ready to prepare the paperwork necessary for submission.

Questions about the Academic Publication Process: Responses by Norman Denzin[15]

In July 2007, I emailed Norman Denzin, one of the most prolific and award-winning writers and editors working in the qualitative world, the following questions about the publication process. Here are the questions and answers:

- What, if anything, do you find useful for authors to say about their work in cover letters? Do cover letters influence editors?

    I pay very little attention to cover letters—the text should show, not tell, and stand on its own.

- Do you ever receive letters of inquiry prior to the submission of an article/story/essay? If so, are they useful to you?

I receive many letters prior to submission, but prefer not to work w/ e-submissions—though I will make a preliminary judgment based on an abstract.

- What is the average length of time required for the review and initial decision about a submission?

  3 weeks is my goal.

- Does "revise and resubmit" usually lead to publication? Do you have a rough estimate of how often that determination leads to publication? Or what the average turnaround time is for a revised piece?

  Yes, it means I'm/we are committed to working with the author—the time table is set by the author—how soon they get r and r back to us—in some cases the r & r will be reviewed in house.

- What are the three or four reasons you find most often reappear in rejections of narratives?

  1. tells, not shows; less is more; be good not original;
  2. [the] writing does not meet Emily Dickenson's rule—it does not take off the top of my head, it DOES NOT bring chills and goose bumps to my arms, AND DOES not make me cry;
  3. it is self-indulgent;
  4. it does not convince me that this story, if published, could make the world a better place to be in.

- What are the three or four most important things you want potential authors to know about the publication process?

  - Principles before personalities;
  - It is always more than just a manuscript;
  - Never take criticism personally; when asked to revise do so, do not become defensive.

- Is there anything else you want to share that will be valuable for potential authors of narratives?

  - Believe in your work your voice and the value of your work;
  - Dare to take risks for you have nothing to lose

Third Submission Question: How Do You Get an Editor Interested in Your Work?

There are two proven ways to get an editor interested in your article. The better of the two is to phone or email her or him and ask. Try out the idea on the editor. Find out if there is any interest. If the editor has a particular slant, you can refocus your work in the direction to meet her or his criteria and biases (which will never be in the submission guidelines) or decide to submit it somewhere else. You can also find out which journal editors are enthusiastic to hear from you and which would rather you did not submit at all.

The second method is to write a compelling cover letter. Writing a cover letter is an important step when submitting unsolicited academic articles for publication consideration. According to Steven Gump, the cover letter should accomplish three goals:

1. establish the author's credibility;
2. help ensure that the manuscript is seriously considered for publication; and
3. initiate a positive rapport with the editor and editorial staff of the journal.

How do you accomplish these goals?[16]

My best advice is to *think about your submission from an editor's point of view.* Editors receive hundreds, maybe thousands, of manuscripts. Their initial task is to determine whether the piece fits the mission and scope of scholarship represented in the journal. Their second task is to assign it to reviewers. The cover letter should assist the editor in accomplishing both tasks in a timely manner.

Academic journals typically welcome submissions from anyone—students, graduate students, post-docs, college- or university-affiliated scholars, independent scholars, and members of the general public. The task of journal editors is to determine, from the diverse array of submitted manuscripts, uneven in quality and often spanning a wide range of topics and methods and writing styles, which ones are best suited to the scholarly mission and readership of the journal.

Editors are generally selected because of their status as senior scholars and the respect peers have for their work. Editors almost always have served as associate editors and guest reviewers prior to their selection as editor, so they are usually quite familiar with not only the process of academic reviewing, but also the important role reviewers serve as mentors to young scholars trying to break into the game; they are also familiar with what is the "right" manuscript for their journal.

Good reviewers provide more than evaluations of manuscripts. Because they understand their role as mentors, they offer helpful advice about the manuscripts they read, including suggestions for ways to improve the quality of writing in it.[17] Editors collect reviews from their advisory boards and guest reviewers and then interpret the comments to provide thoughtful suggestions to authors for improvements and revisions. In the end, only editors—not reviewers—make final decisions about publishing your work.

Editors, in my experience, are both fair and wise, but they are seldom polymaths. They don't know everything and fortunately they don't pretend to. This is why academic editors rely heavily on the advice of others to judge the worthiness of the manuscripts both within and outside their own scholarly expertise. Most reviewing assignments for submissions are not difficult to make because the topic and method speak directly to the research and theory-building interests of an established community of scholars.

That said, editors have preferences as well as biases. There are market forces that affect their decisions. And, let's face it, decisions about publishing can be political.[18] If there is a 90% rejection rate, it means that many publishable articles do not get published in the journal of choice. How the editor decides which articles to publish from the array of possibly acceptable manuscripts is as much a function of their biases and interests as it is of any objective criteria. For authors of journal manuscripts and the editors (and their assistants) who read them, the cover letter is little more than a cursory document. Via email, I asked Professor Kory Floyd, editor of the *Journal of Family Communication* and a veteran reviewer, about his experiences with cover letters. This is what he wrote[19]:

> The typical letter says little more than "Here's my paper and please consider it for publication." My submission guidelines also instruct authors to state explicitly in their cover letters that the paper is not under review elsewhere (I think this originated with the publisher), so they usually do that.
>
> Some authors also give an overview of the paper in their letter, and some actually begin to argue for its merits (i.e., tell me why I should be interested in the paper). I never really pay attention to these, because I think the paper should speak for itself.

If you follow Kory's advice, the following cover letter is appropriate:

Date
First Name Last Name, Editor
JOURNAL TITLE
Address
Address

Dear Professor Last Name:

Please consider the enclosed manuscript "Insert Title Here" for publication in the JOURNAL TITLE HERE. This is an original work not currently being considered for publication elsewhere. The manuscript makes 5600 words.

I look forward to your decision.

Best regards,

Your Name
Your Title

For work that is considered "novel" or "ground-breaking," editors must rely on the cover letter to supply additional information. Again, think about the two tasks the editor must perform and write the body of your cover letter accordingly. What scholarly conversation does your work hope to inform and why should the editor consider it for publication in this journal? Is it similar to other work published in this journal (or another similar journal), and/or does it follow up on an idea for future research mentioned in an article previously published in this journal? How do its contents match the audience for the journal? Are there qualified reviewers on the journal's editorial board who are particularly well suited to read it? If not, whom among our scholarly community might you suggest?

Assisting the editor in accomplishing her or his tasks ultimately assists you in navigating the publication process. One *caveat*: Never waste an editor's time.[20] There is no need to go into elaborate detail about the merits of your narrative or the glorious impact it will inevitably have on the whole of the human race; let the reviewers do that. Nor should you apologize for aspects of the work that still need to be improved; let the reviewers and the editor do that, *later*. And do not use the cover letter to recite your many splendid qualifications for writing this sort of narrative; no one really cares about your identity, and your qualifications should be evident in the quality of the work itself.

Let's say you have a story about your own experiences with Decompression Syndrome (DCS) as a result of a scuba-diving accident. Yours is an unusual account because you connect your experiences with trauma to a spiritual quest within the framework of deep ecology and because you make productive use of the scientific literature to document the physical bases for your continuing feelings of estrangement from your own body and resulting relational challenges. It is an admittedly unusual story, but you feel that a journal that specializes in trauma and that publishes personal narratives may be interested in it. Don't do this in the body of your cover letter:

> Beneath this piece of recycled wood pulp you will find a remarkable story drawn from the very core of my life. Entitled "Deep" (don't you just love single word titles—so unusual for academic articles! And look—no semi-colon either!!), this narrative account of scuba diving plunges the depths of experiential learning associated with a self at one with the sea and then painfully estranged from it, and from the newly known self, as a result of a diving accident. Drawing on Eastern mysticism, behavioral psychology, and ecology literatures (without footnotes but readers will find them on their own), I explore the "return to origins" Darwinian script that resides inside of all us, but is so under-appreciated.

Instead, try to follow a rhetorically simpler, less odd, and more informative model designed to help the editor do an editor's job:

> Enclosed you will please find three copies of "Deep," my narrative exploration of trauma associated with "decompression sickness" (DCS) a well-documented physical condition associated with oxygen deprivation during scuba diving. Although the medical literature provides a scientific basis for understanding DCS, there is an absence of personal narratives about the effects of the experience and its aftermath. My story seeks to fill that gap by providing an account that narratively connects the quest for a personal experience of deep ecology with an estrangement from the body as a result of near-fatal oxygen deprivation.
>
> My story will appeal to readers of this journal interested in the physical, psychological, and relational effects of the lived experience of trauma. It will also appeal as a story to those interested in how narratives can contribute

new understandings to science, as well as how knowledge about trauma associated with DCS can lead to improved treatment.

This is an original piece of narrative scholarship and is not under consideration elsewhere at this time. The manuscript makes 7506 words and follows the APA stylesheet.

Thank you for your time and consideration of my story. I look forward to learning of your decision.

Before we leave the topic of cover letters, it is important to take into account the likely influences of electronic submission on the future of them. Kory Floyd's response provides a prediction:

My journal doesn't use online submission (yet), but several journals are moving in that direction and I would suspect that cover letters will soon become obsolete. I just submitted a paper to a journal last week and the online submission page gave me a one-paragraph window in which to write my "cover letter," even though the rest of the submission page asked for so much detailed information that the "cover letter" was completely redundant at that point.

As I pointed out at the beginning of this chapter, changes in technology consistently contribute to changes in scholarship and in the submission process. Cover letters may, indeed, go the way of letters of introduction[21] as journals more fully embrace electronic submissions. Nevertheless, the advice given here ought to help you make better decisions about how to fill in those one-paragraph windows.

Interlude:

The Five Commandments of the Academic Publication Process, Without Elaboration

Thou Shalt Know the Submission Guidelines and Follow Them

Thou Shalt Face Rejection

Thou Shalt Revise and Resubmit

With Persistence, Thou Shalt Eventually Succeed

Thou Shalt Not Rest on the Laurels of Success

Fourth Submission Question:
What Is Really Meant by Revise and Resubmit?

Of the commandments given above, the one that most often leads to questions is the third one. "What does revise and resubmit mean, really?" The short answer is that revise and resubmit means exactly that: Revise the manuscript using the advice given by the reviewers and send it back to the editor.

It also means that you should *spell out how you addressed the specific suggestions made by the editor* in her or his letter to you asking for revisions. In some cases, this will mean explaining how you met Reviewer A's objections, or Reviewer B's concerns. In other cases, it will mean explaining how you met those objections and concerns *and* followed the editor's additional guidelines for revision. Either way, don't bother to resubmit unless you have revised accordingly. Bruce Thyer advises writers to send a letter *before* they start revising, outlining what they plan to do in the way of revision. If you receive an ok from the editor, it makes it harder for him or her to turn you down later. They've already agreed to your revision plan.[22]

What if you disagree with an editor or reviewer's suggested revision? Do you have to honor it?" The optimistic but slightly risky answer is "no," not so long as you carefully explain to the editor why you aren't comfortable making that change or how you feel that the *other* changes you have made obviate the need for it. The realistic and far less risky answer is that you should probably follow the instructions. Here's why: The editor will send your revised manuscript to the same reviewers he or she used the first time. Unless they buy your argument (the slightly risky strategy) for not making the change, they probably won't change their minds. Further, even if the reviewers change their minds, the editor still might insist on the suggested changes. Not always, but it does happen.

Revising manuscripts can involve more than one cycle of revisions, even if the revisions adhere to the original editorial suggestions. This may be because once the initial revisions are made, new opportunities for improvement occur to the reviewers and/or new errors have been found that were not caught in the original. You should not be put off by additional requests for minor revisions (they will make the manuscript stronger), nor should you assume, falsely, that requests for additional revisions are only given to graduate students or junior scholars.

It happens to all of us. For example, below is an acceptance letter that Angela Trethewey and I received earlier this year from David Collinson and Keith Grint, the editors of the British journal *Leadership*:

Thank you both for responding to the reviewer's comments and for revising your paper, 'Leadership Reconsidered as Historical Subject: Sketches from the Cold War to Post-9/11'. Keith and I have read through your revised manuscript and found it very interesting. We can confirm that your article will be published in the next available issue of Leadership, which is volume 3, #4 (November 2007). In making final revisions, we would like you to consider the following points:

Overall, your paper takes a very polemical approach, which is fine, but it may help your argument (and be even more persuasive) if you tone this down a little – words like 'maddening' and 'pathetic' (on page 21) may be unnecessarily detracting and distracting from your overall argument.

Could you say something about the global reach of your argument – it may be an appropriate model for a US or western approach to leadership but does it really encompass 'leadership' on a global scale? Would non-western scholars understand the history of leadership in a similar way – or is that your point, that a global model has swept aside cultural differences? Sometimes the argument seems explicitly western or American and other times it seems to encompass the globe.

Please consult and think about citing the paper published in Leadership (1(3), 2005) by Holmberg and Strannegard on 'Leadership Voices: The Ideology of "The New Economy"' – although this paper draws on the Swedish experience, it appears to have various links with yours and, as it is published in the same journal, it would be good to make the connection (you might also find useful Turnbull's extended book review in Leadership 2(2) 2006 which looks at 'post millennial leadership refrains').

The suggested revisions above are all minor ones, but they do underscore the point that even manuscripts accepted for publication can be improved. In our response to David and Keith, we used their original letter to address each of the suggestions for improvement they made. And we thanked them for it. Editing and revising your work is a continuous process of quality improvement and should be embraced in a positive and productive manner.

Why?

Because you want the final product to be as close to perfect as it can be. And because the closer to perfect it gets, the more likely it will have a positive impact on the journal's readership and your tenure and promotion committee.

But what if you feel the reviews either missed the point or require too much in the way of revising? Bruce Thyer suggests that if the request for revisions is too odious or the journal editor too discouraging, take what you think appropriate out of the reviews, revise, and ship it off to another journal. There is more than one "right" journal for any article.

Fifth Submission Question: How Do I Write the Academic Book Proposal?

Scholars who pursue qualitative work in either a traditional humanistic, narrative, or critical/cultural frameworks write books. Some of us write them because we find that the narrative freedom afforded by a book-length manuscript allows us to fully develop a thesis. Others write books because the dissertation whetted our appetite for a topic—and so much work went into it—that not mining it for a book would be a shame.[23] Still others write books because they know they are expected to have a book either published or in press at tenure and promotion time.

And then there are those of us who always wanted to be writers. We write books because it is in our blood. Or something. Maybe we are just vain. But I don't think so. Is it vanity that drives a carpenter to dream of building a house? Is it vanity that makes excellent teachers proudest when students learn?

Academic books are written for a variety of reasons. But they all share a common bond: They are the products of our personal narratives and professional selves. They make full use of a range of our educational and research experiences in the interest of advancing knowledge in a field and they require a level of disciplined practice that goes well beyond the completion of a scholarly article. I'm not just talking about a commitment of *time*. Drafting and honing a long narrative requires a habit of mind as well as a habit of practice. By this phrase I mean that there is a frame of mind, a way of thinking through a book project that differs in kind from the frame of mind required to complete a journal article.

Which brings me to the first question for potential book authors.

Is It an Article or Is It a Book?

The difference between an article and book is in the *size and scope of the question.* Large questions lead to books; small pieces of large questions are the material of journal articles. Although it is an accepted practice to piece together a series of smaller articles to make chapters in a longer book project, and although there are fine edited collections composed primarily of previously published journal articles, most academic publishers (and all trade publishers) are far more interested in *an original book-length work that capitalizes on previous research but does not merely reprint it.*

There are exceptions to this, as there are to every rule. But, in the main, if you think your question is large enough to encompass a book, and if you have done the requisite research to write a book proposal that will interest an editor, then you are committing yourself to a way of living and working for an extended period of time that will be different (not necessarily *better*, unless you always dreamed of being a writer) from your normal habits of mind and practice.[24]

Why is it different?

The capacity to sustain a book length narrative is very much like the capacity to turn a romance into a serious, sustained, intimate relationship. The initial attraction is to an *idea that we have projected onto an imagined world* made real only in its largely romanticized end product: true love, pure commitment, ideal marriage, a critically praised and best-selling published book.

Those of us who author books have all deluded ourselves thusly. All of us who have fallen in love at first sight only to find that the object of our affection fails to live up to our initial expectations have been there as well. Relational theorists posit that often the failure is not the fault of the object of our attraction, but instead is the fictionalized, idealized otherness we project onto them. The same is true for would-be book authors. It is the magical charm of *wanting to have written.* And, having imagined that we have written, then hearing the welcoming applause of the world.

As Gerry Phillips, who over the course of his career wrote thirty-something books, once told me, after I complained about how much work was involved in writing *my* first book: "What did you expect? You finish a book with your ass, not your head." By which he meant that day after day, alone in my room, armed with nothing more powerful than my research notes and imagination, my task was to tap out one letter after another on a keyboard. That's how you write a book: one word at a time, all 80,000+ of them, for a long time.

But as I said earlier, it is not enough to simply commit to long stretches of time to write a book. To sustain the romance, you must also commit to a frame of mind. You must sustain interest in the subject and be willing to sacrifice for it. Friends want you to go out for a beverage, but you are in the middle of an important chapter and fear that if you rise from your chair and go out for the evening you will lose the thread. If you think like that, you probably will lose the thread. But *if* you think like that, you will also never allow yourself to leave your home and you will end up a very sorry person.[25]

Robert Boice has done empirical research and has come up with a similar conclusion.[26] Specifically, he argues that the most productive scholars are those who make writing a moderate, but routine and regimented priority. Those who make writing a daily moderate priority (no more important than eating, sleeping, loafing and inviting your soul,[27] making love, etc.) are more productive over their careers and are more likely to get tenure than those who write in "binges" or who wait to write until the conditions are perfect. His research also suggests that:

- new faculty write more productively in brief daily sessions (one hour to 1.5 hours); and

- new faculty who write in brief daily sessions experience less stress during their first year.

What I am saying here, and what Boice's research demonstrates, is that there is an important difference between obsession and love.

But that love should happen at least a couple to (maybe) four hours a day. Writing "early and often,"[28] as Harry Walcott puts it, is a good way to regularize your writing habits. And Brian Fagan's "write 1000 words a day" mantra from his excellent *Writing Archaeology: Telling Stories about the Past* provides a quantitative metric that some writers find useful.[29]

Love means achieving a balance between your work and your life. Obsession means abandoning all hope for any reasonable balance. To attain and sustain love means recognizing that a book is what you write everyday, for as long as can without compromising everything else in your life to complete it. Believe me, you will be much more satisfied with the final product. You will also live to write another book, another day.

Balance is a desired state of mind, a willful relational achievement, a framing device by which to organize and make sense out of writing and living your life. For academics, that may also be what love is.

Okay, Lover, Let's Say You Think It Is a Book: What Are Editors Looking for?

In an article composed for *The Chronicle of Higher Education*, Dedi Felman, executive editor at Oxford University Press, provides a clear and concise account of what academic book editors look for.[30] She advises you to:

- identify the question driving your book;
- identify why that question matters;
- create a narrative structure;
- make the story your own;
- avoid abstraction;
- understand the true beginning of your story;
- understand the end of your story;
- be fair; and
- give your book a pithy title.

You can locate similar advice on publisher's websites. What I admire about Feldman's list is its emphasis on the *question* driving the story and the *elements of the story* itself. Where does the narrative begin? Where does it end? How can you develop a narrative structure that satisfies readers page by page? Because the book will be sold to a discerning academic market, you must always be fair in your treatment of both the subject matter and differing points of view that populate your account. And, of course, your book needs a pithy title.

This last element is key to the success of your proposal and ultimately to the sales for your book. There are basically two approaches to titling. The first is a straightforward clarity of topic that identifies both the subject matter and audience for the book. Most textbooks and practical guides, such as the one you are now reading, follow this example.

The second method of titling relies on being clever—or pithy. My *Encarta World English Dictionary* defines "pithy" as "brief yet forceful and to the point, often with an element of wit." Pithy titles are perhaps best conceived of in the way that Kenneth Burke conceives of motives for actions: as "shorthand terms for situations."[31] It's a shorthand rich in symbolism that taps into a shared cultural conscience, a source of instant identification that, at the same time, sums the motive for our telling the story in the first place. *A Need to Know* is an example of a title that taps into a shared cultural code for clandestine intelligence and, at the same time, spells out my motive for writing the book: I needed to know more about my family's clandestine history. Similarly, I am the co-editor of a volume titled *Weapons of Mass Persuasion: Strategic Communication in the Struggle Against Violent Extremism*, whose first four words taps into a shared cultural consciousness of "weapons of mass destruction," but with a twist. In both cases, coming up with a pithy title took some hard work.

My message here is simple: Don't skimp on the title. Don't just "call it something" in the hope that the ideas and storyline are so compelling that they will overcome a poor choice of title on the cover. They won't. Editors, like book buyers in Barnes & Noble, become interested in a book (or a book proposal) by what they see on its cover—the title and the author on a proposal: the title, the author, the art, and the reviewers blurbs on the back jacket of the finished product. If these are to their liking, then they open to the first page and begin reading.

With that in mind, let's examine more closely what you should place into a successful book proposal.

What Should Be in an Academic Book Proposal?

As Feldman has already pointed out, what creates initial interest in a book is the *question* you are asking. Editors *differ* on what constitutes an interesting question, and presses differ on how they define their *niche* in the academic publishing market.[32] So if you have ever gotten the blank stare from an editor when you approach her or him with an idea for a book, it could mean one of two things: Either that editor isn't interested in your question or your question just isn't that interesting (or, in the editor's judgment, wouldn't attract enough readers to justify the cost of publishing it).

How do you know the difference?

The difference is seldom, if ever, solely with the subject matter. Good questions can be fashioned out of any subject, and good books are annually written on obscure or arcane topics that the authors have managed to bring to life in fresh and surprising ways. But an important point here is to expand your idea to its **broadest possible question**, which is what will address the largest possible audience. Scholars often think defensively about their story and are afraid to stretch an idea beyond what they are sure they already know, but publishers want books to be as broad as possible. Although the old publishing adage is certainly true: "You can't make a silk purse out of a sow's ear," the problem is not the fault of the author's sow. The problem is in the author's *ear*.

Put simply, the difference is in the success of the *rhetorical and narrative appeal* you generate about the question relative to the subject matter for *a particular editor*. To develop your appeal, my advice is to follow a three-step process:

1. *Research the publisher's list and guidelines for submission:* The publisher's list includes all of the titles they have produced that are still in print. The guidelines for submission detail precisely what the publisher wants to see in the proposal. This list will clue you into the topics and approaches they favor. Be careful, though, as "me-too" books are seldom popular with editors. Make sure your project is original in some clear and consistent manner. Answer these two questions: What does your book contribute to the field that is not already known? Who cares about that? The answer to the first question is key to securing the interest of an editor; the answer to the second is key to securing a publishing contract. Remember: *Publishing is a business and books are products*. There must a viable market or else there is no good reason for a publisher to invest in your idea. By comparison, the reason you write a compelling abstract for a journal article is for the same reason, only it is for a different audience and market.

2. *Talk to an editor and gauge her or his interest in your project:* After you have completed your initial research and developed answers to the above two questions, you are ready to talk to editor*s*. Notice I use the plural and italics on the "s." No matter how well you think you know what a publisher is interested in and no matter how carefully you've worked on your pitch for it, editors often change jobs faster than websites; publishing houses get sold to larger entities; and tastes and interests change. My advice is to line up conference or convention time to talk personally to as many editors as you think might be reasonably interested in your project. The goal of the talk is to get one or more of them to invite your to submit a proposal. Editors spent a lot of time "on the road" attending conferences, and one major reason they go is to meet prospective new authors. Don't be shy, but don't be a pest, either: Mind your manners. If an editor tells you "the book isn't right for us," don't try to talk him or

her out of it. Find out what IS right for them. You may one day have a project that is right for this editor, so keep it cordial. You can curse your luck or the shortsightedness of the editor on your own time, and preferably alone. Similarly, if the editor expresses interest in your idea, follow up with a proposal within two weeks of the conversation. Don't make the mistake of assuming that interest expressed at this year's annual convention will carry over indefinitely. Nor you should think that your idea is "safe" or even that it "belongs" to you. You cannot copyright what is uttered in public space, nor can you assume that no one else is working on a similar idea. If it is a good idea and if it addresses a current issue in the research literature, chances are very good that other people are thinking along those same lines. And editors know both of these things to be true. Time waits for no (wo)man, and neither will a good editor wait for you.

3. *Develop the proposal to fit the publisher's interests and needs* [and this is the same advice I'd give someone writing an article]: Having successfully completed steps one and two, you should be able to write a compelling proposal. Please *follow the guidelines for submission* listed on the publisher's website.[33] Most publishing houses require similar submission materials, but there are important differences among them. Basic to all proposals are:

- Title
- Description of the project (the narrative)
- Market (include main competitors)
- Unique features of the proposed text (and why yours is better)
- Table of contents/outline (extension of the descriptive narrative)
- Details (length/word count, artwork, date of proposed delivery of manuscript to publisher, etc.)
- Author's *curriculum vitae*

Some publishers want to see sample chapters and others want to see outlines. If the publisher wants a sample chapter (or two), don't submit the proposal until you have a good one (or two). Because so much of creative nonfiction depends on your writing ability, your sample needs to really shine. Nothing can turn off an editor more quickly than creative nonfiction that is not particularly creative or compelling. One well-known series of creative nonfiction narratives, "Writing Lives," edited by Art Bochner and Carolyn Ellis, won't review anything less than a full manuscript.

If the publisher wants to see a fully developed outline rather than a sample chapter, give them the fully developed outline. One word about outlines: Just because you sell a book based on an outline doesn't necessarily mean the manuscript you submit will follow it to the letter. But neither should it detour from it overly much. Editors understand that writers change their minds during a project, and that's generally okay. But if you deviate a great deal, you should inform your editor and make sure that the changes you want to make still render the manuscript viable for the intended market.

Conclusion

Submitting work to scholarly journals and presses is an inevitable and often intriguing aspect of the life you have chosen. This chapter has provided some useful resources that should demystify the process and equip you with better ways to succeed in your publishing career.

The life of an academic writer is a life of revisions and resubmissions, of developing and later modifying proposals, and of learning how to separate useful criticism from less useful reviews. If education is the basis for "lifelong learning," then entering the academic writing life is the basis for "lifelong improvements" in the quality and content of our ideas.

Writing for academic outlets isn't easy. Nor is submission of your work ever totally free from anxiety or from the occasional frustration of rejection. But rejection and anxiety can be managed by taking a longer view of your career and by viewing those rejections in relation to your successes. When the good news arrives, celebrate it. When the bad news arrives, don't dwell on it. Recognize that one of the unspoken truths of academic culture is that ours is an enviable life, a wonderful life, but that one of the costs of living it is dealing with constant criticism of our work. Most of that criticism is productive and leads to improved thinking and writing. When it isn't or doesn't, just learn to say "*&%#@ it," and move on.

The best revenge for a poor review is a rich and well-lived life. So keep at it.

Little did I know that when I asked Gerry Phillips that fateful question about journal submissions and then enrolled in Phil Klass's creative nonfiction seminar that I would someday become someone recognized as a well-published scholar. Despite years of hard work learning how to write, and a few more years of learning to deal with rejection and success, I have so thoroughly enjoyed my writing life that I often say it has been "cake." That my ideas have had some impact in my discipline is frosting on the cake.

Activities and Questions

1. Consider your current narrative project. What is your narrative about? Who is your audience? What, if anything, might you want to reconsider about it to broaden your audience to include members of the general public?

2. Assume you are planning to attend your national convention with the goal of speaking to editors about a book project you have in mind. Write out your "elevator speech" or "pitch" about the project. Now list at least three important questions you want to raise with the editors. What do you need to know to proceed with the development of a successful book proposal?

3. Select two titles from your bookshelf that represent the sort of work you plan to do. Construct a book proposal based on their content, approach to the subject, and style of writing. How does your project compare to these? What makes your contribution original? What niche might your work fit? How can you use this comparative information to improve your pitch and your proposal?

4. Select from your files a letter of rejection from a journal editor or conference organizer that occurred at least six months ago. Reread the submission that was rejected. Do the editor's/organizer's comments ring true? If not, compose a letter spelling out your responses. If so (and assuming you haven't already done it), what should you do to redo the piece? Barring that, is there perhaps an alternative outlet that might be more appropriate for it after you have mined the editor/organizer's comments?

5. Select from your files a "revise and resubmit" letter and share it with your class or writing group. Explain how you addressed the

reviewer's concerns and editor's instructions. Read aloud the letter you composed to the editor as a result. Hold a discussion about successful and unsuccessful strategies for moving from "revise and resubmit" to acceptance.

Notes

1. For a brief portrait of Gerry, see (Goodall 2002b).

2. I didn't get a study carrel until I was writing my dissertation and then only by default. My name was on a list. So I write here not from personal experience so much as from observation of those who were truly virtuous.

3. In those days, only geniuses went into doctoral programs. Has this, too, changed?

4. The culturally sanctioned exception to this general rule was when faculty "needed to read (or write) *without* interruption." Graduate students were the "interruption." Department chairs tolerated reading (or writing) at home only if faculty were productive. To be considered "productive" usually meant a published article or two every couple or three years. That would leave plenty of time for smoking.

5. Some of the geniuses in our grad program disputed this rule or rebelled against it. Most of them didn't complete their dissertations. Those few who did graduate, with rare exception later failed to attain tenure unless they took positions at small liberal arts colleges, where tenure and promotion is/was based on high-quality teaching and being a jolly good [*sic*] fellow. Moral: To be disciplined as a writer, or undisciplined as a writer, that is the question! And be wise enough to make your career moves accordingly.

6. I was the second choice after a failed first offer and it was late in the hiring season. I later learned I had been a "desperation hire," which, by that time, was already obvious to me. I was assigned to teach organizational communication (which I had never studied) and serve as the faculty advisor to the student newspaper (which I had never done), in addition to teaching three sections of public speaking during the week and (for extra money) a graduate seminar in administrative science (human relations management) on Saturday mornings.

7. Some would argue that electronic submissions are a source of major change, but I respectfully disagree. Authors still need to write the

paper and a cover letter, etc., and submit it, whether by keystroke and email or postage stamp and snail mail.

8. See his website: http://216.92.255.170/williamtenn/

9. I say this because successful academics are by nature highly competitive and because the competition for journal space is intense. Most respected academic journals have a better than 90% rejection rate. Similarly, for every five book contracts signed by a trade publisher, odds are that only one or two books will actually be produced. Academic presses do expect a finished manuscript, and their completion rates are around 75%.

10. Submission guidelines for academic journals and presses are readily available online via the journal or publisher's website. Read them before you submit anything and contact the editor if any of the guidelines are missing or unclear.

11. For example, the University of California at Berkley admissions office processes over 20,000 applications a year. See http://www.foothill.edu/transfer/essay.html

12. All admirable lifelong learning virtues, no doubt. I'm no more calling them into question than is the admissions counselor I'm quoting. The point is not to critique the ideas, but the way they are rendered.

13. Oh, baby!

14. I especially recommend the International Congress on Qualitative Inquiry, held annually: http://www.c4qi.org/iaqi/home.html. Other academic organizations sponsoring narrative scholarship include the National Communication Association (Ethnography Division), The Society for the Study of Symbolic Interaction, and the International Institute for Qualitative Methodology at the University of Alberta (http://www.uofaweb.ualberta.ca/iiqm/index.cfm), Ethnographic and Qualitative Research in Education, and the Manchester Discourse Power Group (DPR). When you attend conferences, go to the panels, hang out in the hotels, and grab something to eat or drink with those you meet. Attend the general information sessions and subgroup business meetings. Develop a *personal network*.

15. For an extended discussion of what they look for and work they considered exemplary, see Denzin and Lincoln (2001).

16. For a good basic guide, see Gump (2004).

17. Reviewers and editors do not always agree on how to improve or revise a manuscript. And, honestly, not all the advice they give is useful

or even necessary to follow. But most of it is. Do not be dissuaded by a poor review or even a mean-spirited one. Trust the editor to determine which of the reviewers' suggestions should be followed and trust in the power of karma to get even with a mean-spirited reviewer.

18. See, for example, Thyer (1994).

19. Personal communication, July 14, 2007.

20. Donovan (2004).

21. In the 18th and 19th centuries, visiting scholars presented "letters of introduction" to gain entry to universities, social circles, and professional societies. Today, business cards and email do the same basic work.

22. Please see Thyer (1994).

23. Notice I do not say, "Turn the dissertation into a book." In all but the rarest of cases, that sort of talk is folly. Dissertations are a unique (and, in my view, an obsolete) genre. Although it is advisable to take the work done for a dissertation and recast it entirely for a wider academic audience, please do not make the common error of asking editors to read your dissertation (unless they are related to you or dating you, they won't), or mislead yourself into thinking that you will have to do very little work to turn the dissertation into a book. Your dissertation has an audience of four or five committee members; your book needs to appeal to an audience of many hundreds or thousands.

24. It takes between a year and half to two years to write and publish the average academic book. According to Robert Bly (2005) "The average nonfiction book is about 200 pages in typeset, published form, with approximately 400 words a page. That's 80,000 words; about 320 double-spaced typewritten manuscript pages (with computer fonts, the number of manuscript pages becomes less and less important and the word count more so). Your book might be longer or shorter, ranging from 35,000 words (a slim, 100-page volume) to 200,000 words or more" (article available online at: http://www.talewins.com/bly1.htm). If you have less material than that, or more, you should reconsider whether or not you have a book project.

25. This advice may seem at odds with Gerry Phillips's statement about what it takes to complete a book project. But Gerry Phillips, for all his hard work, enjoyed a rich and robust life, including time as a Shakespearean actor, a weekly poker club, and love of time spent

with family and friends. Bottom line: write every day, but not *all* day. And certainly not all night!

26. Boice (2000).

27. I love this line! I modified it slightly from the original. See Walt Whitman (1876). Like this:

> I celebrate myself, and sing myself,
> And what I assume you shall assume,
> For every atom belonging to me as good belongs to you.
> I loaf and invite my soul,
> I lean and loaf at my ease observing a spear of summer grass.

28. Wolcott (1990).

29. Fagan (2006).

30. See Felman (2006).

31. Burke (1984, p. 29).

32. A "niche" can be a political perspective (Routledge tends to sponsor lefty books; Left Coast Press does as well, but has carved out its own niche in qualitative inquiry and archaeology/museums studies) or a niche market perspective (university presses, in addition to their scholarly lists, often feature books that are of interest only to residents and scholars of the states that support them). All publishers are driven by the profit motive and the desire to produce books that are positively reviewed.

33. For example: Left Coast Press (http://www.lcoastpress.com/prospective_authors.php),

    Oxford (http://www.us.oup.com/us/corporate/proposalsubmissionpolicy/?view=usa),

    Peter Lang (http://www.peterlang.com/Index.cfm?vSiteID=74),

    Routledge (http://www.routledge.com/proposal.asp),

    Sage (http://www.sagepub.com/repository/binaries/guidelines/SubmissionGuidelines.pdf).

    University presses are located by typing NAME OF STATE university press into the search engine of your choice.

Chapter 4

Reading and Evaluating Narrative Scholarship
From Appreciation to Contribution

What I Did on My Summer Vacation

Picture me in Ardmore, Alabama, during the long dry summer of 1987.[1] I am, at that time, thirty-five years old with hopeful eyes and just this side of handsome, living largely on my dreams of an epic writing life while doing my lesser daytime job teaching at a local university. The local university was UAH, say U-AHHH, the University of Alabama in Huntsville, the university of "the empty head,"[2] which itself was living largely on its own dream of achieving seriously higher status as a recognized center of space science, engineering, and materials technology.[3]

It was an odd and yet interesting place for me to be me. So I wrote about it. I had recently learned that the genre-crossing style of writing I was doing was something called "ethnography,"[4] although I inflected that style with a one part new journalism and two parts rock 'n roll, the result was a series of nonfiction short stories about living and working in rocket city, complete with its vision of a future made of the confluence of capital and technologies and conservative, Christian politics.

As I say, it was an odd and interesting place for someone like me, a critically and culturally oriented nontechnologist with a wide liberal stripe and no Baptist desire with a headlock on my heart. Odd and interesting for someone like me, trained in communication theories and qualitative research methods, with creative and biographical writing as my research tools. Kenneth Burke told me, over dinner one night at Mark Twain's house in Hartford, Connecticut,[5] that this odd juxtaposition of method, opportunity, community, and madness provided me with everything I needed to enact "perspective by incongruity."

I never forgot that comment. I turned my own particular "perspective by incongruity" into a reason to explore an art form by writing from that perspective about Huntsville. It was a critically informed cultural take on the community, its secret Star Wars command and its public shopping malls; its software start-ups and its bottomless military funding; its new venture capitalists and their old gothic Southern neighborhoods, where there was still a reasonable likelihood that the nice retired gay person who read the Atlanta newspaper on their front porch under the magnolia tree down the street in the late afternoons was also keeping captive a crazy relative in the attic while investing that relative's money in illegal arms deals in Nicaragua.

Huntsville was a critical cultural nexus, where the seemingly ordinary mixed it up with the truly strange. How to convey that?

I chose this "new" style because there was no way the old style of traditional academic reporting couldn't handle the "it" that was there and then. It was no longer possible for me to accurately *represent* the culture, for accuracy in this government town was both a political fiction and a strategic deflection away from what was really going on, just beneath the surfaces of talk.

I needed to develop a style of writing that was capable of bringing readers into the symbolic dimensions of a constructed storyline, the seeds planted into everyday conversations by naming things that would only later blossom into patterns, the patterns themselves only evident further on. I needed to connect those symbolic patterns to human mysteries by exploring the confluence of capital and desire, the contradictions of love and work and money amid the lived complexities they lived through and often for. It was necessary to move away from strict reporting to *evoke* the local nuances, the everyday ironies, the high subtleties of language that marked the side-by-side "plural present" of the given place, of the particular people, and of the velocity of change and of the emotional work of the time.

Perspective by incongruity no longer seemed so strange to me.

What seemed strange was the fact that the manuscript that came from those rich engagements was roundly rejected. I thought—no, I *knew*—I was doing the right thing in my writing, but academic editors from sea to shining sea told me "no." No.

No?

Oh, they *liked* it. They praised the boldness of it. They thought the quality of the writing was good, *original* even. But I was assured there was no apparent scholarly market for that sort of genre-crossing narrative writing, not about organizational cultures, not about communities, not about government work or summer conferences.

By then, I had pretty much decided that if I couldn't bring this sort of writing to my scholarship, and this sort of scholarship into the field, that I ought to seriously consider leaving the academy. I figured I had the summer to think it over.

The long dry summer of 1987.

Then a miracle occurred, or maybe just an odd thing, but either way what happened saved me from myself. I received a phone call from Kenny Withers, the executive editor at Southern Illinois University Press. He said, "I have good news! I'm publishing your book."

I thought he had made a mistake. "But you rejected the manuscript a few months ago," I offered.

"I know that," he replied. "But I've had a recent change of fortune and so I've changed my mind."

He could probably feel my smile through the telephone line.

"I will ask that you make one change to the present manuscript."

"Oh? Okay," I said. "What?"

"I want you to add a final chapter that ties what you've written in the previous chapters into ongoing conversations in the research literature."

I felt deflated. Hadn't one of my arguments been that narratives *were* theoretical contributions? Hadn't I already bowed enough to scholarly tradition by including a comprehensive list of references (admittedly under the rock 'n roll label "influences")?

I don't remember what I said to Kenny but I do remember his response. He said, "Look, I know what you've written will be *appreciated*. The writing is strong enough. But I want to help you find a way to show how this style of writing makes a *scholarly contribution*. In the end, that will serve you a lot better. And you might sell a few books."

So I wrote that chapter. Grudgingly. Read that chapter and you will see how grudgingly. It begins:

> I did not want to write this concluding chapter.
>
> It was composed at the insistence of my editor upon the advice of at least one of my reviewers. These individuals felt that to adequately address an academic audience I would need to bring the book to a final place like this one, where I could "tie into" the existing literatures, comment on the

usefulness of the study and its subversive style of writing, and make some overall estimate of what I have learned.

Perhaps they are right.

My reluctance to give in to their insistence grieves even me. After all, I was reared in academic traditions of scholarship. I know how important it is to make an argument, document it with material drawn from the literature, and show the relevance of your own small brushstrokes against the larger canvas of inquiry. I know this, but I can't do it.

Not their way. At least not here.

Casing a Promised Land celebrates a form of resistance to that argumentative impulse. What I set out to do was to show, to reveal, to represent; what is asked of me now is to tell about, to theorize, to prove or at least to argue for. At the heart of my purpose was to demonstrate that the conventions of scholarly writing could be challenged, that news could be made that did not so much tie into the literature as untie from it. That a story could do what narrative theories, organizational theories, and rhetorical theories had not done.

To write the sort of concluding essay that is required here is to suggest—no, worse, to endorse—that it is needed. Naked storytelling is maybe all right as a sideshow, but the real point of this book is best dressed in traditional academic clothes. At least wear the old school tie!

That last paragraph was fun to write, but this book is a first step and first steps often involve compromise.

You are now reading mine.

Maybe I'm afraid they are right. Besides, I know I want to see the book published and if this is all it takes to accomplish that, well …

This is the part where the detective cops out. Not entirely, mind you. But enough to suggest to the reader he isn't pure. Enough to remind himself of it too.

So I give. At least a little bit. A compromise.

It goes like this[6]:

That chapter is not the best chapter in the book. Writing done grudgingly seldom is. But in the end, just as Kenny predicted, the advice he gave me about including it has proven exactly right.

There is a little more to this story.

The "change of fortune" Kenny referred to was his sale of the paperback rights to a book by William B. Ober entitled *Boswell's Clap and Other Essays: Medical Analyses of Literary Men's Afflictions*. Because a university press is a nonprofit organization, Kenny needed to write off his profits from the sale against projected losses by signing books he liked, but didn't think would earn back the investment he made in them. My book was one of them. Actually, he later told me my book was at the head of his list of books he felt wouldn't make a dime.

There wasn't a market, you see.

Happily for both of us, he was wrong. *Casing a Promised Land: The Autobiography of an Organizational Detective as Cultural Ethnographer*[7] sold well enough to justify two more editions and is still in print. It was reviewed widely and well inside and outside of the academy, including a prize review in the *Los Angeles Times Book Review* under the title "Philip Marlowe, Private Ethnographer." It became standard reading in graduate seminars.

Perspective by incongruity. From the other side of the story, it's still the right name.

I had proven (at least to myself and a few others) that I/we could write scholarship in narrative forms and create audiences for my/our writing inside *and* outside the academy. There may not have *been* a ready market for this sort of writing, but there soon became one.[8]

I've learned to take a larger, if somewhat less exalted view of it.

After all, where would I be now without Kenny Withers? Indeed, where would I be now without his sale of paperback rights to an obscure scholarly treatise on an esoteric topic? Indeed, where would I be now without Mr. Ober's interest in the repeated bouts of gonorrhea suffered by the journalist James Boswell?

With facts like these, who needs to write fiction?

Not me. But writing scholarly books like *Casing a Promised Land* did (for me) and does (for you) raise questions about the relationship of facts to fictions, particularly when the form of the story reads a lot like a novel. Which is to say writing stories raises questions about how stories make contributions to knowledge, which then raise additional questions about the scholarly value of truth claims in relation to qualities of evidence revealed in narratives.

Let's examine those issues in light of recent arguments.

Narratives as Evidence

First things first: Stories, whether fictional or factual (or "factional"[9]), are literary expressions of and about the human condition. No one would seriously dispute the claim that novelists (particularly the great ones) open up rich worlds to their readers and that within those worlds we may come to learn more about social life, or professional life, or love, or politics, or economic injustice, or racial inequality, or the intricacies of class warfare, etc., than we learn reading even some of the best social science or analytical philosophy on the same subjects.[10]

There is no lesser beauty to a fictional truth than to a factual one. Unless, of course you've claimed the fiction was a fact.[11] Then, if your deception is exposed, you will be publicly guilty of misrepresenting the truth and misleading your readers. Your credibility will be compromised and with it, your career.

What does lessen narrative beauty crafted in the service of truth is a badly told tale. To borrow Walter Fisher's well-known criteria, either the narrative doesn't "hang together" as a story and/or else it doesn't "ring true."[12] If readers disbelieve the story, they doubt its *veracity*. If they doubt its veracity, so, too, do they discount the value of any perceived beauty associated with its expression.

Nor is "truth" somehow compromised because the prose or poetry used to construct it is drawn from the imagination. We all imagine worlds in order to enter them, whether the source of our imagining is Shakespeare's sonnets or Schrödinger's cat. Imagination is essential to discovery and discovery is how we begin to create knowledge.

The only thing other than outright fabrication that compromises truth is insufficient *evidence* used to support it. Viewed this way, narratives *seemingly incur an additional burden of proof*: If authors of these narratives seek to be taken seriously as scholars, we need to satisfy the evaluative scholarly criteria for evidence *in addition to* the literary criteria we use to evaluate good stories.

But *is* this the case?

Perhaps not. Donald Polkinghorne offers a comparison of traditional and "reformist" (including narrative) social science on the issue of evidence and finds that the criteria used to evaluate the *believability* of arguments is remarkably similar.[13] Both groups expect the evidence given to support the claims advanced, regardless of whether the evidence is in the form of story or statistics. In both cases, the arguments we advance are *probable*, not certain, and therefore the common standard of reasonableness applies. Put simply: Is it reasonable to agree with the author(s) that Z is true (or, narratively, that this is why or how something happened) because of X and Y?[14]

Polkinghorne claims that within the community of science, both traditional and reformist writers *must be accountable to readers* who raise questions about the validity of their conclusions based on the evidence provided. For narrativists, "the differences in people's experienced meaning and the stories they tell about this meaning and the connections between storied texts and the interpretations of those texts" (p. 471) are the two sources of evidence-to-argument concern. He elaborates:

> The disjunction between a person's actual experienced meaning and his or her storied description has four sources: (a) the limits of language to capture the complexity and depth of experienced meaning, (b) the limits of reflection to bring notice to the layers of meaning that are present outside of awareness, (c) the resistance of people because of social desirability to reveal fully the entire complexities of the felt meanings of which they are aware, and (d) the complexity caused by the fact that texts are often a co-creation of the interviewer and participant. (p. 480)

Polkinghorne sums the two responses narrative authors make to these possible objections: Some of us rely on the story itself to convey the richness and detail necessary to meet the criterion of reasonableness; others provide a concluding section (similar to the Discussion section in a traditional scholarly article or the final chapter that Kenny Withers asked me to write) that *contextualizes* the themes of the narrative and connects them to ongoing scholarly discourse.

Polkinghorne does not suggest that one method is "better" than another, but rather concludes: "This basic idea of validation placed the judgment of the worthiness of a research knowledge claim in readers of the research. It is the readers who make the judgment about the plausibility of a knowledge claim based on the evidence and argument for the claim reported by the researcher" (p. 484). So the judgment of the relative (scholarly) truth and (literary) beauty of a narrative rests solely with the evaluation of the readers.

That conclusion rings true to my experience.

The Society for the Study of Symbolic Interaction (SSSI) affiliate of the National Communication Association (NCA) announces an annual competition for the Ellis-Bochner Award for best published article, essay, or book chapter in Autoethnography and Personal Narrative Research. The SSSI-NCA Affiliate welcomes nominations/submissions of published works that advance, reflect, and/or expand perspectives on autoethnography and/or personal narrative in the spirit of Ellis and Bochner's scholarship. Submitted works will be evaluated in terms of the following criteria: (1) originality; (2) creativity and quality of narration; (3) evocative writing; (4) engagement with human emotionality and subjectivity; and (5) significance of contribution to the field and/or to social justice. The award review committee welcomes publications that experiment with novel forms of expressing lived experience, including literary, performative, autobiographical, poetic, multi-voiced, dialogic, and co-constructed representations of lived experience.

Evaluation will be administered by the following review committee:

Dr. Ron Pelias, Southern Illinois University
Dr. Laurel Richardson, Ohio State University
Dr. Carol Rambo, University of Memphis
Dr. H.L. (Bud) Goodall, Arizona State University

Eligibility: Single and co-authored works published in any academic or trade outlet. To be considered, a submission must have a publication date within the two calendar years prior to the year the award is given (2005 and 2006). The award winner will receive a cash award and the Ellis-Bochner Award plaque, which will be presented at the 2007 Annual NCA Convention.

What Do Critical Readers Want, Or: What Makes a Narrative Good?

Why do readers turn to narratives? Is it simply for the pure satisfaction of spending time in the company of a well-voiced writer who can tell a good story? Yes, sometimes.

Is it because the narrative will provide you with ways into lives that you otherwise cannot or will not encounter in any other way? Yes, sometimes.

Is it because you are interested in the craft, and you will learn to write better by reading more? Yes, sometimes.

Is it because it affords you a way to imagine yourself anew? Yes, sometimes.

There are as many self-indulgent reasons to become an avid reader of narratives as there are avid readers of them.[15] All of these reasons come fully equipped with the reader's own personal criteria for what makes a "good narrative" good. But as a scholarly reader and as a scholarly writer, all of the above reasons come with one additional requirement for that narrative: *to make a contribution to the field.*[16]

Of course! You say. That's obvious.

Is it?

Let's assume you read the above call for nominations for the Ellis-Bochner Award. Let's further assume that you can think of a piece or two that you would consider nominating. You read over the criteria: (1) originality, (2) creativity and quality of narration, (3) evocative writing, (4) engagement with human emotionality and subjectivity, and (5) significance of contribution to the field and/or to social justice. You are pretty sure you know what the first four items mean. But when you arrive at number five—"significance of contribution to the field and/or to social justice"—my guess is that you pause. How would you evaluate *that*?

For as long as I can remember, debates over narratives and contributions to knowledge have centered on questions of how we should evaluate them. What makes a good narrative a contribution to knowledge? That is the question.

We seem to have agreed on what makes a bad narrative bad (e.g., failure to meet Fisher's criteria; failure to provide sufficient evidence in support of claims; poor writing quality as demonstrated by telling rather than showing; lack of pay-off for the set-up; poor character development; etc.), but not, within the context of our academic community, on what makes a "good narrative" also a good contribution to knowledge. Go figure. Must be that scholarly critical orientation, eh? What Kenneth Burke, via Thorsten Veblen calls an "occupational psychosis" or "trained incapacity" to see beyond, or differently from, the language of criticism we've been taught to use.[17]

You might have noticed that my name appears on the call as one of the evaluators. That name recognition might, therefore, lead you to conclude that I own one of the four secret decoder rings[18] that unlock the meaning of that phrase, the other three belonging to my other three colleagues. But I can assure you that no such secret decoder ring exists. I can also assure you that the four of us charged with evaluating the submissions likely differ at least somewhat on how we interpret that phrase or what it means to us as we read the submissions. We may even argue about it.

I can also safely say that I doubt there ever will be a consensus opinion on the matter. Not for the four of us this year, not for the narrative community at large, and not among scholars worldwide. The determination of the value of *any* contribution to knowledge—narrative or traditional—will always rest with the readers, and readers will always have their own ideas about that.

Editors are readers. The novelist Zadie Smith, in an essay called "Fail Better," says: "Reading, done properly, is every bit as tough as writing,"[19] and I have never met a good editor, or reviewer, who didn't embody that deep understanding. They each have their own internal logics guiding their appraisal of narratives. They each bring their own skill set and preferences into play, much as a skilled amateur musician approaches a complex piece of music.[20] Your text is to them a composition, but it must be read in the right way—played with passion and grace—to be appreciated or better—to be considered a contribution to the field.

In the Ellis/Bochner award example, we see how a small group of North American reviewers established touchstones for how manuscripts may be reviewed in light of the goal of the award and the (admittedly, maybe necessarily ambiguous) criteria. But how the manuscripts *are read* is entirely of a different quality than the terms comprising the criteria we use to evaluate them.

Reading precedes, organizes, and shapes the process of evaluation. And how a piece may be read is not something that can be prescribed.

Consider this:

I asked Professor Robert Krizek for his views on how he reads and evaluates narrative manuscripts. Bob has participated on a variety of editorial boards for scholarly journals in the areas of communication, sport, health care, and the ethnography of community. He is a fine writer himself. Recently he was asked to review submissions for a special issue of a communication journal featuring narrative nonfiction. Here's his response to my request for information about what he looks for in a manuscript:

> To begin I think this (evaluating stories) is something those of us who write them do instinctively or intuitively—we feel that this makes a good story, this doesn't make a good story. But we should be able to go beyond gut feelings and critique born of intuition, and articulate what it is that we want in a story whose purpose is to impart knowledge primarily to a scholarly audience. … [I]f I were to list my criteria they would be fidelity, coherence, a relevant point/purpose (in the case of Communication scholars the purpose to some greater or lesser degree would be the imparting of knowledge or a sharing of an understanding about human communication), and experiential anchors.
>
> To begin, a story must have fidelity and coherence (to borrow Fisher's language).[21] For a story to have fidelity it must ring true/be believable or at least plausible for the audience/reader. Plausibility requires that the story should in some way relate to our experiences or at least tap into our range of imagery. In contrast, for a story to be coherent it must hang together well. The "hang together well" for me means that there not only is a plot (and all that is associated with a good plot) but also (and here's a key) a plot that is relevant for the context of the audience/reader. A story is always told for a specific audience for a specific purpose (A POINT!!) and, therefore, the audience for the story has expectations about both the form and content of the story. A good story respects those contextual expectations in the presentation of its point.
>
> Related to coherence, and perhaps the linguistic device that blends coherence and fidelity, is this notion of plot. A good story must be more than a chronology of events. To be a good story—one capable of sharing knowledge and understanding, it must address events in a way that often ignores linear sequence to make the events more interesting in order to facilitate achieving its point. The plot, characters, setting, and action all fit together in a way that the audience can perceive as plausible and in a way that achieves a purpose. Stories weave time, events, and people in ways that chronologies don't.
>
> Related to fidelity, and perhaps also coherence, is the notion of experiential anchors. A good plot just isn't quite enough. Somewhere in the story the author must provide experiential anchors, those extremely lucid moments of thick, rich description that invites and allows the reader full access to the story.[22] For me the strength of story as a way to share knowledge is that the power (to understand) lies with the reader not the writer. In more traditional research reports the writer/researcher holds the power. "Significant results were achieved" or "there are six basic categories revealed by the data" are common ways that writers/researchers

display this power. In narrative reports the power shifts to the reader and in order for the reader to be fully invested in this power, he or she must engage the story both intellectually and emotionally—enter with both the mind and body. The writer can only create the conditions for this engagement to occur, he or she cannot demand it or even ensure it. What he or she can do, however, is provide the reader with clear images (show don't tell) that anchor the reader in various and significant moments in the story. It is that thick description, the smell of freshly mowed grass or the feeling of being lost that anchors the reader in the experiential moment and allows them to engage the story in a meaningful way.

If all of this gets accomplished—fidelity, coherence, a point/purpose, and experiential anchors—then there is a possibility for" transferability" (to borrow Lincoln and Guba's[23] term or maybe it was Guba and Lincoln's[24] term). Through transference the reader may understand, absorb, and apply knowledge to her life that the author introduced through a story removed from the here and now. Oh, that reminds me of another criteria for a good story—the finesse and clarity with which an author leads the reader in and out of real time to story time. This movement from real to story back to real time enhances and often clarifies purpose. These movements act like transitions for time travel. Reissman[25] taught me about this. ...

As more and more narrative works hits the pages of our journals we should be able to articulate our reasons for why this story worked and this story didn't because in many instances that will be the difference between what gets published and what inhabits the bottom of our file cabinets.

Fidelity, coherence, a point/purpose, experiential anchors, transferability, and finesse in leading readers in and out of real time and story time. By way of comparison to the criteria established for the Bochner/Ellis award, we find solidarity on key ingredients. We could sum both views on the criteria for evaluating narratives thusly:

Editors want to see original stories that display creativity and quality of narration (e.g., fidelity, coherence, finesse) through evocative writing that provides the possibility of transference while engaging the intellect as well as human emotionality and subjectivity and that makes a point/satisfies a purpose through the significance of contribution to the field.

Although there is an emerging general pattern in these descriptions as to what editors, when working as readers, want to see in a narrative, there always will be some ambiguity involved in how writers make decisions about trying to meet or (preferably) exceed these criteria. So how should you deal with the ambiguity of evaluation? Here are my suggestions:

1. *Create the criteria you want readers to use within the context of your work:* The first rule of evaluating manuscripts is the same rule

regardless of format or genre: Did the author accomplish her or his goal? This means that it is helpful for readers to know what your goal is; it also means that you know what one critical metric is. Make sure you *accomplish* what you say you are trying to do.

2. *Be explicit about how your work connects to ongoing issues in the marketplace of ideas*: Remember that editors want to see work that makes a point and contributes to the field. Those are editorial goals and your job is to meet them. We have discussed textual strategies used by successful writers to signal to readers how and why their narratives fit into ongoing conversations: the use of an abstract, or a framing device, footnotes, or a conclusion section. Regardless of the method selected, be clear about the contribution this piece makes to that conversation.

3. *Understand that the textual choices you make will influence readers to evaluate your work in particular ways*: The nonnegotiable criteria for evaluating stories organize discursive reviewing practices around key terms: fidelity, coherence, experiential anchors, transference, engagement of the intellect as well as human emotionality and subjectivity, and, of course, finesse. Although it is hard to examine your own writing using these metrics, it is a good practice to try. It is even a better practice to ask others to help you (see below).

One additional observation: I once had this up close and personal experience with reviewing. It was a bit of irony, really, that was related to the "textuality" of my story: I submitted it to an academic journal only to have it rejected by one reviewer who wrote: "This looks too much like something Buddy Goodall would have written. Try to develop your own original style." Fortunately for me, the editor had a sense of humor and simply passed along the comment without insisting that I follow the advice. My point in telling it is that how we construct our narratives influences how readers bring in *their own interpretive resources* to make sense of them. I use the trademark * * * at the ends of sections[26] as well as a few one-sentence paragraphs. I later learned that seeing those devices on the page triggered the reaction for that reviewer.

4. *Realize that not everyone will like what you write nor will everyone approve of the narrative form you work within*: The corollary is equally true: You don't like everything written by others, nor do you approve of the writing in some of what gets published. People differ

in their tastes and in their tolerances. Accept it, but don't be ruled by it. Instead, "lay down a path in walking."[27]

Left Tackles and Chemistry: The Importance of (Some) Writing Groups

Rachel Toor was an editor at Oxford University Press and Duke University Press prior to launching her own narrative nonfiction career.[28] In a column for *The Chronicle of Higher Education*, she explains the importance of improving the quality of your writing by soliciting honest feedback from other writers.[29] She also points out how difficult that can be, particularly in today's extremely busy academic world. She writes:

> There is never enough time to do the teaching, advising, and writing that is part of the job; finding energy to help a colleague often gets lost between the intention and the undertaking. Asking someone to read a paper, an article, or a book manuscript is, let's face it, an imposition. No one really wants to read unpublished work. And the effort that goes toward polishing someone else's work is often, even if asked for, underappreciated. ... [M]ost of us wouldn't show our work if we didn't think it was good. What we want, if we're being honest, is the correction of some typos and a pat on the head. Once someone notices problems, we have to fix them, which is hard work and not as much fun as scrubbing the toilet. But for most of us, once the initial sting of good and right criticism has passed, we put our heads down and get back to work. And we are thankful to the reader who has saved us from ourselves.
>
> So what can an aspiring (or, for that matter, an established) writer do?

Toor points to a wonderful example—the writing group—that emerged at Duke in the 1990s. Although writing workshops and summer institutes have a long history, this group of four women simply made time in their busy lives to read and comment on each other's work while pursuing their academic routines. The result was four powerful and well-received memoirs: Alice Kaplan's *French Lessons*, Cathy Davidson's *36 Views of Mount Fuji*, Jane Tompkins's *A Life in School*, and Marianna Torgovnick's *Crossing Ocean Parkway*.

Writing groups, such as that at Duke, tend to work best when there is a both a common genre and common theme tying the individual works together. The four books that emerged out of the Duke group were all deeply rooted in personal experiences of cultures and languages. They brought academic theories and perspectives on gender, class, and ethnicity to the writing and they did so in ways that reached a much broader public audience.

In Rachel Toor's view, each of these women served as a "left tackle"[30] for each other: "Someone who allows you to do what you do best. Someone who protects you while you take risks. Someone who guards you from dangers you can't see." Every writer needs a left tackle. Or three or four of them.

Every writer working in a group needs every other person in the group to care as much about what *you* are writing as they care about what *they* are writing. If not more so. Group members must be able to separate their natural interest in their own work from a professional interest in seeing *you* succeed with *your* work. Friends, editors, and spouses/partners often get a heartfelt word of thanks for their contributions to books (whether or not they served as "left tackles" or in some other valued capacity), but writing groups seldom get credit. Why is that?

I think it's a chemistry thing. To find a good left tackle *group* means that all of the group members must be capable of watching out for, and coaching, each other. Talking to each other openly and honestly without the fear that *what needs to be said* will be perceived as hurtful or mean-spirited. Of course it helps if what is said *isn't* hurtful or mean-spirited, and even among well-intentioned professionals, "words of prey" sometimes fly. Not everyone takes criticism well. Nor will everyone always get along, for whatever reason. We all have bad days. So, at least in my experience of running writing groups, it helps a great deal if some clear rules are articulated early on. One of those rules must be "we are committed to helping each other achieve her or his writing goals; we know there will be times when that goal is tested; and when those times occur we are all committed to the quality of forgiveness."

As I said earlier, finding a left tackle or a left tackle group is a chemistry thing. Writing groups are *discussion* groups made up of passionate, imperfect human beings. While chapters are passed around and read (or posted and commented on), the real work in a discussion group is deciding *what can be said*, indeed, what *must* be said, about the work without unnecessarily offending the listener or allowing something that could and should be better handled stand as-is. And that requires a certain indescribable *social* chemistry.

You have probably observed that I am moving from an individual perspective on what makes for good narratives to a social perspective on what makes good narrative scholarship. In the final section of this chapter, I want to move a little farther into the public sphere by reminding all of us that narrative can serve a powerful tool for enacting social transformation, empowerment, and justice. "Narrative has the power to expose, break open, and revise unjust systems."[31]

Writing as Activism/Action

Beyond reading and writing narratives for self-satisfaction and self-improvement, writers also want narratives to *have impact beyond ourselves and a few of our colleagues, family members, and friends*. In that regard, we all write, as George Orwell cogently expressed it, for four reasons "that exist in different degrees in every writer":

1. *Sheer egoism*: desire to seem clever, to be talked about, to be remembered after death, to get your own back on the grown-ups who snubbed you in childhood, etc.

2. *Aesthetic enthusiasm*: Perception of beauty in the external world, or, on the other hand, in words and their right arrangement. Pleasure in the impact of one sound on another, in the firmness of good prose or the rhythm of a good story. Desire to share an experience that one feels is valuable and ought not be missed.

3. *Historical impulse*: Desire to see things as they are, to find out true facts and store them up for the use of posterity.

4. *Political purpose*: Using the word "political" in the widest possible sense. Desire to push the world in a certain direction, to alter other peoples' idea of the kind of society that they should strive after.[32]

Orwell concludes his essay with the observation that every writer is a product of whatever is happening around her or him at the time. In his case, "The Spanish war and other events in 1936–37 turned the scale and thereafter I knew where I stood. Every line of serious work that I have written since 1936 has been written, directly or indirectly, against totalitarianism and for democratic socialism." As Orwell's personal account of his own motives suggests, political narratives and events going on around us invite us to act. This reason for acting is also a reason for writing and reading, particularly for those of us in academic cultures who claim a critical/cultural stance. For example, Bent Flyvbjerg, in *Social Science that Matters*, writes that:

We may successfully transform social science from what is fast becoming a sterile academic activity, which is undertaken mostly for its own sake and in increasing isolation from a society on which it has little effect, and from which it gets little appreciation. We may transform social science to an activity done in public, for the public, sometimes to clarify, sometimes to intervene, sometimes to generate new perspectives, and always to serve as eyes and ears in our ongoing efforts at understanding the present and deliberating about the future.[33]

For Flyvbjerg, the vehicle for accomplishing a social science that matters is telling powerful stories that address values and issues of power. In that vein, Norman K. Denzin's *Flags in the Window: Dispatches from the American War Zone*[34] offers an alternative vision of "the long war" that brings a passionate critical perspective to bear on issues that have been dramatically influenced by the Bush Administration's policies and actions, particularly those in Iraq. Denzin takes as his task the reevaluation of the meaning of values such as democracy, science, patriotism, civil society, and authority. His contribution is both a fine story and a scholarly engagement with vital issues of the day that make social science matter to a broader public audience.

Of course, bringing a political perspective to matters of war is not the only way to make social science have greater public impact. One of the virtues of a body of feminist and performance scholarship has been its committed activism on behalf of a number of worthy awareness-that-leads-to-action causes, from worker rights to gay rights to social justice to ethnic violence to human trafficking to women's health care to abuse and addiction issues.

Feminist scholars have long been interested in producing scholarship that actively and productively intervenes in and provides resources for women's everyday lives. The provision of women's health care, for example, has benefited from decades of feminist research and advocacy. This includes the early second-wave feminists who produced the now famous *Our Bodies, Our Selves* to recent work that aims to reduce the access barriers that women of color and working-class women continue to face at home and abroad, or to critique and transform the medicalization of women's bodies and to empower women to reclaim their embodied experiences of illness, infertility, menopause, pregnancy, and other medicalized processes.[35] Recent work has also highlighted the value of narrative in reforming emergency medicine.[36]

Addressing real-world issues and problems brings with it the often fragile and conflicted politics of writing and performing narratives wrought of personal experience. For example, at a Qualitative Inquiry conference in 2005, Lisa Tillman presented a powerful and provocative indictment of some members of the gay community's lack of support of the Kerry/Edwards presidential ticket in Florida.

The audience responded to the performance in divergent ways.[37] Keith Berry, for example, said he felt "scolded," and wondered whether "evaluation trumps understanding" as a goal for autoethnography. He admits that others in his department as well as those present at the performance felt that Tillman should be free to express her experiences in any way she felt necessary. At the same time, he offers the following assessment of what he considers a larger issue about the relationship between "experience" in autoethnographic work, the "provocative" verbiage used to reveal it, and the relationship between criticism and creativity:

> I have learned to be fearful of simply leaving others to work through abstractly communicated ideas about vital social issues on their own. It is painful to allow others to "live their own story" when doing so drastically calls into question and refashions the ongoing constitution of my own. I have become concerned with provocative discursive moments like these, in that the ability to be good at writing (in this case, autoethnographically through poetic verse) seems to rely on minimizing verbiage. As a result, the extent to which we can complicate ideas is lessened.
>
> And these ideas need complicating. There's too much at stake. Granted, overly scrutinized ideas can limit creativity, but less circumspectfully relying on categories can minimize fairness, coherence, and, in effect, greater awareness. Provocative can be sexy, yet sometimes sexy feels dirty.[38]

Berry's publication of his views invited a response from Lisa Tillman. She writes:

> Delivering "The State of Unions" in that way to that audience sparked a lively, layered discussion. But at what cost and to whom? To this day, I pause reflectively and compassionately when reengaging the responses of gay male audience members, who felt "implicated," "scolded," even "gay bashed." Keith Berry's questions (what of my participants' responses? what of my role as rhetor?) stay with me. I believe in judging research practices as he (2006, p. 3) suggests: "by their impact and efficacy."
>
> Ethnographic dialogue must proceed from a reflexive stance of mutuality, empathy, and understanding (which perhaps I did not sufficiently communicate in this polemic). At times, that dialogue will include the expression of hurt, betrayal, and anger about and across our dominant and marginalized identities. Our responsibility as autoethnographers and performers includes making space for the range of responses our expression

evokes—and to respond with a heightened and better informed commitment to equality and justice.39

As the politics of narratives moves more directly into the public sphere, the question of "what constitutes a good narrative?" becomes more complicated. As the conservative rhetorician Richard Weaver once succinctly put it in the title of his most controversial work, *Ideas have consequences.*[40] Evaluations of political speech will inevitably be political themselves. Criticism may not trump creativity, but neither will creativity alone be a reasonable defense of provocative ideas.

This debate over Lisa Tillman's "State of the Unions" performance evokes questions raised by Joan Scott in her highly controversial and provocative essay, "The Evidence of Experience."[41] In that essay, Scott, a distinguished professor of history, writes:

> Experience is at once always already an interpretation **and** something that needs to be interpreted. What counts as experience is neither self-evident nor straightforward; it is always contested, and always therefore political. The study of experience, therefore, must call into question its originary status in historical explanation. This will happen when historians take as their project not the reproduction and transmission of knowledge said to be arrived at through experience, but the analysis of the production of that knowledge itself. Such an analysis would constitute a genuinely nonfoundational history, one which retains its explanatory power and its interest in change but does not stand on or reproduce naturalized categories. It also cannot guarantee the historian's neutrality, for deciding which categories to historicize is inevitably political, necessarily tied to the historian's recognition of his or her stake in the production of knowledge. Experience is, in this approach, not the origin of our explanation, but that which we want to explain.[42]

For Scott, one criterion for evaluating narratives of experience—and perhaps the most persuasive—is how that experience is historicized, contextualized, and questioned. For her, and for Berry, it is not enough to speak *from* experience; those experiences must be scrutinized for how and why they were called into being.

For me, what Scott calls for and Berry is moving toward is a more fully reflexive account of personal experience. However, in the realm of political action we must be careful not to privilege the historical and critical at the expense of the creative work—what Soyini Madison calls "dangerous ethnography"[43]—that is designed to productively irritate, provoke, and make messier those categorical aspects of lived experience that otherwise go unchallenged. That said, neither should we lose sight of our overarching vision to use narratives to *improve our communities.* Alienating those whom we hope to influence doesn't accomplish that goal. In Della Pollock's words, we need to find or make space for work of "the performative I" that also empowers an "ethics of sensuous coalition and a politics of errant possibility."[44]

As the Tillman/Berry debate points out, to attain that worthy goal without sacrificing the conversational and dialogic qualities of narrative ethnography will be challenging. The more political the ambition, the more passionate the engagement, the more volatile the prose, the more likely newer, harder questions will be asked about our motives as well as the scholarly value and worth of some of our work.[45] This latter challenge imposes evaluative criteria well beyond those associated with traditional aesthetic or artistic or ethnographic assessments of narratives.

This is not new. But it can be risky, particularly for untenured faculty and graduate students, and it should remind those whose work moves in this direction that scholarship done as activism works at an emerging intersection of personal experience, institutional boundaries, public expectations for publicly and privately supported research and teaching, and legal challenges to academic freedom and tenure.

But there is yet another concern, another challenge, that emerges from research and writing that is politically engaged, particularly when it is done with intimate others, friends, colleagues, and students. It is even a challenge for research and writing done about family members, friends, colleagues, and students who are dead.

It is a challenge that moves us into new discussions of *relational ethics.*[46] Carolyn Ellis, a pioneer in this area of inquiry through her own collaborative research and research she has inspired in her students and done with her husband, suggests that the criteria we use in conducting research and writing about intimate others must be drawn "from our hearts and minds." By this phrase, she means that we need to "acknowledge our interpersonal bonds to others, and take responsibility for actions and their consequences," mindful always of our position of privilege and power as the eventual authors of those narratives. She concludes her essay with the following sage advice:

> They say they just want to write their own story. I tell them that self-revelations always involve revelations about others (Freadman, 2004, p. 128).
>
> I tell them they don't own their story. That their story is also other people's stories. I tell them they don't have an inalienable right to tell the stories of others. I tell them that intimate, identifiable others deserve at least as much consideration as strangers and probably more. "Doing research with them will confront you with the most complicated ethical

issues of your research lives." I tell them they have to live in the world of those they write about and those they write for and to. I tell them they must be careful how they present themselves. "Writing about your depression and suicide attempt while taking sick leave and trying to earn tenure?" I ask, aghast, and the former student replies, "Yes, I have to write myself out of my depression." She does, and gets a teaching award the next year (Jago, 2002).

I tell them our studies should lead to positive change and make the world a better place. "Strive to leave the communities, participants, and yourselves better off at the end of the research than they were at the beginning,"

I say: "In the best of all worlds, all of those involved in our studies will feel better. But sometimes they won't; you won't." I tell them that most important to me is that they not negatively affect their lives and relationships, hurt themselves, or others in their world. I tell them to hold relational concerns as high as research. I tell them when possible to research from an ethic of care. That's the best we can do. "But what about those who kept secrets from me, who hurt me?" they ask, and I reply, "Write to understand how they put their worlds together, how you can be a survivor of the world they thrust upon you."

Sometimes I say, "I don't know."

I warn that they are not therapists so they should seek assistance from professionals and mentors when they have problems. I tell them I am not a therapist, but that I will be there for them. I seek to make my relationship with my students similar to what I want their relationships to be with those they study—one of raising difficult questions and then offering care and support when answers come from deep within. I tell them we will take each project on a case-by-case basis, and I promise to be available to discuss each step of the way. I tell them that every case has to be considered "in context and with respect to the rights, wishes, and feelings of those involved" (Freadman, 2004, p. 124).

I tell them that not only are there ethical questions about doing auto-ethnography but also that autoethnography itself is an ethical practice.

In life, we often have to make choices in difficult, ambiguous, and uncertain circumstances. At these times, we feel the tug of obligation and responsibility. That's what we end up writing about. Autoethnographies show people in the process of figuring out what to do, how to live, and what their struggles mean (Bochner and Ellis, 2006, p. 111).

I tell them that there is a caregiving function to autoethnography (Bochner and Ellis, 2006). Listening to and engaging in others' stories is a gift and sometimes the best thing we can do for those in distress (see Greenspan, 1998). Telling our stories is a gift; our stories potentially offer readers companionship when they desperately need it (Mairs, 1993). Writing difficult stories is a gift to self, a reflexive attempt to construct meaning in our lives and heal or grow from our pain.

I tell them I believe that most people want to do the right thing, the sensible thing. As human beings, we long to live meaningful lives that seek the good. As friends, we long to have trusting relationships that care for others.

As researchers, we long to do ethical research that makes a difference. To come close to these goals, we constantly have to consider which questions to ask, which secrets to keep, and which truths are worth telling. That's what I tell them. Then I listen closely to what they say back. (pp. 25–26)

As those of us who conduct qualitative inquiry become more self-reflexive about the practices of living with and writing about others, and as our maturity about the quality and power of personal narratives continues to grow, challenges to our sense of relational ethics and professional best practices are ripe for constant reexamination and discussion. There may never be consensus, but living with and questioning the tensions that define our craft is part and parcel of our moral obligation to use what we know, and what we do, to improve or perhaps to change the world.

But there is good news at this busy and at times confusing intersection. Think of it as a Burkiean comic corrective: As scholarship becomes increasingly public, engaged, and provocative, it will also be increasingly populated by scholars who no longer have to rely on a dead journalist and his case of the clap to break into print.

Activities and Questions

1. Using the criteria for a good story, critique the opening narrative about my experiences finding a publisher for *Casing a Promised Land.* What works well in it? What could be improved? What specific suggestions would you make to me about it?

2. In a piece done for *The Chronicle of Higher Education*, Rachel Toor (yes, the same Rachel Toor quoted earlier in this chapter) suggests that writers need to consider what gives readers pleasure, not just what our needs are to divulge information.[47] She points out that the best stories are written by authors that readers would like to spend personal time with, sharing a long walk, a dinner, or a conversation. In this way, she says that writing successful narratives is, like good teaching, an art of seduction with the erotic always in play. Discuss this principle of good writing and good teaching as it relates to the

material in this chapter—both the personal narrative that opens it and the resulting discussions of evidence, criteria, and relational ethics.

3. In much the same way that you might consider how your narrative will unfold in terms of its structure and storyline before you compose it, think about the criteria you would like your readers to invoke while reading your narrative before you write it. How can you provide criteria-earning triggering devices in the narrative itself? How do you let them know what you hope to accomplish in the telling of the story?

Notes

1. Ardmore was actually just my mailing address. The town of Ardmore is in northern Alabama above Huntsville, close to the Tennessee state line. I lived out in the country between Ardmore and Huntsville on Schoolhouse Road.

2. That was because the symbol of the university is the blue outline of a Spartan head with nothing in it. The university officials thought it meant that nothing was in it because at UAH everything was possible, but still.

3. Which, I am proud to say, it has. Princeton Review lists it as a "Best Southeastern College" and U.S. News & World Report places it among the best science and technology schools in the nation. This is no big surprise to anyone who knows Huntsville, as it has long been the home of missile technology since Warner von Braun brought his German rocket team over after WWII.

4. Nick Trujillo proclaimed that I was writing ethnography after I read my first chapter from the book on Huntsville to the Alta Conference on alternative approaches to organizational communication in the summer of 1986.

5. I don't want to convey a false impression about my relationship to Kenneth Burke. I had attended a talk he gave at the Eastern Communication Association and seeing that no one had arranged to take him to dinner, I volunteered. It was a wonderful evening for me because I got to ask him all kinds of questions about himself and his work that I had wondered about since grad school. I didn't realize at the time that "having dinner with KB" would also serve as a set-up that I would pay off many times in retelling the story, or that what he would tell me would serve as a guide to writing about Huntsville.

Note to newbies: Take some risks; volunteer; ask questions. You just never know what might happen.

6. Goodall (1989a, pp. 133–134).

7. Goodall (1989a).

8. I wasn't the only person writing this way who contributed to the acceptance of this method, but mine was the first book-length manuscript coming from the communication field done in this "new" style. Within that field, Tom Benson had published a long article, "Another Shootout in Cowtown" in 1980 (but then took so much heat for it he never wrote in that style again), in *The Quarterly Journal of Speech*, and Mike Pacanowsky had published (at my insistence) an article during Tom Benson's editorship of *The Quarterly Journal of Speech*, "Slouching towards Chicago" in 1988.

9. This refers to works of literature that combine real historical figures with fictional plot elements and characters.

10. This particular observation has been made by a variety of learned others. See, for example, Sennett (1982); see also Rorty (1979).

11. James Frey learned this lesson the hard way when his supposedly true memoir *A Million Little Pieces* was shown to have fictional scenes in it: http://en.wikipedia.org/wiki/James_Frey. Although Frey erred and was publicly shamed, the literary category of "memoir" is generally considered a subcategory of autobiography and may contain fictional elements. Gore Vidal's comment about the difference between the two is instructive: "a memoir is how one remembers one's own life, while an autobiography is history, requiring research, dates, facts double-checked" (Vidal, 1996). Frey's example points out how important it is for authors to be honest with readers; many best-selling memoirs contain fictional elements and no one complains about them so long as the writer describes the book as a combination of fiction and fact. For examples, see Kingston (1989). However, the "tell the truth" mandate is itself highly problematic; for an excellent discussion based on interviews with scholars who have authored creative nonfiction narratives and memoirs, see Owen, Mcrae, Adams, and Vitale (forthcoming).

12. Fisher (1984).

13. Polkinghorne (2007).

14. Another way to think about our demand for evidence and the criterion of believability in academic papers is captured in two statements often attributed to the social scientist Harry Stack Sullivan: "First you tell people what you're going to say, and then you tell them what you're not going to say, and then you say it, and then you tell people what you didn't say, and then you tell people what you said. ... At the end of my life I came to realize that during my whole academic career I had been writing as though my reader were a paranoid idiot." Whether Professor Sullivan actually said these things is hard to track down; see John Emerson's site: http://www.idiocentrism.com/fake.htm

15. Self-indulgence is not necessarily a bad thing. We consume that which brings us pleasure, that which delights the imagination and moves the will. Nothing wrong with that!

16. See Richardson (2000a).

17. Burke's (1965) discussion is on page 7 of his *Permanence and Change*. For a fuller account, including the controversy it generated, see Wais (2005).

18. I got this phrase from Kathy Miller, professor of communication at Texas A&M University.

19. See Smith (2007).

20. Metaphor derived (but modified) from Smith (2007).

21. Fisher (1984).

22. "Thick description" is a Clifford Geertz term; see Geertz (1973).

23. Lincoln and Guba (1985).

24. In Guba and Lincoln (1989).

25. Reissman (1950), among others.

26. This is a technique I "borrowed" from the noted American novelist and short story writer, Barry Hannah.

27. Verela, Thompson, and Rosch (1991). This is a principle of "mindfulness," which encourages a focus on the present and a preference for enlightened action over naysaying and negativity. In other words, prove the value of your writing by doing it.

28. See her bio at: http://www.racheltoor.com/Bio.html

29. Available online at: http://chronicle.com/jobs/news/2007/07/2007072701c/careers.html

30. A "left tackle" is vital to the health, quality of play, and well-being of American football quarterbacks, most of whom are right-handed and therefore can be blindsided by defensive linemen on their left-hand side. For a detailed explanation, please see Lewis (2007).

31. Madison (2005, p. 211).

32. From Orwell (1946).

   33. Flyvbjerg (2001, p. 166).

34. Denzin (2007a). For an excellent sampling of other qualitative scholars who have engaged these issues, see also Hartnett and Stengrim (2006) and Taylor, Kinsella, DePoe, and Metzler (2007).

35. Pollock (1999); see also Turner (2004); Parry (2006); and Ott and Geist Martin (2003).

36. See Eisenberg, Baglia, and Pynes (2006).

37. See Berry (2006). See also Tillman (forthcoming).

38. Berry (2006, p. 7).

39. Tillman (forthcoming, pp. 14–15).

40. Weaver (1984).

41. Scott (1991).

42. Scott (1991, p. 797).

43. Madison (2007).

44. Pollock (2007).

45. See, for example, Goltz (2007a). Dusty Goltz wrote and performed "Banging the Bishop: Latter Day Prophecy" in the Empty Space Theatre at Arizona State University, but only after a major public controversy over an advertisement for the performance was found "deeply offensive" by members of the Church of Latter Day Saints. The script may be found in Goltz (2007b).

46. Please see Ellis (2007).

47. See Toor (2007).

Chapter 5

Success in the Academy

The Attempted Symbolic Kill of a Storyteller: A Cautionary Tale

"This story will have a happy ending."[1]

Chris told us we needed to know that going in. He was right. That said, my apologies to any reader who may find a close parallel between this story and your own. I can only hope your story will also have a happy ending.

But there are no guarantees. You should also know that going in.

The story begins when I hired Chris out of his doctoral program. He was, and is, a narrative ethnographer, a creative nonfictionist, who brings a unique background in philosophy, religious studies, and communication to bear on issues of family communication, identity, and secrecy. During his "job talk," he presented a narrative that was well received by the faculty, save one person who shall remain nameless.

He got the job and moved his family to our fair city. I served as his department chair for three years before moving to my present position. During that time, he was an exemplary faculty member and received high marks from his students as a teacher. He began publishing his stories in academic outlets and worked on a book proposal. When I left that job, he seemed perfectly poised for tenure and promotion.

In the three years between my leaving town and Chris's tenure review, he continued to do excellent work. He volunteered to serve as graduate director, despite being untenured. He received high marks for teaching and his research continued to attract and develop a readership among qualitative researchers, narrativists, organizational, and family communication scholars. He attracted the attention of Art Bochner, who invited him to submit his book proposal for consideration in a prestigious series. He was praised by Norman Denzin for a presentation he made at the 2nd International Congress on Qualitative Inquiry. Readers around the country began using his published work in their seminars, occasionally dropping him personal notes of thanks. In his final review prior to his tenure-earning year, he received a unanimous endorsement from the faculty. He spent the summer working on his new book, by then contracted for the prestigious Ethnographic Alternatives series.

She who shall not be named, as a senior faculty member, was appointed to oversee and guide the construction of Chris's tenure portfolio. Depending on who you talk to, that may have been where the unraveling began. But perhaps not. It could have begun earlier, when he vigorously defended narratives as theory-building work in a faculty meeting and (as some say), he didn't read the situation as politically charged. Or it could have begun later, when, after the death of a close relative and some deep soul searching, Chris entered a "dark time" and wasn't "as easy to be around" as he had been. Who knows?

His tenure portfolio was submitted in September and he received a unanimous endorsement from his faculty, save one person, the same person but you have probably guessed that by now, who, once again, shall not be named. At Chris's university, a unanimous decision on a tenure nomination at the department level translates into assured clear sailing up to the provost's office, where the actual tenure and promotion decision is made. But even one vote against a candidate—it was only one vote—and the tenure "nomination" becomes a tenure "case" and must be reviewed at every level: the college committee, the dean, the university committee, and, finally, the provost.

That is when and where things fell apart. The vote from the college committee and endorsed by the dean was 8 to 1 against him.[2]

Chris was speechless. Devastated. He didn't understand how this could have happened to him, but neither could he accept it. He wrote a brief, stunned email to the external reviewers and a few friends to inform them of the negative decision.

We, too, were uniformly shocked, surprised, and unable to make sense of it. Then we got angry. How had this process gone so horribly wrong? Because tenure decisions are confidential, there is no easy way to find out. As Kenneth Burke would tell it: the order (university) protects its secrets, one of which is how it decides tenure and promotion. Or, in this case, tries to deny it.[3]

We made inquiries. Chris told us what little he knew. Reviewers and friends organized a protest. I wrote a letter to the provost asking for a reconsideration of the decision. Art Bochner talked to the department chair and to the dean. Roy Wood, a former provost at Northwestern, wrote to the provost. Carolyn Ellis, Norm Denzin, Ron Pelias, and David Weber added their voices to the growing chorus of complaint. Other faculty, both in his department and elsewhere on campus, contributed their views on the injustice that we felt had occurred.

Certain facts then emerged.

The first fact was that Art Bochner had been disqualified as a reviewer because he was the editor of the book series in which Chris's book was contracted.[4] To add insult to injustice, the college committee did not inform Chris of this decision before their vote, nor was he given an opportunity to name another reviewer to replace Bochner.[5] Bochner, before merely angry, became incensed.

The second fact that emerged in a conversation about the decision among Chris, his department chair, and the dean was that there was no question that his teaching and service were exemplary; nor was there any concern about the number or the scholarly outlets where his published research appeared. For anyone else coming up for tenure and promotion, what was in his file would have been enough. *More than enough.* This was truly confusing to all of us.[6]

In that same meeting with the dean, Chris discovered the third fact, the cruelest cut and cause of his denial of tenure: "I have failed to offer a compelling case in my dossier that my research adds anything to the disciplinary conversation in communication studies, or advances theory, or moves the conversation about relational or family communication forward. I have not convinced the committee or the dean that my work, as an alternative, expands the field."[7]

What?

This "fact" was simply untrue. The letters from the external reviewers *attested to the exact opposite* of it: Chris's work was original, his voice creative, his research insightful, and all of it made a contribution to knowledge! How much clearer could his contribution be?

Chris composed a letter to the provost asking for a reconsideration of his case. I reprint parts of the letter below, with names of university officials removed:

It was with shock and deep disappointment that I read (the Dean's) memo regarding my tenure case. The fact that I have been denied tenure was stunning enough given the strong evidence in my favor (excellent annual merit reviews, strong publication record, exemplary teaching and service, and strong outside reviews), but the extreme characterizations of my work and the intensity of the negative vote, along with the reasons given for not recommending me for promotion and tenure, were baffling. Narrative Inquiry, ethnography, and autoethnography have a long (and storied) history in the field of communication studies, and are widely accepted as legitimate research methodologies. Moreover, they are considered as among the primary research methodologies in the areas of relational and family communication. And this is, in fact, the first time during this process (either in the department or even in my refereed publications) that I have heard the criticism that my work does not connect in any meaningful way to communication scholarship. ...

I would like to set the record straight. ... My research clearly moves knowledge in a new direction ... a performative direction, a direction that stems from an epistemology that sees knowledge as praxis rather than as an object or a product. These research methodologies proceed by a logic that I would hope my peers at this university would value. The new narrative methodologies do not proceed via a traditional social scientific approach (hypothesis-test-conclusion), a linear-causal predictive view of reality, or a positivist or neo-positivist paradigm grounded in prediction and control. My scholarship does not seek to be work that, "generates data, tests predictions, or leads to explanations" (criteria cited _____ memo) though it clearly accomplishes goals that other methodologies cannot. ...

These are long-established distinctions, and in my field at least, accepted. In short, the large body of qualitative/interpretive/narrative research and scholarship with which I engage in scholarly conversation is coming at knowledge from a different perspective than that of the orthodox/traditional social science paradigm. So the idea that it should generate data, test predictions, or lead to explanations misses the point of the research. ...

According to the reviewers and editors of my published work, I have consistently met the criteria by which new narrative scholarship is judged within my disciplinary community. Since I was also trained in a traditional social science paradigm, I understand why someone might say that it does not meet traditional social science criteria. It purposely does not. But I ask that someone please look at my research from the perspective in which it is written and through the lens of the goals it is trying to achieve. ...

The memo goes on to say that I have not discovered anything, and have nothing insightful to offer. I fear this is a misunderstanding of my work. This form of scholarship does not tie knowledge up, like an object, in a neat package, and summarize key points in a list at the end of the work. ... That said, I have discovered much along the way, and have been praised for doing so. I have discovered that disruptions, like 9/11 or deaths in the family or other traumatic events, in the flow of everyday life can be read and engaged as springboards for dialogue and creative work, and for a reorientation of family and relational communication patterns. In my piece entitled "Disruption, Silence, and Creation: The Search for Dialogic Civility in the Age of Anxiety," I have extended dialogue theory to bring forward the interruption as the key moment in the making of what the top theorists in our field call "moments of meeting (Cissna and Anderson, 2002). And I have discovered that stories are the opening to possibility in these moments of trauma, with a storied methodology being a primary textual act that can serve to make real change in our social world. In other words, I have discovered that families and other close, enduring relationships often suffer in silence and thus lapse into secrecy as a result of these traumatic moments, and that researchers have not found ways to uncover anything more than the dysfunctional dynamics of this secrecy, but that the natural storytelling urge, invoked in close relational research praxis, can serve as a counterbalance to that dark, secretive, depressive energy that can overwhelm even the healthiest relationships in the face of loss. In other words, I have discovered that the relationship between the "researcher" and the "researched" is critically important in the discovery process. ...

Finally, the memo calls into question the choice of outside reviewers. (Department Head) made these choices because they are the top names in our field, and not just in my area of the field. These are three of the most respected scholars in communication studies, nationally and internationally. The memo goes on to question my connections to them. These people were chosen first because they are the giants in my area of inquiry. Of course I know them. It is a small world we inhabit. But I know them not because we are friends but because they have heard, read, and admired my work, and have approached me at conferences to discuss it. They have asked to use my work in their courses, and have sought my advice on how to use it, including in doctoral-level courses on new narrative methodologies. I do not invite them to my home; I do not call them or see them outside of conferences. I communicate with them by email on business related matters. We know each other through our work. ...

Nowhere in the Promotion and Tenure Guidelines does it say that anyone has to justify methodological preferences. This has never been stated to me before as a criterion by which I must proceed. The burden of proof, as I understand it, is on me to establish that my scholarly voice is being heard by an audience, that I am making a significant contribution to the disciplinary conversation, and that I am developing a national reputation as a respected scholar. That seems to be clearly demonstrated both by my work and by the letters in my dossier. ...

> I hope that this letter will help to clarify some matters. I ask that you reconsider the College's decision and appoint a committee to review my case that has members who are familiar with narrative scholarship. I hope, as I have always, to achieve tenure and promotion at ____. It is a fine institution, and I consider it my academic home.

On February 27, Chris was home in bed with the flu and a case of laryngitis when his department head called with the good news: "You got tenure."[8] Although he did not receive any details about how the final decision was reached, Chris was grateful to those of us who protested the initial decision as well as to his colleagues, save she who shall not be named, for their unanimous support throughout the process.

I told you this story had a happy ending.

But I also believe it is a cautionary tale for anyone who writes narrative ethnography or who relies on narratives as evidence of scholarship.[9] And there are important lessons in it. As you read the following sections on the tenure process, think about what we may glean from Chris's case as you prepare for a tenure and promotion process as well as a life in today's complex (and often conflicted) higher education environment.[10]

Tenure

Tenure is one of the most misunderstood and highly controversial concepts in higher education. It emerged historically as a protection for employment and academic freedom during a time when major donors to elite universities often exerted undue influence over the selection and retention of faculty, as well as their research agendas.[11] By placing the responsibility for hiring and retention of faculty in the hands of the faculty (rather than senior administrators who had to be responsive to the wishes of donors), and by contractually guaranteeing faculty who are granted tenure the legal right of academic freedom to pursue/express/ publish ideas wherever they may lead, tenure protects faculty with controversial political, professional, or social views, including providing protection for those who express views contrary to the established policies of the universities that employ them. Tenure also encourages an intellectual environment where the freedom to pursue any idea—not just "safe" ideas—is valued, which is one important way in which colleges and universities serve as protected cultural spaces so vital to the interests of a democratic society.

Tenure also protects colleges and universities, as the awarding of tenure is a considered a faculty benefit as well as a legally protected "property right."[12] Faculty often remain at the institutions that grant them tenure, although recent evidence suggests that this may not be as advisable due to the "loyalty tax" associated with spending one's entire career, or even a major portion of it, at one institution.[13]

Tenure is, in the public mind, often equated with permanent job security. Because it is difficult to revoke once it is awarded, most people believe that receiving tenure guarantees lifetime employment, and, for most faculty members granted tenure, it effectively does guarantee it. But, unfortunately, it has also led some unscrupulous individuals to become seriously unproductive after they receive tenure. The image of a "retired on the job" faculty member with a "fat" state-supported salary[14] who only shows up sporadically to teach from yellowed lecture notes[15] and who conducts little or no research[16] has contributed significantly to a public perception of tenure as an antiquated institution that ought to be abolished or at least significantly reformed, particularly at state-supported institutions in the United States. Although this stereotype does not, in any way, represent the vast majority of hard-working academics, I am sorry to say that on every campus where I've been employed, it does characterize a small number of people. The academy is not alone in its occasional tolerance of unproductive employees, but the issue of tenure is often debated on account of it and has faced (and is facing) serious challenges to its continued legitimacy.

Challenges to Tenure

Although tenure has not been abolished in the United States, it has been reformed and it can be revoked. State-supported institutions, in particular, have had little choice. They, and the Boards of Regents that govern them and the legislatures that fund them, must be responsive to taxpayers, however ill informed those taxpayers may be on the issue of academic freedom and tenure, because taxpayers support them.[17] For this reason, tenure is no longer a guarantee of lifetime employment. It may be revoked due to financial exigency (e.g., when entire departments or institutes are eliminated because officials have determined that they are unworthy of continued state investment or that they can no longer support themselves through grants and contracts) or for "just cause," which generally means not performing up to established standards, however fuzzy those standards may be or how they may have changed since older faculty members received tenure twenty or thirty years ago.[18] Nor is tenure now necessarily the full protection of academic freedom to say whatever the hell you want to, as Native American activist and former Ethnic Studies Professor Ward Churchill discovered.[19]

Post-Tenure Reviews

These days, it is common in state-supported institutions to conduct post-tenure reviews, or regular examinations of a tenured faculty member's teaching, research, and service contributions in relation to the mission and established productivity standards of the host institution.[20] In the state institutions where I've worked, post-tenure reviews are *mandatory for all tenured faculty members*, although the procedures for conducting them among those institutions vary. At Arizona State University, for example, post-tenure reviews are conducted annually, based on a random selection of tenured faculty. At other institutions, tenured faculty can expect to be reviewed every three–five years or even longer.[21]

Committees composed of tenured senior faculty members (selected by the provost and/or dean) conduct post-tenure reviews. The tenured faculty member being reviewed submits his or her portfolio (much as in tenure and promotion decisions) for evaluation, sometimes accompanied by a personal statement that frames the material, sometimes accompanied by letters of support from colleagues, peers, and/or (in some cases) external reviewers. The committee reads, deliberates, and decides.

In the institutions where I have worked, the vast majority of tenured faculty—because they have continued to be hard-working, valued, and productive members of departments—are found to be either "satisfactory" or "exemplary." However, if a tenured faculty member is found to be "unsatisfactory" in any one or more of the three evaluation areas (teaching, research, service), then an "improvement plan" must be hammered out between that faculty member and her or his department and dean. Tenure may be revoked and the faculty member dismissed if he or she fails to meet the goals established in that document.

The point I want to underscore is that tenure is *not* the last time you will be held accountable by your peers and your host institution.

Too often, new faculty members think of the tenure decision as the final hoop to job security (and eternal happiness). Tenure should be thought of, instead, as an important ritual and rite of passage from junior to senior faculty status, but not the final destination of an academic career or the final hurdle to a richly imagined (and fictional) lifestyle of studied and bemused leisure.

The Future of Tenure and the Entrepreneurial Business Model

Even with the reforms to the tenure process already in place, the days of tenure may be numbered. Leaders of academic institutions are noticeably and vocally less supportive of tenure than they have been in the past.[22]

In part, this shift in thinking has occurred because state legislatures and donors have required that institutions of higher learning become more business-like and more financially accountable, usually under the rallying cry of encouraging colleges to become more "entrepreneurial." It is instructive to think about the implications of adopting such a business model in higher education.

This new business model based on entrepreneurialism is predicated on the economic idea that a free market economy prospers best under conditions of less regulation and intense competition. To become entrepreneurial requires establishing a teaching and research infrastructure that supports the creation of new business ventures; takes calculated risks based on the needs of local, state, regional, national, and global markets; and is able to capitalize on the university or college's unique "embeddedness" within a community.[23]

It is hard to overstate the cultural changes that adopting entrepreneurial thinking in the academy have created or required. Whereas the "old" culture of the academy was widely regarded as the last remaining vestige of "medieval feudalism,"[24] this new culture of entrepreneurialism has ushered in what one reviewer calls "predatory capitalism."[25] Put succinctly, power that was once held by feudal lords and ladies because of their relationship to the prince (i.e., deans or provost) or king (i.e., president or chancellor) has been replaced by power determined by the relationship of every faculty member, program, and administrator to new money.

Traditional academic life—once the province of thinkers, tinkerers, scientists, poets, writers, and prophets who were rewarded because they published monographs in academic journals and highly esoteric books with academic presses—has become a radically altered province peopled by the same overbrained motley crew, but who are now required to think of themselves as "knowledge entrepreneurs." This means that faculty members are asked to engage in new strategic initiatives designed to create or apply theoretical principles and research to external audiences beyond the traditional readership of academic journals. We are also asked to create new ways of working in interdisciplinary or transdisciplinary groups in order to tackle big questions and to go after bigger grants and contracts. In addition to the usual virtues of excellence in the classroom, traditional research productivity, and good citizenship and service, a faculty member is also expected to seek external funding to support research and teaching. Nowadays, we are informed that, under these new business rules, research quality will be measured not so much by traditional publication (although traditional publication is still required and considered important) as by the impact of the research and the notoriety of the writer.

Although some faculty and administrators struggling with the impact of these changes long for a return to the not-too-distant-past academic culture that, for most of us, was already quite challenging, there is no good reason to believe that will ever happen: *Change never carries us backwards in time.*

Furthermore, good things have happened under the new entrepreneurial model. Medieval feudalism may make for intriguing novels, but it also makes for very poor lives—unless you happen to be the prince or king. Or one of the favored sons and daughters of nobility. Or perhaps the fool.

Beyond issues of power were and are issues of regulation and control. Under academic feudalism, new ways of organizing were strongly discouraged. Tradition reigned supreme; interdisciplinarity was frowned on. New methods of research and writing were, as Chris Poulos found out in his own medieval drama, suspect. Junior faculty were often treated as apprentices until tenure was awarded, and there was little opportunity to teach advanced courses because senior faculty "owned" them.

But, most importantly, the entrepreneurial model encourages a way of thinking about teaching, research, and service that newly connects individual faculty members to the world outside the academy, which is the world that supports us. And which is the world that needs our ideas, our innovations, our activism. As universities and colleges find new and improved ways of serving our publics, those publics will find new respect for the value of theories, research, science, and the stories we offer to enrich, enliven, and enable their lives.

That is my hope. And, as I have learned, that is also a hope embraced by the entrepreneurial business model. But that model has also had—and will continue to have—important consequences for how we think about evaluating faculty members and especially how we evaluate tenure cases.

Tenure as a Return on Investment

As a result of moving to a more entrepreneurial business model for running the organizations they lead, college presidents have learned to think of tenure in almost purely business terms: The state (and/or donors) has made an investment (I), and therefore is entitled to a reasonable rate of return on that investment (ROI). The investment includes your salary and benefits, but also the cost of department office space (including utilities), secretarial/research support, and sponsored travel. The ROI is calculated using a variety of metrics, but let's say, for purposes of illustration, that it includes the number of students you teach (e.g., what we informally refer to as "The Spielberg Metric": *asses in seats*) and their (as well as peer) evaluations of the quality of your performance; the relative frequency and prestige of your papers, publications, and grants; the scholarly (and public) impact of your research; and the perceived value and quality of the service you provide to the department, college, university, community, and scholarly community.

Although high-quality teaching is important and quality service and good citizenship are expected, *most tenure cases are made on the basis of research productivity* (more on this later). In one institution with which I am intimately familiar, tenure is largely based on the I/ROI formula, and that formula is used to project the likelihood of a continuing reasonable rate of return in the future. Since this business model was introduced at this institution, the average rate of tenured faculty dropped from 98% to 70% and "the bar" for gaining tenure has been significantly raised, and not just mathematically. When the president of this institution was asked in a public forum, "What does it take to get tenure?" his answer was "that you are the best in your field."

But calculating the ROI on faculty members and insisting they be "the best" in their field is not the only business reason that tenure may become a relic during your lifetime. *Freakonomics* authors Steven D. Levitt and Stephen J. Dubner, themselves tenured faculty members, make this case against it:

> What does tenure do? It distorts people's effort so that they face strong incentives early in their career (and presumably work very hard early on as a consequence) and very weak incentives forever after (and presumably work much less hard on average as a consequence).
>
> One could imagine some models in which this incentive structure makes sense. For instance, if one needs to learn a lot of information to become competent, but once one has the knowledge it does not fade and effort is not very important. That model may be a good description of learning to ride a bike, but it is a terrible model of academics.[26]

Additionally, some legal scholars have pointed out that the principle of academic freedom itself has been under attack in the United States since 9/11. Mark C. Rahdert, reviewing three recent Supreme Court decisions involving the application of the concept, concludes that the Roberts court: "would support punishing student speech that conflicts with important institutional values, punishing faculty speech that occurs in the course of employment, and punishing the university itself if it fails to comply with external commands regarding the conduct of its auxiliary activities."[27] He goes on to point out that legislation has already been introduced in several states to ensure "intellectual diversity" by creating affirmative action-like guidelines for promoting a balance of "underrepresented views" in faculty hiring, teaching, and scholarship.

But, at least as of this writing, tenure survives intact throughout the United States. There are about 280,000 tenured professors in the United States, and seven out of ten faculty members who come up for tenure get it.[28] Of those 280,000 currently with tenured appointments, only fifty–seventy-five per year have it revoked.

So don't panic. But do prepare. Think entrepreneurially. Be aware of how you will show a return on the investment made in your hire. Equip yourself with knowledge of the tenure process at your host institution (both at the department and university levels) and begin assembling your tenure portfolio from the day you accept your job.

How to Prepare a Tenure and Promotion Portfolio

As a writer creating a structure for a storyline, you have learned to think of plot from a reader's point of view. *Apply that same thinking to the construction of your tenure portfolio.* You are crafting a story about yourself and about your contributions within the general mission and core values of your host institution.

Your themes are excellence in teaching, excellence in research, and, if not excellence, then at the very least, yeoman level of service. Let's examine each of these areas in more detail.

What Should a Tenure Portfolio Contain?

This is a question you should ask your department chair soon after you arrive on campus at the beginning of your first year on the job. I cannot stress enough the importance of having clear guidelines for what you should be doing and accumulating as evidence from the time you begin your career at X college or university. And beyond knowing what you should be doing and accumulating is the even more important task of actually following through on it. Too often, junior faculty put off the organization of a tenure portfolio until the summer prior to the tenure decision, and in many cases this is too late for them. Fortunately, most universities and colleges do a much better job of guiding junior faculty than used to be the case, but no university or college can do the job for you.

For purposes of illustration, I have copied from the provost's website at ASU our current tenure and promotion portfolio guidelines:

General Guidelines for Faculty for the Preparation of Review Materials for Promotion and Tenure Reviews for 2007–08

The following material should be submitted as PDF documents on a CD-ROM:

1. Table of Contents for the materials in candidate's submission. Include a listing of four publication titles or titles of the other documentation of research, scholarship, and/or creative activities.

2. A statement of not more than four pages written by the candidate to put past work into perspective and to outline future goals. The statement should help reviewers see relationships among the individual's teaching, research, and service and how these activities have built the foundation for continued professional growth.

3. The candidate's current curriculum vita presenting such information as research publications, scholarship and/or creative achievements, service, grants, and papers presented, etc. Refereed and non-refereed publications should be distinguished. Joint authors of articles should be listed in the order in which they appear, and the nature of one's role in research projects and other joint efforts should be clearly described (e.g., use an asterisk to identify the author making the major contribution to the paper or project).

4. A copy of up to four publications or other material reflecting the research, scholarship and/or creative activities of the candidate. A portfolio documenting creative activity may be submitted as one of the four pieces of evidence.

5. Review materials of teaching and instructional activity:
   - A summary table of courses taught, the number of students in each, and a summary of student evaluations including scale, mean, and standard deviation;
   - A statement of teaching philosophy and any professional development activities undertaken in relation to teaching and instruction;
   - Instructional materials as specified by the unit;
   - Supplemental materials providing evidence of instructional effectiveness may be submitted for up to two (2) courses, e.g., syllabi, copies of major tests and assignments, reading lists, websites, CDs, etc.

Contents of external review packets submitted to the unit/college to be sent to external reviewers:

1. Current curriculum vita;

2. Personal statement (optional, unless required by unit/college);

3. A copy of up to four publications or other material reflecting the research, scholarship and/or creative activities of the candidate (a portfolio documenting creative activity may be submitted as one of the four pieces of evidence.

Be sure that all information received after the file has left the unit/department is forwarded on through each review level to the University Vice Provost to be added as an Appendix to the candidate's file. A brief statement should be written at each review level stating whether or not the new material would change their earlier recommendation in any way. Also, please notify the University Vice Provost that additional materials are on their way to be added to the candidate's case file.

I present the above guidelines in full because they are representative of guidelines at similar research-intensive public universities in the United States. One way in which ours may differ from your university or college is in the specific requirement for only *four* publications to be included in the portfolio (most colleges and universities require all of them).

One additional piece of information concerns the external reviewers. At ASU, we require ten letters from distinguished faculty at or above the rank to which the candidate aspires. Many institutions require only three–five. In either case, these reviewers are typically drawn from peer institutions (e.g., colleges or universities with similar institutional profiles, missions, and rankings) and should not have had any (or very little) personal knowledge of the candidate beyond her or his publications. This means that dissertation advisors, coauthors, and friends (however distinguished they are) should be avoided. It also means that early in your career you need to start thinking about how to use published work and conference participation to facilitate a professional network of readers interested in and supportive of what you write about.

Reminder: Chris Poulos developed a strong network of supporters through his published writing and convention participation. When he ran into tenure trouble, it was his *network* that volunteered to help him. Don't forget it.

The Personal Statement as a Framing Device

Recall how important a framing device was to the construction of audience interest in your story? Very important, right? Now think of the personal statement at the front end of your tenure portfolio as a framing device. What you choose to say in these few pages[29] serves as the set-up for everything that follows from it.

This is the key: You need to write a personal statement that ties together (preferably in a seamless fashion) the *overarching agenda* that drives your teaching, research, and service. That overarching agenda should be directed to answering a BIG question that is perceived to be of critical importance by scholars and by the general public. Of course, this advice is most useful *before* you accept a position because it gives you six years to develop the supporting story. But if you are already well into your tenure track job, the advice is still useful.

Why?

Because unless you teach at a very small liberal arts college marked by a high degree of collegiality, most of the scholars and administrators who read your file beyond those in your immediate department will know absolutely nothing or close to it about who you are, what you do, or why you think doing it is so damned important. They won't care a whit about the struggle for identity you endured growing up as a smart person who wanted to write among dolts who didn't like to read, or that you worked *so very hard* in the best schools to get where you are today. Or that your dissertation advisor was INSERT NAME OF FAMOUS SCHOLAR HERE. Or that you are a truly nice person. Or, so rumor has it, that you are good in bed.[30]

Wake up!!! The personal statement is a story crafted for an audience. Know your audience? I doubt it. Nor will you, most likely. College- and university-level tenure committees are rotating service assignments, and the chances that you will know the people selected for it are slim. The larger the university or college, the slimmer your chances become.

Close your eyes. Imagine a college or university committee made up of some of the faces you've seen in meetings on campus, people who are older but not well known to you. One person you may have heard described as an "eminent physicist"; another is someone called "a biodesign expert" said to be on the brink of a major discovery; and then there is that gender studies faculty member you've maybe talked to once or twice who has a joint appointment in history and philosophy and who everyone says is "scary smart."

Now imagine a few others, tenured senior professors who seem to be part of the backbone of the university and who come from every walk of life. Now throw in a new dean, a political scientist recently arrived from an Ivy League school, a long-serving provost from chemistry, and a president with a Ph.D. in the history of science and a law degree.

These are very different people. If collected together in a bookstore, these committee members likely would be interested in very different titles. So what can you do to make them interested in *your* story?

Think about it. They will be people with busy lives and their own beliefs, academic values, theoretical commitments, research methods, and interests. They are generally highly competent individuals, even if one or more of them seem to be socially dysfunctional or to have "gone round the bend." It doesn't matter. Their task is to make a recommendation on your tenure case. They are, for the most part, honest, hard working, and fair minded. But they may not have a clue about you or what you do. Like Chris Poulos's college committee, they want to make the best decision for the institution, which means that their job is to ensure that not only are they recommending someone who will continue to prove worthy as teacher/scholars, but someone who fits the mission and vision for the university and will be a major asset to the university or college community.

But I stress: They may not know you or what you do. So how do you craft a personal statement capable of attracting their interest and support?

Let's begin with the big picture, which, for academics, is always about theory and research. Some of them may have heard of "qualitative research," but others probably won't. Some of them may fully grasp the interpretive turn in the social sciences and the role of narratives in theory development; others may not. One or two of them may have deep personal and/or professional reasons for skepticism when asked to read prose published in an unfamiliar journal that resembles a short story and equate it with a refereed journal article in a prestigious scientific outlet. One or two of them may admire narrative *theories* but find it difficult to justify actual narratives as scholarship. And one or two of them will not only be deeply familiar with creative nonfiction, but also active and perhaps even well-regarded practitioners of it who may think it very odd that you didn't bother to make their acquaintance during your pre-tenure years and/or who didn't know that people in your field actually did this sort of writing.

And we haven't even approached the *topic(s)* you write about yet.

But even as imagined avatars on this printed page, people like these will be your readers. Your evaluators. Although some of them (most notably those in your immediate department) may have at least some native interest in your story and have formed a positive view of your tenure case, most readers beyond that local decision point will be wholly without clues about how to connect the dots *until you provide them*. Furthermore, the higher up the administrative ladder your portfolio travels, the more likely readers will be to rely on external metrics to judge the worth of your research (more on this later).

So pay attention to the personal statement. Write it as you would write a perfect framing device for the story that you want your readers to read as they sift through the evidence of excellence further on in your portfolio.

Don't ever assume they will understand what you mean; it's *your responsibility* to tell it to them in clear, straightforward, non-jargon-laden language.

And never, not once *ever*, believe that they will automatically connect your narratives to ongoing theoretical or methodological discussions, or that they will see—without being clearly documented—that your work contributes significantly to the literature in your field and to the marketplace of ideas.[31]

Remember Chris Poulos. Remember the third and final objection raised by the dean to the contents of his tenure portfolio. *Even with supporting evidence to the contrary*, the dean said that Chris had failed to make clear in his personal statement the relevance of his scholarly contributions to the committee—well, there it is. That she who must not be named should have warned him about that, well—there but for the grace of God go *you*, my friend.

So please consider yourself officially warned.

Now let's briefly examine the contents of what should be in your portfolio.

The Curriculum Vitae

The *CV* is one of the most important documents you will create, not just for a tenure and promotion file but also for future employment opportunities. A *CV* differs from a résumé in that it is generally longer (more than two pages) than a résumé and focuses on academic training and expertise, publications, and presentations. A typical academic *CV* includes the following information:

NAME
Address, City, State, Zip
Telephone/Cell Phone
Email

EDUCATION: *List undergraduate and graduate institutions attended in reverse chronological order.*

Graduate Institution
City, State, Zip
Degree Received
Date of Graduation
Dissertation Title

Graduate Institution
City, State, Zip
Degree Received
Date of Graduation
Thesis Title

Undergraduate
City, State, Zip
Degree Received and Major/Minor
Date of Graduation

EMPLOYMENT HISTORY: List in reverse chronological order; include position titles and dates. For each entry, provide one or two sentences describing your responsibilities and two or more sentences describing your accomplishments.

2005–present   ABC College
Department of Communication
1112 East West Avenue
Yourtown, State, Zip
Assistant Professor of Communication

Responsibilities: Taught undergraduate courses in rhetoric and performance studies; graduate seminar in qualitative research methods. Served as artistic director for the department.

Accomplishments: Created new hybrid course in critical/cultural studies that combines online and traditional classroom delivery; received grant to support research project on "constructing the performing self"; won Outstanding Teaching Award for the College, 2007.

REPEAT FOR EACH INSTITUTION.

PUBLICATIONS: List in reverse chronological order using a consistent style sheet. Note: Only list works that are in print or in press, and if the latter, include the date of its acceptance. If the article or review is available online, include the URL.

Books:

Refereed Articles:

Book Chapters:

Book Reviews:

Convention and Conference Papers:

Other:

HONORS AND AWARDS

SERVICE: List in reverse chronological order

Department/College/University

Community

Professional

REFERENCES: List three–five persons familiar with your work and give complete contact information for each of them.

It is important to update your *CV* often (at least once every semester) and to *always make a back-up copy of it* in case the original is lost or the computer crashes. Seems obvious, doesn't it? But have you backed up your *CV* lately? How about the rest of the contents of your hard drive?

Go do it. *Now.*

Pay attention to the language used to describe everything included on your *CV.* Remember: You are telling readers a story about your life and consistency of theme and organization of details matter. Most readers will accept that graduate students and newly minted doctorates will have publications and papers that fall outside of what eventually becomes an area of focused expertise. But it is wise early on to develop a core area of teaching, writing, and service that will add up to the personal statement you want to forward to your evaluation committee(s).

Teaching

The teaching section of the tenure portfolio should include:

- syllabi for all courses taught;
- tests and other methods of evaluation used;
- creative exercises/handouts/class activities;
- summaries of teaching evaluations from students; and
- peer evaluations (where possible).

Depending on the requirements and traditions at your school, the teaching portfolio may also include:

- books, articles, and convention papers authored on issues of pedagogy;
- textbooks; and
- resources for teaching that you've developed (e.g., online materials, podcasts, blogs, interactive programs, etc.).

Evaluations of teaching effectiveness are essential to any tenure decision, *even when the host institution views research productivity as the most important category.* No university or college can afford to tenure ill-prepared or ineffective classroom teachers, which is one reason why most institutions put serious money into on campus resources to develop teaching skills, particularly (but not exclusively) for junior faculty.

Take advantage of them.

Research and "Impact" Measurements

Colleges and universities exist for the discovery, discussion, and distribution of knowledge. As such, it is both right and fitting that our institutions hire, evaluate, and retain scholars who contribute new knowledge, facilitate discussions of knowledge, and disseminate their work via publications, presentations, and performances.

Research is an expected part of the job, and for most academics it is one of the most pleasurable aspects of living and working in a university or college community. Research that leads to publications, presentations, and performances is integral to the social and professional construction of academic life. Moreover, published research is how individuals make their mark in the world of ideas, so it should come as no big surprise that evaluations of research productivity are critical to evaluations of tenure and promotion.

As a person who has spent over thirty years as an academic, over twenty of them spent as an administrator, I can say unequivocally that standards for evaluating research in relation to tenure decisions have changed academic culture. In part, the cultural change has been driven by "big picture" economic factors related to the business model discussed earlier. Universities and colleges were asked to become less dependent on state funding and more dependent on external research dollars, thus creating an environment where reduced teaching loads to support research (but *not* less quality in teaching) and more research productivity (e.g., grants, contracts, publications, and impact) was and continues to be encouraged.

And in part the cultural change occurred because graduate students, in addition to becoming educated in advanced theories and research methods, are "professionalized" by (not simply acculturated into) research-intensive departments, complete with a focus on having clear research goals coming into them and with an earlier expectation for competitively selected professional presentations and publications going through and out of them, these days often producing impressive *CV*s prior to receiving the terminal degree.[32]

But, as with most things bright, shiny, and academic, there is a dark side to this story. New faculty members at most institutions are expected to "hit the ground running" as productive teacher/scholars while they spend the first year or so getting acquainted with their new surroundings and colleagues, as well as being personally engaged in an ongoing and somewhat exhaustive round of cultural and relational sensemaking. The more strategic among them have anticipated that the first year on the job is often the most difficult, so they have "timed" the submission of articles and papers accordingly, "saving" work done during the last year of graduate school so they might use it during the less productive first year on the new job. In "professionalizing" graduate students, they learn to behave this way because we have also taught them that most universities and colleges don't or won't "count" published work done prior to their arrival at the new host institution, so during the final stages of doctoral study they should only submit what they feel will land them at the type of host institution they want to work in.

It's a bit deceptive, isn't it?

Yes it is. But perhaps it is necessary given the relatively short length of time between initial hiring and tenure evaluation and the relatively high standards for publication guiding tenure decisions. I say "relatively short" because one fact of academic life is that the reviewing cycle for journals, although normally six–eight weeks, can be as long as twelve–eighteen months. Delayed decisions on submissions can be maddeningly frustrating for junior faculty members in their fourth or fifth year, who have a handful of "revise and resubmits," who face long turn-around times, and who are painfully aware they have precious little time before the tenure clock runs out.

Standards for promotion and tenure, too, are ever higher. Although it is dangerous to speculate or generalize about "what it takes to earn tenure" generally,[33] it is true that at the institutions where I've worked, there was a *minimum expectation* for one or two refereed articles in good journals[34] per year and a book (or two, if one book was fashioned out of a dissertation[35]) published or in press at tenure time.[36]

A list of convention and conference papers on the *CV* won't save you. Convention papers—although important steps on the road to academic publication—don't count for very much at tenure time, unless (a) they win Top Paper awards, and/or (b) they lead directly to grants and/or publications.

Finally, it is important to think strategically when considering a publication outlet. Ideally, you want the majority of your publications to be in higher status, bigger "impact" journals. But this is not always going to be the case, nor is it always necessary. Excellent work can appear in lesser journals, and evaluation committees at the department level spend considerable amounts of time reading the publications to arrive at their own conclusions about them. Beyond the department level, the relative status of the journal will carry as much or more weight than what you have written, mostly because readers will be less conversant with concepts and methods that are foreign to them.

Although there are exceptions to the rule I'm about to articulate, it is generally the case that higher status journals have national and international readerships. For interdisciplinary journals and journals that have highly specialized readerships, or journals that are unfamiliar to you, check the journal's website for its impact rating (see below) and try to find out what the average turn-around time is for submissions.

If you are a new Ph.D. and want to turn your dissertation into an article or two (or three), try to locate a seasoned editor who is willing to work with you. Talk to editors at conferences and conventions, or, failing that, make a phone call or two. Based on what you find out in those conversations, write a cover letter in which you explain that you are trying to work a dissertation into an article and admit that you may need some help. Don't make the mistake of assuming that the editor won't know your submission is drawn from a dissertation. Believe me, in all but the rarest of cases, all the earmarks of a dissertation are on it.

Allow me one personal example. I had a recent conversation with Cheree Carlson, the current editor of the *Western Journal of Communication*, and she explained to me that as a regional journal editor, she often works closely with new Ph.D.s to tell them how to make better informed choices about what to omit and what to include from a dissertation. "They are trying to pare down a 300-page document into 25–30 pages, and often that means they cut out exactly the wrong sections." She went on to say that dissertation earmarks include long literature reviews, references that black out the author's name on a series of convention papers, and thanking three or four senior faculty members from the same academic institution, but not the one from which the author currently hails.

I must also point out that in most cases you will be better off trying to get two or three refereed articles out of your dissertation than a book. If you want to write a book based on your dissertation research, that's fine. It will be a commitment of time and energy, but you should have a solid enough background in your subject matter to complete it. But simply "turning your dissertation into a book" is more of an academic fable than a reality. Books and dissertations serve different purposes and address different audiences. The dissertation gets you a doctorate; a book helps you get tenure and promotion. A dissertation is designed to please three, four, maybe five people on your committee and the formatting storm troopers in the graduate school; a book must reach a considerably larger audience. And, for the *coup de grace* on the subject of books and tenure, most universities and colleges require published reviews of your book—not just the raw fact of its publication—to give serious points to your tenure tally.

Bottom line: Turn chapters from your dissertation into published articles in refereed journals and think about a book as a "new" project. Also plan to complete the book by your fourth or, at the latest, your fifth year in the tenure cycle so there is enough time to include published reviews in your portfolio.

Before moving on, I want to say a few words about the concept of "external metrics" for evaluating the impact of published research.

What are "external metrics"?

Two metrics for academic journals have become quite popular among senior administrators and some department chairs: the "impact" ranking of the journal in which your work appears and the "citation index" that reports how many times your work has been used as a reference in other scholarly articles.

For the impact measure, each academic journal is ranked in the *Thomson Scientific Journal Citation Reports* according to its preferred classification (Communication, Interdisciplinary Social Science, Humanities, etc.).[37] If you are curious about how the journals you publish in (or are considering submitting work to) are ranked, go to the individual journal's website to check it out. For example, here is the 2006 listing for *Qualitative Inquiry*[38]:

2006 Ranking: 31/58 in Social Sciences, Interdisciplinary

2006 Impact Factor: 0.514

Some academic journals don't list their rankings on their websites. But that may change because of the increasing pressure to find some way to locate some external, nonsubjective measure of the "impact" of one's research.

The other metric often used is *Citation Index*. The basic idea is that if others cite your work they use it and therefore value it, and this metric for measuring impact provides statistical data about the number of times your work has been cited in scholarly publications.[39] *Google Scholar* provides data designed to accomplish the same thing for books and articles. If you want to test it, just type "Google Scholar" in your search engine and when it pops up, type in your name or someone else's name.

For those of us write and perform narratives, these measures of impact contain important lessons and key decision points. One lesson is that our work likely already is, or will be evaluated by these metrics, regardless of how we feel about it. Another lesson is that this fact of institutional life is *not necessarily a negative thing* for those of us who write and perform narratives. The decision points emerging from that lesson involve thinking through (and then acting on) two important questions[40]:

1. How will what we write be used and cited by others?
2. How can we use knowledge of these metrics to our advantage and to the advantage of narratives generally within our scholarly and public communities?

How you respond productively to these two questions can point to and light the way out of the otherwise darkened ambiguous passage that we too often associate with tenure and promotion. *How?*

Think of it this way: One reason colleges and universities have confidence in external metrics to measure scholarly impact is that those metrics provide a common objective reference against which any and all contributions may be compared. Why is this important?

Because although it is true that appraising the aesthetic quality and scholarly worth of a story may be fairly accomplished only by readers who approach it *as a narrative* (rather than as a "finding" in a strict social science sense of the term), judgments of quality are notoriously subjective and opinions among even knowledgeable readers often differ. So how should an evaluation take those issues into account?

Interestingly, what these external metrics do is *accept that subjectivity and differences of opinion will exist but ultimately they don't matter*: A controversial piece can have great impact *because it is controversial.* The more often it is cited, the better.[41] So, examined one way, using impact measurements actually works to the advantage of cutting-edge scholarship, even if the worth or "rightness" of that scholarship is hotly contested. From an institutional perspective, *the more often a scholar's name is associated with an idea, theory, or research finding that is deemed worthy enough to warrant criticism and debate, the better.*[42] All the better if what you have contributed turns out to have been more worthy of praise than criticism and/or if what you have written becomes nominated for a big prize. Institutions benefit because this sort of notoriety indicates that important work is being done at that place, which, in turn, attracts better students and better scholars to it.

Service

As I have repeatedly said throughout this chapter, tenure is based on teaching and research. No one gets tenure based on good departmental citizenship, volunteering to chair a Homecoming committee, or serving as a manuscript referee. Yet, that said, you must commit to doing those things as well.

Nor should doing them, and doing them to the best of your ability, be thought of as a waste of time. It isn't.

But wait, you cry! If this entrepreneurial business model asks me to think differently, why wouldn't I consider these activities—which aren't going to help me get tenure—as a gigantic time suck?

Because, that *isn't* what I said. Read more carefully. I said no one *gets* tenure based on service, but I never claimed that service wasn't necessary or even quite important. In fact, quite the opposite.

These activities *are* going to help you get tenure. Remember a few pages back when I asked you to imagine the nameless faces you pass on campus who will probably be members of your college and university level evaluation committees? One common failure among junior faculty is that they don't get out of their own departments enough, don't spend time with others on campus outside their immediate faculty, and, as a result, don't know the people who will be asked to evaluate them.

Hmmmm. Wouldn't it make sense to develop those relationships? Although you must be careful about the time you devote to service as a junior faculty member (you'll be asked to do a lot more of it once you get tenure), it is equally important to fulfill at least one important service role in your department per year. After your third year, branch out to other committees at the college or university level. Become well known for showing up for meetings on time, thoroughly prepared for whatever the assignment is. Avoid negativity in all aspects of university life. Be a force for constructive change. And remember this: Whenever someone asks you what your research is about, make sure you have your "elevator speech" about creative nonfiction handy.[43]

Now to the matter of service to the profession.

Recall that I said tenure cases require several external letters of evaluation from distinguished senior faculty serving in peer institutions? Don't you think it might matter a great deal if you become known in your professional community *before* you come up for tenure? Beyond that, volunteering to read papers for a conference is an excellent way to see what other people are contributing and to learn more about topics that you may want to explore in greater detail. Attending business meetings for interest groups is also a good way to meet others and build a network. As you get closer to the tenure year, don't be afraid to volunteer for offices in your professional organizations. Put yourself up for election if you need to. By the time you are ready to assemble your tenure portfolio, you should have at least one important entry for each category of service: department, college or university, community, and profession.

In sum: Think of committee service as a way of broadening your social connections at the departmental and university levels, and think of serving as a reader or reviewer or office holder as a way of deepening your professional networks.

Summing Up: What's Your Story and Who's Your Audience?

Success in the academy is less of a mystery than it often appears to be. But to become successful means staying in the game, and staying in the game means securing long-term employment, preferably with tenure. For this reason, I devoted much of the advice given in this chapter to understanding the tenure process within the evolving, and ever changing political and economic realities of higher education in the 21st century.

I began with a specific story about a specific man at a specific university, but I hope you see that the story was more than just about Chris. It is a story—a mystery story, really—about success in the academy, a success that rises above the initial evidence and symbolic kill of tenure denial and shows that in the end, the institution, when prodded a bit from the outside, did the right thing.

However, it is also a story about life in the academy that could have turned out quite differently *without changing anything about the evidence*, or anything about the characters, because in a mystery sometimes the same clues that make things work out one way, if read differently or if ignored, or if not read at all, well, can make things turn out quite differently. The lesson here is the story-within-the-story, the letter that Chris authored to his dean objecting to his decision but, at the same time, a letter writer who seized the opportunity to do more than object, but instead to teach people unfamiliar with creative nonfiction how to read it and how to connect stories to theories. Perhaps if Chris had been advised to do that in his personal statement, none of this would have been necessary.

But there is a lesson, too, in that omission. It is a lesson about the critical importance of using the personal statement as a strategic framing device, a set-up for all that follows in the tenure portfolio, a way of beginning a story for an imagined audience made up of the nameless faces you pass everyday on campus, but that one day will be asked to consider your worth and value to the institution.

For this reason, I began the advisory sections following from Chris's story from an institutional perspective on the tenure process. I explained that tenure is the most important decision an institution makes about an individual faculty member; that the institution/state has made a significant monetary investment in you and your scholarship and deserves to see a fair return on that investment; and that (as in any business) only the highest performing faculty will help make the institution competitive. I began this way because these are elements of the plot you must learn to master, to connect your professional dots to, and to write about.

Finally, I provided some practical advice about what to include in your tenure portfolio in the traditional categories of teaching, research, and service. Although each institution has its own ideas about this or that related to the material contents, I provided a general framework that may be adapted to your specific situation and some strategies for navigating the tenure process.

Good luck!

Activities and Questions

1. Discuss Chris's story. What lessons do you derive from it as they might apply to your own institution and work?

2. There has been a lot written about the "corporatization of higher education" that underscores the importance of thinking about tenure and promotion as a political process not unlike those that characterize moving up a corporate ladder to a position of relative security in a global company. But there has also been criticism of this corporate model on the grounds that higher education has always served as a protected cultural space for work that cannot be done elsewhere, including work that challenges existing notions of power, economics, beliefs, and hierarchies. Discuss this issue with the goal of providing advice to incoming graduate students about how they can best prepare themselves for the world of future work in the academy.

3. Collect each other's CVs and circulate them a few days prior to your next class meeting. Use part of that session to critique them and

offer suggestions for improvement. Develop a list of dos and don'ts based on your analysis of the most successful ones.

4. Find out what is considered an exemplary case for tenure and promotion in your field at your institution. If possible, locate examples of the CVs of the most recent successful candidates. What can be learned about the local values of your school based on these cases?

5. Start writing your own narrative about your own program of research. Keep it on file and update regularly. This narrative should provide an account of what you study and why it is important, the conceptual underpinnings of your scholarship, and what contribution(s) and impact it has made to theory, method, and/or practice.

Notes

1. These are Chris Poulos's words, and what follows here is drawn from Chris's story, as he described it in a panel on the subject of tenure and promotion at the 3rd International Congress on Qualitative Inquiry, Champaign-Urbana, IL, May 4, 2007.

2. Being denied tenure is the university equivalent to what Kenneth Burke terms "a symbolic kill," hence, the title of this section.

3. It is intriguing to apply Burkeian thought to university life and to the decision-making process. For an expanded discussion of performance appraisals from a Burkeian perspective, see Goodall, Wilson, and Waagen (1986).

4. This is not a normal practice, at least in my experience. External reviewers are carefully selected, and disqualification generally only occurs if the reviewer is personally connected (dissertation advisor, coauthor, close friend) or is or has been intimately related to the candidate. Editors of book series, particularly those not personally affiliated with candidates, are generally not disqualified.

5. It is standard practice to at least allow another external reviewer to be named in place of the original choice.

6. Symbolic violence in organizations can be either personal or impersonal. In this case, the college committee no doubt assumed it was acting rationally and in the best interests of the university and that furthermore their impersonal decision was based on an "objective" reading of the material in Chris's portfolio. From a Burkeian-infused organizational power perspective, there are no particularly evil people

in this scenario, only a bureaucratic order empowered by its secrets and so-called objectivity *to act* against others who do not share the same values, commitments, or beliefs as they do.

7. Personal email communication, December 1, 2006.

8. Personal email communication, February 27, 2007. Readers will undoubtedly notice that the loss of voice associated with laryngitis is itself a symbolic indicator of how deeply Chris felt about this "attempted murder." He had been unable to write as a result of the initial decision, a condition worsened by both the flu and his deteriorating situation.

9. David Wright offers another "cautionary tale" about the role of Institutional Research Boards and creative nonfiction. See Wright (2004).

10. I realize that most of the material in this chapter applies only to North American universities and colleges. As I have little experience elsewhere, I didn't think it prudent to comment on appointments in universities or countries with different systems for continuing employment or those without tenure.

11. See Chait (2002).

12. See De George (1997). See also Van Alstyne (1993).

13. See Stone (2006).

A "loyalty tax" happens when faculty choose to remain at a host institution instead of moving to another institution for more money. By remaining at the host institution, unless the offer is matched, and such matches typically only happen once, the faculty member loses out not only on the higher salary but also the accrual of retirement monies. Another way to think about it is that new jobs are highly competitive and require institutions to offer highly competitive salaries to recruit and attract the best talent. So if you work at a state institution that only offers minimal annual merit increases in pay and that—as most states do—fails to offer any increase in thin revenue years, for every year you remain at that institution, you are likely to fall behind the regional and national averages. Equity adjustments for loyal faculty are fairly rare, and the best way (ironically) to boost pay is to go out on the job market and get a better offer in the hope that your host institution will match it. See Cahn (2006).

In my experience, there is also a gender dimension to the loyalty tax; women who are brought in at lower salaries than their male counterparts seldom make up the difference. Furthermore, women—particularly single mothers—often remain at institutions where tenure is granted because they have a social and professional support network established and the thought of trying to build a new one is daunting. See Fogg (2003).

14. Although most PhDs know that our salaries often pale in comparison to those of lawyers, physicians, and hedge fund managers with similar or even lower levels of education, the public perception is that faculty are well paid for what we do.

15. And, while I am milking the negative stereotype, some of the public also believes that faculty holds students captive to left-wing political views and radical anti-American sentiments.

16. Actually, the research we conduct is often negatively equated with time devoted to teaching, which, in my experience, is what most taxpayers want and expect from college professors. For those of us who conduct research and publish our views on controversial political or social issues, well, the very idea that we should be *paid* to do that from public coffers is often perceived as insulting.

17. In fact, states often only support a small portion of a university or college's budget, anywhere from 12%–30% in most states. The remainder of the budget must be earned through grants, contracts, and licensing fees.

18. Tenure may also be revoked for "moral turpitude," or gross violations of community standards usually associated with felonies.

19. Ward Churchill was fired from a tenured position at the University of Colorado at Boulder after officials found that Mr. Churchill's record "shows a pattern of serious, repeated, and deliberate research misconduct that fell below the minimum stand of professional integrity, involving fabrication, falsification, improper citation, and plagiarism." Churchill argued that he was being punished for remarks he made comparing some victims of 9/11 working in the World Trade Center to "little Eichmanns." However, the Regents decision to revoke his tenure and fire him "focused on his professional activities, not his statements about victims of September 11, 2001"; see Gravois (2007).

20. See Haworth (1996, p. A15).

21. But post-tenure reviews are separate processes from annual reviews conducted to assess teaching, research, and service performance.

I say this because I've often had to correct my neighbors when they assert that, "once you get tenure, you don't have to be accountable to anyone." That is simply untrue.

22. See Fogg (2005, p. A31).

23. For more on this concept and the changes it has brought to academic cultures, see Slaughter and Leslie (1999). See also the video presentation on the entrepreneurial spirit at ASU: http://www.asu.edu/ui/entrepreneurship/

24. The lifestyle was often lampooned in academic novels; see, for example, Russo (1999); Smiley (1996); Hynes (2002); and any of the works of David Lodge.

25. Ryan (1998).

26. See their blog at: http://www.freakonomics.com/blog/2007/03/03/lets-just-get-rid-of-tenure/

27. See Rahdert (2007).

28. For a quick review of the history, statistics, and arguments for and against tenure, see http://en.wikipedia.org/wiki/Tenure

29. Institutions differ on the preferred length of personal statements. In general, three–five pages generally suffice. At Arizona State University, the provost provides "exemplars" of personal statements and vitae of successful tenure cases; you can access it online at: http://www.asu.edu/provost/promotion-tenure/exemplars/index.html

    One of the files on that page is that of Dr. Sarah Tracy, whose creative nonfiction narrative was highlighted in a previous chapter.

30. This last comment may seem flippant and irrelevant. I hope, for your sake, that it is. Because of the cloistered nature of decisions about tenure, the "secret" that precedes the symbolic kill, you should expect that your character and reputation will be discussed and may figure into the outcome. It is, in this respect, still very much like a medieval drama.

31. I recommend that tenure-track faculty working using personal narratives as a method of inquiry and creative nonfiction as a style of writing present an array of published work: at least one theory piece about narratives, at least one methods piece on the specifics used to inform a study, one pedagogy piece on or about teaching narrative inquiry, and at least one or more stories that demonstrate the academic values espoused in the theory and methods papers. By

providing readers unfamiliar or skeptical about the academic value of creative nonfiction narratives, this array of theory, methods, pedagogy, and applications—framed, of course, by a compelling personal statement that explains their connections and makes clear their value to the field—leaves little to the imagination and nothing, in principle, to object to.

32. Not all graduate students opt for the research intensive (or R-1) life, but, as a one of our doctoral students recently commented to me: "I wanted an R-1 education, but not an R-1 life." Accordingly, she paced herself, balanced her work with her life, and got an excellent job at a state university where teaching and research were equally valued, and being a good citizen was not relegated to "also-ran" status at tenure time.

33. Find out what it does take to get tenure at your institution by reading the official documents, attending new faculty sessions, and talking with senior faculty and your department head.

34. By "good," I mean Tier 1 (journals that have national or international readerships and high impact ratings) or Tier 2 (journals that have regional or highly specialized readerships and middle-to-high impact ratings). Publications in Tier 3 (e.g., state journals, graduate student–edited publications, and non-refereed outlets) count for almost nothing.

35. Remember, work done at prior institutions doesn't count at your host institution. If your dissertation required substantial rewriting, it will count for something, but not for as much as a book you produce on your own beyond the dissertation.

36. Make sure you include the acceptance letter in your portfolio. Also, in the best cases, the book has not only been published, but also favorably reviewed; place the published reviews in the portfolio, too.

37. The *Thomson Scientific Journal Citation Reports* is not a free service (although your university should be able to let you use it via a license fee or through the library), but you can check out the website: http://scientific.thomson.com/products/jcr/

38. One reason for the relatively "middling" ranking for *Qualitative Inquiry* that is otherwise held in high regard internationally by qualitative scholars is that *QI* has an "open review" policy, rather than a "blind review" policy. For some traditional scholars, this policy of knowing the names of your reviewers is unscientific. One result of this policy

is that *Thomson Scientific Journal Citation Reports* ranks the journal lower than others that have blind review policies.

39. Of course, a lot could be thought wrong with this way of thinking, particularly for writers of narratives and performance scripts. For one thing, it encourages us to *avoid publishing work without notes and references*. Those references are what are counted in the external metrics. Similarly, it makes us *think differently about the practical politics of publication and institutional rewards*: If we want others to cite our work as having had impact on them and their scholarship, then we ought to be willing to cite their work as having had an influence on ours.

40. Resistance, although always fun to discuss, is unlikely to be of much use.

41. Conversely, it is all the worse for your career if you write and even publish pieces that are *not* cited by others. Your stories may be "beautiful" and "true," but they will be seen as lacking *impact* if not cited. This is a hard truth to acknowledge, but given the business mentality associated with tenure and promotion decisions in higher education these days, publications that lack impact are likely to be seen as simply mere vanity. This logic also applies to work done in the "harder" social sciences, where decisions regarding tenure and promotion are often determined by whether or not (or to what extent) research is supported by external funding. In either scenario, an external metric is the mediating influence. As a vice provost for research at an otherwise pleasant institution once explained it to me: "If your research is not funded, how can you call it research? Who cares about it?"

42. There are exceptions to this general rule, as was the case with Ward Churchill's writing. But in general, if your name is mentioned in the public sphere because of your scholarship, that is a good thing from an institutional point of view. For example, being quoted in major newspapers and magazines, or having your work used by important opinion leaders, or appearing on talk shows are all public sources of "impact" that are vital to the image your host institution is developing in the marketplace of ideas.

43. An "elevator speech" is the twenty–thirty second pitch you would give to the president/CEO of an organization on behalf of your work. Think of it as selling a major motion picture producer or publisher on the idea for your current writing project.

Chapter 6

Success beyond the Academy
Becoming a Public Scholar

Going Public, Then

In June 1966, *Esquire* magazine published "In Cold Fact," a piece by Phillip K. Tompkins, then an assistant professor in the Department of Speech at Wayne State University.[1] The narrative was a public rhetorical criticism of Truman Capote's "nonfiction novel," *In Cold Blood*. Tompkins had read the novel and had concluded that it was not entirely, well, *factual*. Tompkins writes[2]:

> I knew something of the case—the murder of four members of the Clutter family in Western Kansas, my home state. Small but obvious factual errors jumped out at me from the pages of In Cold Blood. More importantly, a former student of mine at the University of Kansas, Lowell Lee Andrews, appears in the book on death row, waiting with the two Clutter killers, Perry Smith and Richard Hickock, to be executed by the State of Kansas. The characterization of Andrews was greatly overdrawn. It became clear to me that a new literary genre required a new critical method, a form of rhetorical criticism.

Tompkins began his research by flying back to Kansas. He read newspaper files, interviewed local authorities and members of the media, read the transcript of the trial, and even discovered a confession by one of the killers. In his view, "the evidence clearly contradicted Capote's account in crucial ways." His colleagues urged him to "go public."

So he did. *Esquire* agreed to publish the article under two conditions: "I would first have to demonstrate the inaccuracies in the book; second, I would have to explain *why* Capote changed the facts." As he later found out, he would also have to undergo the most thorough scrutiny of the facts in his article that he had ever experienced.

The piece was published and generated some wider public interest. National newspapers and magazines discussed the piece; Tompkins was interviewed about it and presented a paper at a national convention on the topic. It has since been reprinted in *The Quarterly Journal of Speech* as well as in one anthology, one book about Capote's book, and a volume of literary criticism. Going public had clearly attracted a wider public audience for his work, and, so far as I know, it has been the *only* piece of rhetorical criticism published by a communication scholar in that magazine.

Tompkins wrote well on topics of public concern and brought his scholarly resources to the task. He demonstrated the utility of a form of public rhetorical criticism to the then "new" journalism. He had contacts in the New York publishing world through his exposure and could have used those contacts to continue to publish for the mass market. But, for many years after that, he chose not to. Why?

One large clue is in the chilly reception he received in academic circles. He writes:

> Despite the wide circulation of the article, and my technical commentary on it, the head of my department at the time said he would pay no attention to an article that could be read in a barbershop. I heard indirectly that he and the other senior professor in the department would give much more weight to an article in *The Speech Teacher* than in *Esquire*.[3]

Tompkins returned to publishing his work in traditional academic outlets. He enjoyed a "super-star" career as one of the great scholars in organizational communication, including work as a consultant to NASA and author of books on aviation safety, the *Challenger* and *Columbia* space shuttle disasters, and, since retirement from the University of Colorado at Boulder, he has been a tireless and effective advocate for the homeless. He has, interestingly enough, also published columns and letters to the editor in mass market circulation newspapers and magazines, including *The New Yorker*, the *New York Times*, the Denver *Post*, and others. Thinking back now in response to the question "Why don't modern scholars engage in public scholarship more frequently," he writes:

My own attempt to engage in public scholarship was not valued by people in a position to evaluate my performance. I thought then and now that they were wearing academic blinders. In addition, and this may sting some current academics, since retiring from everyday campus life in 1998, I have worked as a volunteer at a homeless shelter once a week. I spend more and more of my time as a member of advocacy organizations that hopes to end homelessness in Denver. That experience makes me think of some academic scholarship with a word I once heard Kenneth Burke use: "Precious." I think he meant by that expression the kind of paper or journal article that would be of interest to only a handful of pedants around the world, and with no possible application to the concerns of ordinary human beings.

If current communication and rhetorical theories are as powerful as some believe, persons in our discipline ought to be better than those in others in reaching the wider audiences.[4] Audience adaptation is, so far as I know, still a cardinal communicative canon. Communication scholars ought to be able to communicate. There is a dirty little secret, however, in the academic world that must be articulated here: Rewards are determined by the discipline, not the university. The college or university committees and bureaucrats respect the disciplinary evaluations of individuals while making tenure and promotion decisions. One must be willing to risk a negative, if unfair, evaluation by the discipline if one communicates beyond it, particularly to the general public. Some intellectual snobs think of this as a form of pandering.

Going Public, Now

In the last chapter, I discussed the new entrepreneurial business model that is driving so much of the change in higher education. One by-product of that model has been that universities have learned that to compete in today's global marketplace of ideas, scholars must reach wider public audiences in addition to the narrow audiences within their specialties. Not just qualitative researchers, but researchers and writers in all academic fields.

I would be lying, though, if I said that there has also been a sudden universal happy embrace of public scholarship by various scholarly communities. Some senior scholars, feeling the known (and prized) worlds of academic status slip away under the new systems of rewarding scholars who attain a public presence, resist and rebel. The dwindling away of the textual authority of the scholarly monograph; the diminution of departmental power based on an emerging culture of big grants and academic celebrity; and the passing of known ways of doing scholarship and being an academic in the world—well, under these cultural and political conditions, when the sheer velocity of the changes is overwhelming and the future is in doubt, some of the best of us resist the new, even when it is no longer in our best interests, or our discipline's, to do so.

But there are other market forces driving the demand for public scholarship and for a reward system to support it. In a report titled "University Publishing in a Digital Age,"[5] the following passage illuminates the idea that information technologies support a much broader definition for what constitutes scholarship as well as providing digital formats for it:

> In American colleges and universities, access to the Internet and World Wide Web is ubiquitous. Consequently, nearly all intellectual effort results in some form of "publishing," whether via a blog or Web page, "a working-paper Web site or institutional repository," or a more traditional peer-reviewed journal or monograph.
>
> Scholars—especially younger faculty members—have been quick to adapt. "They want 24/7 access, and they want to access content remotely," the report observes. "Behavioral changes ... have taken place quite rapidly, much more so than universities have adapted the ways they produce and qualify scholarship."

Perhaps you chuckled at the beginning of this book when I mentioned that there were "still dinosaurs" when I was in graduate school. That was a long time ago, but the dinosaurs are still with us. Now some of you are finishing graduate school. They aren't the same dinosaurs, but they are dinosaurs nonetheless.

Perhaps you chuckled again when you read the section about how the self-correcting typewriter was the last gasp of an older world when my friends in the computer center forecast a new digital age on the academic horizon via something called "personal computing." How personal computing changed everything. How it still does. And my guess is that you might have shaken your head in wonder and thought: That kind of change will never happen to me. But an even bigger change is happening in academic culture. *Now.*

And you have a choice to make: to become a dinosaur, or not to become a dinosaur. That is *your* option.

The future of scholarly publishing is where the public sphere and the entrepreneurial business model of academic culture meet. Increasingly, all of the available evidence suggests that regardless of your academic area, attaining a public voice, supporting your research with websites, with blogs, with interactive media, and reaching the public through live appearances as well as digitally mediated ones will be the norm. Although academic culture struggles to cope with the changes, those of us who acquire the skill set will master the game.

Fortunately, there have been many positive signs associated with academic culture change, despite the fact that dinosaurs are still among us. My own discipline, for example, now publishes an e-zine[6] designed to bring communication theories and research to the attention of a wider reading public. Scholarly presses more readily seek out creative nonfiction manuscripts, and even those that remain proudly traditional expect a quality of learned writing that makes what was once "precious" far more accessible.[7]

Things *have* changed. And they will continue to change. Good narrative writing that reaches across disciplines and into the world is the new gold standard, and creative nonfiction is the preferred style of this brave new genre. Democracy and the academy are finally well met.

Constructing the Academic and Trade/Crossover Author Self

I first wrote for the trade market back in the mid-1980s. These were two "self-help" books based on original academic research, both co-authored with my friend and former mentor, Gerald M. Phillips.[8] At that time, Gerry was represented by the literary agent Gloria Stern, and as a happy result, she also agreed to represent me. Ms. Stern hoped to make Gerry into "the Isaac Asimov of the social sciences," by which she meant that she hoped to channel his prolific writing in the academy into prolific writing for the trade market. "Prolific" for Asimov takes on a whole new meaning. By the time of his death in April 1992, Asimov had authored or edited over 500 books, and his work was represented in nine of the ten Dewey Decimal System categories.[9]

Gerry Phillips continued to write prolifically for both academic and popular markets until his death on April 26, 1995. He wrote, coauthored, or edited two, sometimes three or four books a year, in addition to many articles, reviews, and letters-to-the editor.[10] He was an early and vigorous pioneer and advocate of the Internet and became what today we call a "blogger" long before that term was in common parlance. He never achieved Ms. Stern's dream of becoming the "Isaac Asimov of the social sciences," but he had a long and wonderful career as a writer, teacher, and Internet pioneer. Today, two major awards are named in his honor: the Gerald M. Phillips Award for Distinguished Scholarship in Applied Communication, from the National Communication Association, and the Gerald M. Phillips Award for Mentoring, from the American Communication Association.

Gerry taught me a great deal about the importance of constructing an identity for public consumption, lessons he learned from Ms. Stern, from publicists, and from many others in journalism and entertainment business since his first television appearance on *The Johnny Carson Show*. "Goodall," he once told me, "nobody wants to see just another boring academic on television. And, I'll tell you this: if you are boring on television, even once, you'll never get a second chance."

I looked at him, no doubt wearing a dumb expression.

He went on:

> Listen, before scholars turned inward and created journals as the primary vehicles for the dissemination of knowledge, before we divided up the study of communication into narrow specializations, we had to cultivate a public audience to drum up interest in our subjects and to pay the bills. I'm talking Plato, Aristotle, the Sophists, all the way up to the early 20th century. So our forebears gave public lectures and made presentations to instruct and to entertain public audiences. These talks were always a mixture of scholarship, opinion, and a whole lot of theatre. Not much has changed except the technology, not if you want to cultivate a public audience.[11]

What he was telling me was this: In a mediated entertainment and news environment, you don't get brownie points for being "just another boring scholar." We have to *earn* the public's interest. We must earn it by being more than just smart. If you want to become a public intellectual, if you want to appeal to a wide public audience, you need to be well-informed, yes, but also smart enough to recognize that the engaged public life is a series of *performances*, and then you need to learn how to construct and deploy an appealing performance *identity* constructed for your intended public audience.

The second time I ventured into the public sphere was for fun and profit, and it happened as a result of a bet. I was by then an academic ethnographer and pretty much resolved to a writing life of academic publication.[12] It was a good life and rewarding work, *but*.

But *what*?

But this: I also had developed an interest in the celebrity authors who populate daytime television. If you watch early morning or midday or late afternoon news shows, for example, almost every day there is an author on to discuss *whatever*. For large national markets, those celebrity authors who write best-sellers have agented book deals that include these sorts of appearances to promote the books. But for smaller markets with their own news and entertainment shows who follow the same basic format, the "celebrity authors" I was interested in were mostly midlevel writers, some self-published, some academics, and their fifteen minutes of fame often occurred after ominous reports of flu outbreaks and just before locally produced segments on gardening tips.

We were then living in Greensboro, North Carolina. I was teaching and head of the department at UNCG, and I joked with my friends and colleagues about seeing these people on television and having a bad case of author-envy. In our media-saturated world, my envy was a kind of illness, probably. The malaise of the overlooked and underread. But there it was. I couldn't ignore it and it wouldn't go away.

I'm not always the hero.

One day, a neighbor of ours named Renee came into the house as I was preparing dinner. I love to cook and am proud to say that I excel at it.[13] Renee made some polite comment about the dish and said something like "I wish my husband could cook like that."

I assured her that he could. I pontificated a bit. Cookery, as Socrates observed, is akin to rhetoric. It is a skill set that can be developed by almost anyone, although, as Socrates failed to concede but I do, there are masters of the art and science of it, and then there is everyone else—the mere openers of cans, the sad eaters of microwave dinners, the "arrangers" of pretty foods prepared in upscale shops and bought on the way home, the "I only grill red meat" men, the "I only make reservations" women, etc.

(This was a friendly dig: Renee was one of *those* women.)

But for those of us who like to eat and who have studied cooking, who prize finding new recipes and fooling around in the kitchen, and who, in fact, collect rare cookbooks and go out of our way to try out new spicings. ... Well. We add a little something extra to the basic culinary skill set. We are, I told her, the Attic orators of the kitchen crowd.

I'm afraid I went a little too far.

One thing led to another. By the end of the conversation I had bet Renee I could teach her husband how to cook. By the end of the evening, fueled by good wine and high spirits, I had bet my wife I could write a book teaching all the men on earth how to cook.

. By the next morning I awoke to discover that I had talked myself into it, more or less.

But I knew I needed something more than an idea for a cookbook. I needed a hook. There are a million cookbooks. How could I make mine stand out? What did I know something about that would make a cook-book for men sell? How could make myself into a ... (here it comes, God help me) a celebrity author on talk shows?

What made me different from other would-be cookbook authors was my background in communication. What made me interested in writing a cookbook for men—who notoriously don't cook—was that I knew what would motivate men to want to read it: Sex. *Of course*. Men who know how to cook have one of the best romantic resources on earth at their disposal. "Would you like to come over for dinner, let me cook something for you?"

It was the perfect marriage of (bad boy) motives and my cookbook opportunity.

Food Talk: A Man's Guide to Cooking and Conversation with Women[14] was published in 1998. The book combines recipes written in "guy speak," with practical advice about romance drawn from the gender and intimate relationships literatures. I created mythic manly narratives around the food categories and talking points for dates. It was, if I do say so myself, clever, upbeat, and funny, and it had great original cover art and good recipes.

It was accompanied by a speaking tour that fulfilled my celebrity envy in ways that made me wonder why I ever had the envy in the first place. The celebrity author life is *tough*. Tougher still for a first-time cookbook writer. Not only did I have to squeeze my carefully scripted sound-bites and celebrity performance of self between the flu outbreaks and gardening tips, but my long-suffering wife and I had to produce the dishes at oh-dark-thirty in the morning before the early morning shows, using the small kitchen facilities available in places that cater to people who usually eat out.

We existed for three months primarily on fast food and little sleep on the road in a Toyota 4-Runner surrounded by pots, pans, overnight bags, and books. We had to. We were driving from venue to venue, shuttling between talk show appearances, radio interviews, and bookstore signings from New York City to Fairbanks, Alaska, from Los Angeles to Atlanta. I learned that it was and is a tiring and unhealthy way to live. I know now why most celebrity authors *hate* the book tour.[15]

But no complaints.

It was also, at times, a lot of fun. We met interesting, talented people and made a little money, although not the elephant money we had hoped for. We were slightly ahead of the market (trade market publishing success is "a casino"[16]: one part product, one part planning, four parts luck, and if there is a best-seller casino God, that God is in the timing of the release and the absence of notable competitors), as two books with very similar themes followed on our heels, both of them making a much bigger splash.[17]

But I won my bet with Renee, if not my wife. A few good men learned the joys of cooking and more than a few women—who gave the book as a gift to their boyfriends, spouses, or relatives—got more than a few laughs and a free dinner out of it.

For me, being a celebrity cookbook author and romance advice giver was a lark. I also learned a great deal about creating a media identity and appealing to popular audiences as a performer. I learned how to handle interviews,[18] read aloud the same selection over and over and over again with truly simulated feeling, and sign autographs in personally meaningful ways. You have no idea what requests for inscriptions some people make or the value of making sure you ask them how to *spell* their names.

By the time I published *A Need to Know: The Clandestine History of a CIA Family* in 2006, I was prepared to do what had to be done to make my book successful. In the interim more changes had occurred, and in addition to what I knew from prior public exposure, I needed to acquire additional skills to do well in the rapidly expanding world of Internet sales, web identity, podcasts, and literary blogs. In the remaining sections of this chapter, I'll share what I have learned.

Audiences and Communities beyond the Academy

Close your eyes.

Yeah, I know. This is the second time I've asked. But this will be even better than the last time I asked you to close your eyes. This is all about *you*.

Imagine a crowded mass market bookstore on a Friday night in late September. The lights are suitably bright, the smell of fresh roasted coffee and something chocolate fills the air. You arrive a little before the scheduled signing is to begin, dressed for success and a little nervous, and meet with the store manager, who tells you that she has made sure that copies of your book are available at the signing desk. If you need anything, just ask.

You need nothing. You have done this before. You came with your book, the marked-up oral reading passages highlighted, and a bottle of water in your hand. You move to the lectern and begin. There are perhaps twenty or twenty-five persons whose eyes are upon you. Now comes the test: Tell me who you see.

Who are these people? What do they do for a living? Discount your relatives and friends from the university. Who are the *others*?

What are they doing *here*? Is this just a regular event in their lives (some people show up for all book signings, not interested in reading the book at all, only to buy it at a steep discount, get you to sign it, and then put it up for sale at a premium price later on eBay; others frequent bookstores on Fridays looking for a date, etc.).

Why are they (potentially) interested in you and your book? Or, more to the point: Are they *really* interested in your book?

Now the important question: How many copies will be sold tonight?

Now open your eyes.

Ah, the profit motive rears its ugly capitalist oink face after all, yes? In truth, for all the romance you may associate with writing and publishing, the bottom line is still the bottom line. Book publishers are interested in *sales*, not in you, or at least not in you as a person until you make them some money. Oh, an editor may *like* you, find you amusing or interesting, controversial or cool, but editors don't keep their jobs because of the people they like. Unless the people they like make them money.

Figuring out who your audience is and what they want from you is vital to your success. This is as true for gaining tenure as it is for creating a public self and identity as an author. In either case, you need to close your eyes and imagine who is listening and what they want to hear, before determining what might be the best way to appeal to them.

My third venture into trade publishing was far more personal and at the same time international in scope. After years of being in denial about the true nature of my father's government work and in response to some pretty basic questions put to me by our son, I decided it was time to use my research and writing skills to confront the past directly and to discover the truth behind how I grew up.

My father was a spy. I had grown up in a clandestine family. We kept secrets. We even, if not most especially, often kept the most revealing secrets from each other. In the end, the secrets we kept and the politics of the clandestine life destroyed us as a family. This is the one book I had not wanted to write, but it was also the one story I could no longer afford to run away from.

My son had a need to know. So, as a result, I, too, had a need to know.

My wife, Sandra, had always wanted to know. But, moreover, she knew I needed to know if I was ever to bring some resolution to my family story. It had haunted me for years.

Had I approached this research and writing task purely as an academic task, I would have thought of the project differently. I would have conceived it as an article, perhaps a case study, on the long-term effects of secrecy in families. In fact, I had recently read a book on the subject that contained the expression "toxic secrets" that begged for an application to my story.[19]

But in my mind, the story I had to tell was a book. It would be part history, part memoir, and part speculation—a perfect combination for creative nonfiction. The audience I imagined when I closed my eyes was made up of three distinct groups: people, mostly men, who read spy novels and spy stories and spy memoirs; cold war history fans, particularly those fans who had a keen and abiding fascination with Harold Adrian "Kim" Philby and James Jesus Angleton, two of the main characters in my father's secret life; and, finally, academics from a variety of fields who shared an interest in autoethnographic/autobiographical writing, particularly those who read about families.

Knowing my audience was composed of these three groups of readers helped me make some decisions about how to tell my story. Having been an avid reader of cold war spy stories and spy histories, I knew that almost all spy stories from that era follow the same basic storyline: patriotic young men veterans emerged from the end of World War II knowing there was a new enemy on the horizon—international Communism—that had to be defeated. They volunteered for clandestine service and served their country well, often with distinction, only to learn that they are being betrayed not by the enemy, but by one of their own kind, usually for political protection or personal political gain. They try to fight back against the injustice, but find that fighting back is useless. Spy organizations are bureaucracies. Those in power will do anything to maintain or expand their power. In the end, the tarnished hero "retires" from active service as an embittered soul and then begins a long, slow spiral of despair and alcoholism that ends in a sudden and often violent death.

Every spy story that ends badly is essentially the same story.

I knew the story well. It was my father's story, too. The plot I needed to adopt was linear chronology, modified only by a preface that began with where I first knew I was entering a mystery: my father's untimely death and my confusion as a result of learning that the man I had thought I knew and loved had been also someone else—a cold war spy.

So, contrary to my usual practice,[20] I wrote the preface first. I needed a framing device that would appeal to the readers I had identified. And I needed to seed this opening framing device with set-ups that would lead to pay-offs, with symbols that readers couldn't fail to read as signs of what was to come. That I would return to this preface innumerable times to add or change details was something I knew going in, but I needed a hook for the story, the hook that had reeled me in so many years ago and that had pointed to the mystery at the heart of it, and I needed to write that mysterious beginning for two very good reasons.

First, I needed to write, from the heart, exactly where the story began. I needed to do that work so I would know where to go from there, because there were choices involved. Should I go backward into the deep past and recover my father's and later my mother's narratives? Or should I jump to the present, where the story ended, with me revealing to my son and to my wife what I learned from this journey into the past? If I chose the former method of telling the story, the linear chronology would be my guide as well as my guard, and the story would either end up a tour through the past or, depending on what I discovered doing the research, I would become of prisoner of it. I knew that trap only too well. So I was wary of it.

If I chose the latter approach, that would involve another sequence, a *reverse* chronology. But try as I might, I couldn't envision how to do it that way. I didn't yet know how the secret-story-within-the-cover-story that I didn't yet fully know *went*, much less where or how, exactly, it ended. So, in the end, I chose the linear chronology.

The second reason for writing the preface first was I needed something to sell to an agent or publisher. I knew that in trade publishing of this variety, the fortunes of my book proposal would rise or fall based on composing a compelling query letter, which meant finding a compelling hook for the query letter. I also knew that finding an agent was as difficult, if not more so, than locating a publisher.

I knew this search for an agent would take time. And during that time, I would be researching and writing the rest of the book. Which meant I needed to begin the process of researching an agent early, and yet not *too* early. Because if my pitch worked, the agent would want to see the manuscript or at least some sample chapters.

This thinking went into a process of researching agencies, limiting the ones chosen for queries to those that specialized in historical narratives, and particularly to those individual agents who represented espionage books. I was targeting agents, thinking of them as an audience for my pitch.

The Agent as Audience

To find a suitable agent requires a good deal of research and a lot of time spent composing the pitch, known as a query letter. Unlike academic publishers who may increasingly find cover letters or queries to be less useful than the submission itself, agents and trade publishers often make decisions based solely on query letters and proposals.

Allow me to dispel some myths about finding an agent.

First: Not just "any" agent will do for you, nor will you have an easy time finding one. Instead, it is wise for you to think about the highly competitive market you are entering and to cater your search to those agents who specialize in selling work in that market. There are several published guides to literary agents that are updated annually and these make good resources but not necessarily definitive ones, as agents change affiliations or stop accepting new clients out of cycle with the publications that list them. Unless you can get a personal introduction from a well-published friend or mentor, your best resource for finding an agent is the Internet.[21]

Even with the speed of the Internet, this quest for an agent is a time-consuming and often frustrating enterprise, so you need to begin by asking yourself whether you actually *need* an agent. If you are publishing in scholarly journals and want to write a textbook or a scholarly book, you don't. If you want to write for local or regional magazines, you don't. If you want to sell your book to a major trade publisher and that publisher only accepts agented manuscripts, you do. For obvious reasons. If you think you have a story that not only will make a great bestseller but also a fine movie, you do. For obvious reasons, too, though, make sure the agent you choose handles both books and film rights, because not all agents do. If you plan to have a long and prolific career writing creative nonfiction for trade markets, you do. In fact, if you fit into this latter category, have a track record of publications, and can prove you can write for a defined trade audience, you are an ideal candidate from an agent's perspective.

Remember the oink? Publishing is a business, and the best agents are a combination of business managers, tough-love editors, legal representatives, and effective salespersons. If they can represent five authors, each of whom puts out a book a year, that's ideal. The money is steady, and, assuming their authors aren't hounding them every day for news, life is good. If they have to represent fifteen authors who average a book every three years, it can be thin times between paychecks. Particularly if they also represent authors who hound them every day for news. So, think about who you are from an agent's perspective, and when you think about that question, be honest about how prolific you intend to be. Remember: From an agent's perspective, the best indicator of future success is your track record of past success.

The next question to ask yourself is what *market niche* you plan to write for. Although there are large agencies (which you may or may not find attractive) that represent work across the vast expanse of the fiction and nonfiction publishing universe, the *individuals* in those agencies who will read your query all have much smaller, more well-defined book interests and market specializations. For example, the person you want to contact may only talk to certain editors at a given number of publishing houses, or she or he may only represent authors who are likely to appeal to *a* specific editor at one specific house, at least *this* year. Everything else, for her or for him, is a waste of time.

And a waste of time is a waste of money.

And this is a business, oink, which means money may not be everything (fame is good; notoriety excellent), but it is the only thing that pays the bills. It doesn't matter if you may be the next J. K. Rowling.[22] If what you want to write doesn't fit what the agent feels he or she can fairly represent and make a profit on, you don't get a contract. You may not even get an answer to your query.

206

Assuming you have worked through the above questions and still want to pursue a literary agent, what should you do? I know you want an answer to that question, but hold on. I'm not quite ready to answer it yet. Let's narrow it down a little more.

First, have you already written the book? This is important because if it is a work of creative nonfiction in the areas of fiction, general nonfiction, history, biography, or memoir, and if you have written a compelling query, you will be asked to submit a full proposal and sample chapters from your work or, in some rare cases, the completed manuscript. If you submit a full proposal and samples and the agent or publisher likes what you've done, you will then be asked to submit the whole manuscript *immediately*. That won't be the time to say, "I haven't finished it yet."[23]

If, on the other hand, you are writing a self-help book or if you are trying to turn a research study into a mass market work of nonfiction in the usual academic categories found in mass market bookstores, you may be better off *not* having completed the manuscript but have a full-blown proposal ready to ship along with two or three sample chapters. Agents specializing in those areas often like to work closely with the author to fashion a proposal for a specific publishing house, and that means (in most cases) altering what the author might want to do to suit the needs of the market.

You are now ready to find an agent.

Here's what to do. First, visit the websites of the list of agencies you've compiled and make sure that you have assembled and ready to ship precisely the items they ask for. If they want a query first and nothing else, prepare to write the query. If the agency wants a query and fifty pages, prepare the query and fifty pages. Not sixty pages. Not thirty-five. Fifty. If the agency requests a query and two sample chapters, but not the first chapter or last chapter, then do it.

Next, you will want to create a computer file listing all of the agents (and their contact information) you plan to contact, what they require, what you send to them (and on what date), and what their response to it was/is. I use a Word file with a table and columns. Works fine for me.

So, to review, let's assume that you have completed three important tasks:

1. asked yourself the hard questions and been honest about the answers;

2. researched the market and articulated your niche; and

3. researched agents and publishers and made a computer file of potential targets, their requirements, etc.

You are now ready to proceed to step 4: Write a compelling query letter and a proposal.

Writing a Query Letter

Remember those hard questions you needed to answer about yourself and your publishing goals? This is the place where your answers will come in handy. Why?

Because everything you have told yourself about yourself as a writer—novice or mid-level career or advanced—and everything you know about how you see your career as an author (one book only; a book every three years; a book a year) and everything you have articulated about the target market for your book will be used to write a compelling query letter. Note: You can write a compelling letter from *any* of these standpoints, but when communicating with an agent and publisher you need to be clear about them.

There are many high-quality guides to writing query letters.[24] Fiction or nonfiction, all of them stress these key essentials:

- one page is best; two pages maybe, but it is a risk; no spelling or grammar errors;

- address it personally to the agent you want to read it;

- four paragraphs in length:

  1. *hook*: A catchy one or two sentence explanation of the book, its length in the approximate number of words followed by a brief description of the audience for it and why this book has "the inside track" on it;

  2. *synopsis*: What is in the book, why it should appeal to the target market;

  3. *your bio*: What are your credentials for writing the book (including your educational creds if they relate directly to the subject);

  4. *closing*: Like this: "Thank you for your time and consideration. I have enclosed (whatever is asked for on the website). I look forward to hearing your decision."

In these guides you will also find lists of key dos and don'ts[25]:

The Dos:
- Do address your query specifically to an agent.
- Do state the title of your book.
- Do mention the word count and genre of your book. Insert those at the end of your first "hook" paragraph.
- Do mention exactly why you're approaching Ms. Agent. Try to compare your book with other books that Ms. Agent has represented in the past.
- Do adopt a professional, serious tone.
- Do keep your query to one page only. Unless it must be two. But understand that two is usually one page longer than an agent will read.
- Do format your query using standard business letter alignment and spacing. That means single-spaced, 12-point font, everything aligned along the left margin, No paragraph indentations, but a space between each paragraph.
- Do list your phone number, mailing address, and email address
- Do include a self-addressed stamped envelope (SASE) with all snail mail submissions.[26]
- Do have a pair of "fresh eyes" proofread for typos and grammar mistakes.

The Do NOTs:

- Do NOT start off your query by saying, "I am querying you because I found your name in 'such and such' writing guide or Internet agent database." Not only does this take up valuable query letter space, it's also the sign of an amateur.

- Do NOT refer to your work of creative nonfiction as a "nonfiction novel." You aren't Truman Capote.

- Do NOT sing the praises of your book or compare it with other best-selling books.

- Do NOT send gifts or other bribes with your query.

- Do NOT print your query on perfumed or colored paper. Use plain business stationery.

- Do NOT shrink your font down to 9 points so it all fits on one page; a 12–point font is standard, 11 points if you're really desperate.

- Do NOT Fedex or mail your query in a signature-required fashion in order to make your query stand out. It will stand out, but in a very "annoying, overzealous, bad first impression" kind of way.

- Do NOT apologize in your query for being a newbie writer with zero publishing credits and experience. Your goal is to write a tight, alluring, eye-catching query and sound like a professional. If you're worried about your lack of writing credentials, just keep quiet and let the writing speak for itself.

- Do NOT include sample chapters with your query UNLESS an agent's submission guidelines specifically SAY to include sample pages with your snail mail query.

- Do NOT forget to list your email address or contact phone number on your query.

- Do NOT forget to enclose a self-addressed stamped envelope (SASE).

Sample Query Letter[27]

Agent's Name
Agent Company
Address
City, State, Zip

Dear _____:

When my father—H. Lloyd Goodall—died in March of 1976 at the age of 53, I inherited a small gold key to a safety deposit box located in a Savings & Loan in Hagerstown, Maryland. The box contained his diary and a copy of The Great Gatsby. I had never known my father to keep a diary nor did I consider him a literary man. I believed he had retired on medical disability from the Veterans Administration after an ordinary and relatively undistinguished career as a government bureaucrat. I was wrong.

From the diary I learned that my father had been a spy. He devoted his life to fighting a clandestine war against Communism and, in the end, it cost him his life. Along the way he made powerful enemies, but none more powerful than James Jesus Angleton, who, for over twenty years served as the Director of Counterintelligence for the CIA. My father's meteoric rise within the clandestine service; his successful tours of duty in Rome and London during the 1950s;

his fateful encounter with East Germans in Berlin; and his "exile" to clandestine hell in Cheyenne, Wyoming were all the result of his dealings with Angleton. So, too, was his final assignment, bought with his soul, to perform illegal domestic surveillance against the anti-war movement in Philadelphia during the late 1960s. It was here, finally, that the years of stress and duplicity took its toll on his mind and body. And it was here, in January of 1969, that he officially left the clandestine service a broken and troubled man at age 47, on a 100% medical disability retirement.

My story—*In Search of My Father's Shadow: Uncovering the Secret Life of a Cold War Family*[28]—is a work of narrative non-fiction that is part memoir, part historical reconstruction, and part imagination shaped by what I call my "narrative inheritance." The manuscript makes 120,000 words and is ready for review.

My book will be of interest to general readers interested in "ruthlessly honest" memoirs as well as to veteran readers of espionage novels, histories, and personal accounts of the Cold War. I became interested in your agency having read—and very much enjoyed—Hermann and Kate Field's *Trapped in the Cold War: The Ordeal of an American Family,* and hope that my story appeals to you as much as theirs did. Because my book also tells a research story, a third audience for my work will be academics aligned with qualitative methods of inquiry who study organizations, families, and communication in the social sciences.

I am a veteran academic author (18 books, over 100 articles, chapters, and papers) and an acknowledged authority in the field of Communication Studies. I am also associated with pioneering work in the writing method known as narrative ethnography. I have published text, trade, and scholarly works, won several writing awards, and have extensive media experience. This year I was honored to receive a Lifetime Achievement award from the National Communication Association.

I have written a unique book I feel is worthy of your representation. I am interested in forming a longer-term professional relationship with an established agency enthusiastic about broadening the appeal of my work to reach a wider public audience.

Thank you for your time. I sincerely hope my query has captured your initial interest. I very much look forward to hearing from you.

Best regards,

H. L. (Bud) Goodall, Jr.
Address
Phone
email

A final word about proposals: Some agents readily accept—even re-quire—electronic submissions. If they do, and if you query them online, you will likely (but not always) get a faster reply. See their websites for details and, again, *follow the instructions*.

The Trade Market Proposal

Trade market proposals are informative, detailed business documents that contain and expand on the pitch that was in the query. They may be generated for agents or for publishers, but they differ from propos-als generated for academic publishers in small but important respects. Although the individual proposals themselves may differ in approach, style, length,[29] and contents depending on the subject matter and ex-perience of the author(s), trade market nonfiction proposals tend to have similar components:

- a cover letter: Based on your query, the cover letter should include the title; hook; complete description of the contents; word count (and number of photos or illustrations, if applicable); the audi-ence, and why you are uniquely positioned to write this book for that audience; and the expected delivery date of the completed manuscript.
- a table of contents for the rest of the proposal: Complete with page numbers for ease of reference. The contents should include:
    - overview of the book;
    - chapter titles and brief descriptions of what is in them;
    - market analysis (who will read it, what is the competi-tion, why your title is better or will compete well against the competition—but don't be overly negative about other titles), complete with number of sales for competing volumes;

- promotion plan: A good idea because some agents consider this section to be the most important in your document. This should include the details of how *you personally plan to create an audience and promote sales* of your book, including but not limited to mailing lists, potential reviewers, development of website support, willingness to do a book tour and interviews, previous reviews or media appearances, prior work with a publicist, important people and celebrities who will endorse the book, etc.;
- author bio: Normally this *isn't* your academic *CV,* but a tailored version of it that focuses on your credibility to write this particular book for this particular market. It should establish your credibility and provide details of your professional experience, speaking experience (before public audiences and groups), published work in related areas, and media experience; and
- sample chapters: Usually one–three chapters.

It is important for you to be upbeat and passionate about your project, and it is wise to remember that agents (and publishers) appreciate three politeness rituals: (1) to be thanked for their time and work on your behalf; (2) to have their authors follow through *on time* with the promises they make; and (3) to be recommended to others—but not too many others, and preferably only those interesting others who can also increase their income.

Crafting and Marketing a Web Identity

It strikes me as dinosaurish today when I meet a practicing academic who doesn't actively maintain a website. After all, websites are not terribly complicated to create; they provide interested students, colleagues, clients, customers, and audiences access to important and persuasive information about you and what you do; and they are vital to your success as a public scholar.

That said, there is a difference between a university website and an author website. University websites are often controlled by the "branding" office where you work and what they will allow on college and university servers can be—and should be—strictly limited.

By contrast, an author website maintained on a public or private server (but linked to your university webpage) allows far more freedom in design and features, as well as the opportunity for you to personally update your pages on a regular basis. And yes, you must update your pages regularly, if not daily. You want readers to return, right? They will only if there is something new for them to read, look at, or do while they are surfing the net.

Creating an Author Website

Unless you are a skilled graphic artist with web design experience, this task is best contracted out to a professional. Why? Because chances are that in the time it would take you to master the technical design tools necessary to create a competent site, you could write a couple of articles or half a book.[30] Ask yourself: What use of time will have the larger payoff, for *you*?

You can expect to spend way too much money unless you know the answers to five basic questions that any competent professional will want to know before starting to design your website. Those basic questions are[31]:

- WHO is the site for (creator? audience?)? Is this website an act of ego or oink? Some combination of the two?

- WHAT should the site do? Are you trying to sell books, create an image, entertain visitors, or what? Do you plan to sell subscriptions to a blog or charge for downloads of podcasts or chapters?

- WHEN does it need to be accessed? Do you expect people to be able to access it 24/7 or just during regular business hours or maybe just on weekends? Remember, how you answer this question is important, because if you want return visitors you need to regularly update it. Furthermore, being open only during business hours implies a local or regional rather than national or international market, yes?

- WHERE should it be found? Who will host your site, how do you register it, and how can you increase the number of hits to it so that it pops up on the front page of major search engines, such as Google, Yahoo, AskJeeves, or Dogpile?

- WHY does it help you? Back to issues of ego or oink. Be honest.

If you can answer these questions to your own satisfaction and if your answers lead you to conclude that you need an author website, then your next step is to purchase a domain name. *GoDaddy*[32] is a good economical place to do that, and no, they don't pay me to say that. When thinking of a domain name, use something that will last, such as firstnamelastname.com. Think of a domain as the one thing customers will need to remember. Act accordingly.

Your next move is to visit author websites for folks you like to read. See what appeals to you in terms of the design of their website and the features (e.g., navigation buttons, flash pages, photos, counters, etc.). Make a list of the sites you like and the features and share them with your professional web designer. This move will save the person you hire time, which means it will also save you money.

If you *still* want to create your own website, and if you have registered a domain name, and if you have some quality time to spare, then Karen Stewart's design rules will help you. As a matter of fact, we've already covered design rules 1 through 4 and are now up to her Design Rule 5:

5. Create a Site Architecture

- Divide info into categories
  - Try not to exceed 5
  - Try not to use more than 3 sub categories for each main category
- Follow 3-CLICK rule
- Follow Standard Naming Conventions = short obvious names for links
- Do you need room to grow? Make sure you save some

You will note, please, that what you are doing is deciding how your site will "work" for visitors to it. Of critical importance is the "3-Click" rule, which, as you probably have figured out, means that you should design your site architecture so that no visitor has to click more than three times to navigate through it.

Another item of importance is the "standard naming conventions" line. For example, "contact" is for how a visitor to your site can contact you; "books" is for links to your books; "blog" is for a blog; and so forth. Don't get fancy because visitors may not understand and won't want to waste time figuring it out.

Which brings us to Design Rule 6:

6. Start Designing

- Pick your software
  - What do you know?
  - What can you learn?
- Low End: ?? Or try http://www.cnet.com/downloads (search for "author ing tools")
- High End: Dreamweaver (Adobe) or Expression Web (Microsoft)

Pretty self-explanatory. Either you are familiar enough with a software package to use it, or you have to devote some time to learning one. If you are undecided about how much you know and how long you are willing to devote to learning an application, Karen's suggestions are good ways to consider your options.

Make your choice and move on to Design Rule 7:

7. Your Home Page

- The 8-second rule – or – *To Splash Page or Not to Splash Page, that is the Question*
- Clearly identify where we are
- And what the site is about
- For a 14-inch monitor – above the fold

Again, pretty self-explanatory. The idea is to get your website visitor to what she or he wants to get to on your pages as soon as possible. Hence, the eight-second rule. Studies have shown that most people won't wait longer for eight seconds for a page to load. Photos and flashy things and little bunnies that hop across the page all take a lot of time. Either eliminate them or reduce them in size to keep within the allotted eight seconds. A "flash page" is a front page that only contains the most basic information—your name, a small photo, a brief statement—that will lead automatically to the second page where more information is located.

"Above the fold" is old journalism parlance for the news that is important, which always was visible "above the fold." In web design language, it refers to the need to design the pages for a laptop monitor, which means no HUGE typefaces or large photos that would require scrolling down to read.

Design Rule 8 is all about how visitors "learn" to navigate your site. Karen is most insistent that from the time you launch your website until you die (or until it dies), you should not change the navigation scheme. Why not? Because it would be like going home and finding that not only was the furniture rearranged while you were out, but that the rooms were moved, too. It's off-putting as well as confusing.

The rest of this rule follows from the heading. The "I want to go home" line is a reminder that every page (other than the home page, for obvious reasons) should have a "home" button. People hate to backspace. Karen's suggestion to consider including contact information on each page is worth considering, particularly if that information is difficult to recall or connected to the oink factor in some significant way.

8. Introduce a Navigation Scheme and then DON'T F--K with it!

Also known as "Persistent Navigation"
- Same names
- Same location(s)
  - Top of page or side of page
  - Repeat at bottom of page
  - Graphic vs. Text-based
- I want to go home!
- Maybe do this for contact info too

Read over Design Rule 9. Perhaps the only one that requires elaboration is the advice against using "large fields of color outside the banner." Here's the elaboration: Don't do it! Loading lots of color takes time. Simple color schemes are better. And remember that you are murdering the planet if you waste printer toner on needless color copies.

I may have overstated that. But pretend I didn't. The planet will love you.

9. Color

- Think legibility!
  - Don't use day-glow colors – if you must, limit use
  - Don't use colors that clash (lime green with pink)
  - Don't use white type reversed on a black field ;-)
  - Don't use large fields of color outside of the banner
    - People need to print your pages and fax your pages
  - Try to use Web-Safe Color
- Good colors to use? Easy on the eyes and pretty to look at

Design Rule 10 is perhaps the hardest rule to follow when designing an author website. Ironic, even. Why? Because authors like to talk. We revel in words. Limiting our freedom of speech is against our personal and poetic constitution. But, the Internet is all about speed and visuals. So just do it.

10. Nobody Reads

- Eliminate "Happy Talk" – but don't
- Think "fast"
- Show don't tell
  - Use icon conventions
  - Use graphic conventions

Design Rule 11 offers a primer in graphic literacy for author websites. THIS IS A VISUAL MEDIUM SO THINK VISUALLY!! The better your website looks and the easier it is to navigate, the more likely you will achieve your goals for it. Of the subpoints, the line about including a photograph of yourself is key. Visitors want to "see" what you look like. Hence, the photo you use will communicate more than your likeness. It should be a reflection of your personality and voice. More than any other single element on your website, your photograph breaks down the "digital separation" and makes a cool medium warmer, more human.

11. Graphics

- This is a visual medium so think visually!!
- Color, form, depth, motion
- Flash with caution
- Include a logo or repeatable visual design element – but not a lame one
- Include a photograph of yourself – but not a lame one = THIS IS IMPORTANT
- Creative connection with an audience
- Overcome digital separation

That's it. The design "rules" for creating a website. With a little software knowledge and some artistic talent, these rules can assist you in crafting a web identity capable of helping you accomplish your goals.

One final question: Are you *sure* you want to do it yourself?

Creating Blogs and Podcasts for Your Website

In a crowded marketplace, success is determined by finding newer and better ways to capture and hold customer attention. Advertising was invented to do precisely that, following by marketing, which was based on the idea that a campaign is more likely to sell products than a single ad.

Author websites are "advertisements for myself" (with apologies to Norman Mailer). Clever as they may be, they are little more than Internet billboards on the information highway that visitors smile at when they them see but click through very quickly *unless there is some value added* that warrants staying there.

Podcasts and blogs add value to your author website.

In a digital age marked by a consumer explosion of interest in MP3 technology, it is no wonder that canny authors quickly realized that creating their own MP3 downloadable podcasts to market their writing was a good way to grab the attention of web visitors. Who doesn't click on a freebee? What's the worst that can happen—if the podcast is truly bad, just exit and delete. If it has a hook, if it captures attention and then holds it, well, my friend, step right up and get your *very own* copy of the real thing. In other words, it is a great way to sell books on websites, or at least direct the listener to an online outlet where the purchase can be made.

For about a minimal $50 investment and four hours of time, you, too, can create a podcast and launch it on your website.[33] Podcasts have the added advantage of also featuring your own voice, which adds an aural dimension to your identity as an author. So even if you don't net some sales immediately, if your voice is pleasing to the listener and if you provide additional podcasts on a regular basis, you have a way of building relationships with your audience. From a marketing and sales perspective, success is all about building those relationships.

Blogs are also popular ways to gain and hold the interest of readers.[34] A blog is a way to share your thoughts, images, concerns, field notes, and writing with visitors, in the hope that they become *regular* visitors to your site. The keys to a successful blog are to be consistently interesting and to add new material to it often. It is also wise to try to get your blog linked to other blogs and author websites in the global writer's network, including literary blogs that review books and interview authors.

Effective author websites with podcasts and/or blogs are increasingly sought after by agents trolling the Internet for new talent. From an agent's point of view, this resource is better than reading query letters and proposals because it provides anonymous access to the writer in Internet time. If the agent becomes interested, all he or she needs to do is click on the contact information provided and request a manuscript or proposal.

From *your* point of view as an aspiring author, it doesn't get any easier—or better—than that.

I hope it happens that way for you.

Concluding Remarks: The World Needs Our Stories

This final chapter has covered a lot of ground but I hope it provides you with the information you need to work toward becoming a successful public scholar and popular writer of creative nonfiction narratives for intelligent lay readers.

As I pointed out at the beginning of this book, the newest generation of scholars is the best educated and best prepared our doctoral shops have yet produced, but you are emerging into an academic culture undergoing tremendous and challenging changes. Some of these changes will affect how you think about yourself and how you work within the academy. The entrepreneurial business model encourages all of us to consider how we figure into the return-on-investment principle guiding important decisions about our fate. So, too, will entrepreneurial thinking likely affect the decisions we all make about how we pursue narrative scholarship. Some of those decisions will involve how we use what we write to more productively construct tenure and promotion portfolios (as well as evaluate them); to determine the comparative value of where to publish work based on journal impact ratings; and to build strategic networks of narrative and performance scholars who understand the political importance of citing each other's work to counter the potentially negative effects of decisions that weigh a raw number in a citation index as a significant, perhaps singular indicator of the impact of our scholarship.

But we are also citizens who work and compete in a global marketplace of ideas. Universities and colleges that employ us compete in that marketplace for new resources, rankings, and the support of taxpayers and donors based in part on the status of faculty in that larger public environment. For our colleagues in the sciences, major grants and inspired teaching are the gold standard. For our colleagues in the professional schools, grants and teaching are also highly valued, but how faculty research and teaching economically benefits the community, the region, and/or the state also yields high value return on investments. For those of us in the humanities and social sciences who have been perhaps too content to tend our intellectual silos while around us academic culture changed, things are very different.

Ask anyone who works in one of our departments and the story you hear will be much the same. We are continually asked to teach greater numbers of students with fewer tenure-earning positions, more poorly compensated lecturers, and no real increase in budgets. Our research, already undervalued if unsupported by external funding, is too often perceived as an elite or "precious" discourse removed from the concerns of ordinary citizens, and whatever its yield that yield has little or no practical value. We celebrate an absence of oink.

To our critics inside and outside the academy, social science and humanities faculty are odd people. We appear content to talk in academic tongues among only ourselves for comparatively little money. In the classroom we lead our unsuspecting students ever leftward and away from both a proper reverence for oink and for God. Horrors!

Under these economic and political conditions, there is every good reason to suppose that turning around these perceptions will require public leverage beyond the reach of traditional scholarship. It will require placing stories that matter before a public that desperately needs them to survive. To prosper. To enable new and better leaders. To rebuild our cities and to regain our credibility and stature in the world.

If we can do that, if we can make our narratives matter to a world waiting nervously for them, then the parts we play in the necessary moral recovery of our nation, the rebuilding of justice to guide human institutions, ensuring the health of all of our citizens and sustainability of our beautiful blue but tortured planet, our work will attain a value far higher, far richer, far greater than mere gold.

That is how important our stories are.

That is how important our *writing* is.

And that is why I wrote this book for *you*.

Activities and Questions

1. Take a trip to your local bookstore and peruse the narrative nonfiction titles. Select one or two that connect to your subject area. Read them. How do the authors frame or position their narratives for public consumption? What works for them? What doesn't? What can you learn from them that will help you turn an academic story into one suitable for trade markets?

2. Think about how you might be able to expand a current narrative project into a trade book. What would you have to do? Who might be your audience?

3. Research a possible agent for your work using the material provided earlier in this chapter. Construct a query letter that is specifically targeted to the agent's interests. If you are serious about pursuing the project, submit your letter to the agent and record what happens.

4. Develop a podcast and/or a website based on a current narrative project. Discuss with your class the joys and challenges you experience completing the assignment.

Notes

1. Tompkins (1966).

2. Phillip K. Tompkins, "Public Scholarship Revisited," CRTNET. All subsequent quotations from his account are drawn from this electronic document available in the archives of the National Communication Association website (http://www.natcom.org/nca/Template2.asp?bid=207).

3. *The Speech Teacher* was a publication sponsored by the national speech association that featured articles on pedagogy written by academics in the speech field. At the time, it was considered the least prestigious publication put out by the national association.

4. Substitute the name of your discipline and see if this sentence still rings true.

5. See Howard (2007). A discussion of the report via *The Chronicle of Higher Education* is available online at: http://chronicle.com/daily/2007/07/2007072601n.htm. The quoted material is from the *Chronicle* article.

6. *CommunicationCurrents*, available online at: http://www.communicationcurrents.com/

7. Allow me a bit of humor with that great Burkian concept of "precious" scholarship. Although I doubt that any acquisitions editor these days would consider publishing a highly jargonistic, deeply theoretical account written in the old high style of arid academic prose about, um, shall we say, the cultural functions of bodily emissions, Allen's (2007) extraordinarily well-written book *On Farting: Language and Laughter in the Middle Ages* was published to rave reviews, such as these:

> Allen has written the secret history of waste from the Ancient to the early modern world, and—dare I say it?—the hidden history of humankind's relation to the anus. On Farting, in the line of Norbert Elias's Civilizing Process or Erik Erikson's Young Man Luther, begins small and spreads like wind to almost every area of personal, social, and even spiritual life in what is a truly original and significant work of cultural analysis. (R. Howard Bloch, Sterling Professor of French, Yale University)

> Allen takes the fart seriously, refusing to see it either as a marker of abjection or as mere rudeness but also managing to tread the fine line between the portentous and the jeu d'esprit. The book is witty and learned: a tour de force of scholarship and cultural history. (Ruth Evans, Professor of English, University of Stirling, Scotland)

8. Phillips and Goodall (1983) and Goodall and Phillips (1984). You will note that I was still in my "H. Lloyd" period, which had happened when my first editor, Louise Waller, decided that "nobody would buy a book from someone named Buddy Goodall," and, on the strength of my dissertation about F. Scott Fitzgerald, decided to re-christen me in that vein.

9. See the Wikipedia entry for Isaac Asimov at http://en.wikipedia.org/wiki/Isaac_Asimov

    Asimov wrote creative nonfiction, fiction, essays, and literary criticism in addition to over 90,000 postcards. He is perhaps best known for his science fiction *Foundation* Series, but his books on popular science were also perennial best-sellers.

10. He also continued to teach very popular undergraduate courses and graduate seminars on interpersonal, group, organizational, and health communication, advise doctoral and masters students, and participate in theatrical and musical productions. For a partial listing of his work and testimonials from former students and friends, see his memorial page at: http://cac.psu.edu/~santoro/gmp/gmp.html

11. Interestingly, a very similar argument has been made about the discipline of history's inward turn based on journal publications and narrow specializations. See Hamerow (1989).

12. Not that there is anything wrong with that. But it was by then, for me, a pretty safe bet that if I submitted something for academic publication—whether book, chapter, paper, or refereed article—it would be accepted. Furthermore, my work wasn't as "precious" as most scholarship in our field or in related fields. Confession of the Ego, unbridled by the Id: Despite my success in the academy, I knew my readership was limited and I longed for a wider public audience.

13. This cooking habit is not an accident. In college, I worked as a waiter in *The Old South Mountain Inn* until the James Beard–trained chef moved me into the kitchen. From him, I learned the basics of the trade. Later, after I had failed as a novelist and before I returned for a Ph.D., I operated a diner in Philipsburg, Pennsylvania, that

catered to the local clientele of coalminers, insurance agents, and police. For a period of time during my posting to Huntsville, I tried to pick up a new regional cuisine every couple of years, and, of course, at every opportunity I seek out new restaurants and recipes. I am, by my own estimate, at best an enlightened amateur chef.

14. Goodall (1998).

15. There are a lot of complaints, but here is an oral performance piece that I find particularly clever and on target, from the novelist Zadie Smith (2007):

> I have just completed a book tour, which is somewhat like being on safari but without the attendant dangers of thick bush-land, extreme heat, guns, or wild animals. But book tours offer their own perils to the young writer. I have been on an American book tour before. Four things come out of an American book tour:
>
> 1. The writer gains 15 pounds.
>
> 2. The writer can find a minibar within five seconds of opening a door, irrespective of wood-paneling camouflage.
>
> 3. Any original thought the writer ever had—every pretty black mark she ever made on a piece of white paper—is replaced by the endlessly reoccurring phenomena of the writer's own name rising up at them in embossed font on the front of a book they have come to despise.
>
> 4. The writer is reduced to embracing the only creative subject she has left: writing about writing and writers. And, if she is lucky, hair.
>
> You should read the whole performance script. It's hilarious and true.

16. The idea of publishing as a casino is not original. See Boss (2007).

17. This was before the Food Network. Sigh.

18. It is helpful to prepare a script for the interview in advance. Develop eight–ten questions that will allow you to sell the best features of your book at, at the same time, will keep viewers/listeners interested enough to prevent them from finding another station. Be witty, charming, self-depreciating, and by all means, reiterate the title of the book and its intended audience at least twice. If you work with an experienced media interviewer, they will do this for you, but be prepared. Provide the interviewer or producer with a copy of the script prior to the interview. If they don't want to use it, they won't use it. But if they do—and many of them will be thankful for

the help—you will have a much better chance of getting your book promoted in the style and manner for which it was intended.

19. Goodall (2005).

20. I usually write a preface last, after I know what is in the book.

21. There are a variety of guides to writing query letters and getting the right agent for your work. I recommend reading Todd James Pierce's (2007) advice as an excellent primer on the subject. I also recommend the Writer's Net Guide to Literary Agents (http://www.writers.net/agents.html) and the posting "Beware of Dishonest Agents" (http://www.sfwa.org/beware/agents.html) before you begin your search.

22. It is probably worth noting that J. K. Rowling, the best-selling author of all time, was rejected by every major and minor house to which she submitted *Harry Potter and the Sorcerer's Stone* until Scholastic signed it. It is also probably worth noting that those editors who rejected her work were not uniformly sorry they had done so, even after the phenomenal success of the series. Think about that, won't you?

23. This advice may seem somewhat confusing, but agents differ greatly on what they require. For this reason, please *check the agent's website* and give them precisely what they ask for, no more and certainly no less.

24. I particularly like Zack (n.d.). See also Allen (2001) and Flewelling (2005).

25. Drawn, with some additions and deletions, from an excellent source "Agent Query," full of useful information and links: http://www.agentquery.com/writer_hq.aspx

26. This is a must if you ever want to see your material returned to you or even read.

27. This sample is representative of thirty-one I submitted to targeted agents specializing in historical memoirs and cold war stories. About one-third of the agents I contacted requested a proposal and sample chapters from the manuscript. While I was waiting for a decision, Mitch Allen, the owner of Left Coast Press, offered me a contract and I accepted it. I later compiled the results of my agent search and discovered that of the thirty-one agents I initially contacted, twelve requested proposals and/or sample pages/chapters; eight indicated that they weren't interested in the project; and the remaining eleven

never replied. As a side note, one of the agents I contacted who hadn't replied finally did reply with the offer of a contract—but my book had already been published! So it goes.

28. That was my working title for what became *A Need to Know: The Clandestine History of a CIA Family.*

29. Proposals for nonfiction trade books can be thirty–eighty pages in length.

30. One exception to this general rule is if you have expertise in Adobe Professional series applications. If you do, then check out Krug (2005).

31. I am indebted to Karen Stewart for what follows on web design. She's the pro; I'm a mere user.

32. http://www.godaddy.com/gdshop/registrar/search. asp?isc=goox2001au

33. For step-by-step instructions, go to http://reviews.cnet. com/4520-11293_7-6246557-1.html

34. For a listing of the "best" author blogs, see http://www.internetwriting journal.com/authorblogs/

References

Adams, T. E. (2006). Seeking father: Relationally reframing a troubled love story. *Qualitative Inquiry*, 12, 704–723.

Agar, M. (1996). *The professional stranger: An informal introduction to ethnography,* 2nd ed. New York: Academic Press.

Ainsworth, S., & and Hardy, C. (2004). Discourse and identities. In D. Grant, C. Hardy, C. Oswick, & L. Putnam (Eds.), *The Sage handbook of organizational discourse* (pp. 153–174). London: Sage.

Alexander, B. K. (2004). Black skin/white masks: The performative sustainability of whiteness (with apologies to Frantz Fanon). *Qualitative Inquiry*, 10, 647–672.

Allen, M. (2001). How to write a successful query. Retrieved November 5, 2007 from http://www.writing-world.com/basics/query.shtml

Allen, V. (2007). *On farting: Language and laughter in the middle ages.* New York: Palgrave Macmillan.

Athens, L. (forthcoming). Blood is thicker than water: Two tales from *The melting pot boils over. Qualitative Inquiry.*

Baudrillard, J. (1989). *America.* London: Verso.

Behar, R. (1997). *The vulnerable observer: Anthropology that breaks your heart.* Boston: Beacon.

Behar R., & Gordon, D. (Eds.). (1996). *Women writing culture.* Berkeley: University of California Press.

Benson, T. W. (1981). Another shooting in cowtown. *The Quarterly Journal of Speech*, 67, 347–406.

Berry, K. (2006). Implicated audience member seeks understanding: Re-examining the 'gift' of autoethnography. International Journal of Qualitative Methods, 5, 1–10. Available online at: http://www.ualberta.ca/~iiqm/back-issues/5_3/pdf/berry.pdf

Bly, R. W. (2005). The bullet-proof nonfiction book proposal. Retrieved November 5, 2007 from http://www.talewins.com/bly1.htm

Bochner, A. P. (1994). Perspectives on inquiry II: Theories and stories. In M. Knapp & G. Miller (Eds.), *Handbook of interpersonal communication*, 2nd ed. (pp. 21–41). Newbury Park, CA: Sage.

Bochner. A. P. (1997). It's about time: Narrative and the divided self. *Qualitative Inquiry*, 3, 418–438.

Bochner, A. P. (2001). Narratives virtues. *Qualitative Inquiry*, 7, 131–157.

Bochner, A. P. (2004). Interpretive and narrative perspectives in the social sciences. In J. Paul (Ed.), *Research and inquiry in education and the social sciences: Philosophical and critical perspectives* (pp. 65–67). Upper Saddle River, NJ: Prentice Hall.

Boice, B. (2000). *Advice for new faculty members: Nihil nimus*. Needham Heights, MA: Allyn & Bacon.

Boss, S. (2007). The greatest mystery: Making a best seller. *The New York Times*. Retrieved November 5, 2007 from http://www.nytimes.com/2007/05/13/business/yourmoney/13book.html?ei=5070&en=34033faf09efd9e2&ex=1186113600&pagewanted=all

Boylorn, R. M. (2006). E Pluribus Unum (out of many, one). *Qualitative Inquiry*, 12, 651–680.

Burke, K. (1959). *Attitudes toward history*, 2nd. rev. ed. Los Altos, CA: Hermes Press.

Burke, K. (1964). Literature as equipment for living. In S. E. Hyman (Ed.), *Perspectives by incongruity* (pp. 103–106). Bloomington, IN: University of Indiana Press, 1964.

Burke, K. (1974). *The philosophy of literary form*, 3rd ed. Berkeley: University of California Press.

Burke, K. (1965; 1984). *Permanence and change*, 3rd ed. Berkeley: University of California Press.

Burke, K. (1989). *On symbols and society*. Edited, with an introduction by J. Gusfield. Chicago: University of Chicago Press.

Burroughs, A. (2006). *Set of 3 memoirs by Augusten Burroughs: Running with scissors, magical thinking, dry*. New York: Picador.

Buzard, J. (2003). On auto-ethnographic authority. *The Yale Journal of Criticism*, 16, 61–91.

Cahn, P. (May 12, 2006). Will they stay or will they go?" *The Chronicle of Higher Education*, N.P. Retrieved November 5, 2007 from http://chronicle.com/weekly/v52/i36/36c00201.htm

Camus, A. (1991). *The plague*. New York: Vintage Reissue Edition.

Canary, D. & Dainton, M. (2003). *Maintaining relationships through communication: Relational, contextual, and cultural variations*. Mahwah, NJ: Lawrence Erlbaum Associates.

Carr, J. (2003). Poetic expressions of vigilance. *Qualitative Health Research*, 13, 1324–1331.

Chait, R. P. (Ed.) (2002). *The questions of tenure*. Cambridge, MA: Harvard University Press.

Clair, R. P. (Ed.) (2003). *Expressions of ethnography: Novel approaches to qualitative methods*. Albany: State University of New York Press.

Coffey, A. (1999). *The ethnographic self: Fieldwork and the representation of identity*. London: Sage.

Communication Studies 298, California State University, Sacramento. (1997). Fragments of self at the postmodern bar. *Journal of Contemporary Ethnography*, 26, 251–292.

Crawford, J. (2006). *The last true story I'll ever tell: An accidental soldier's account of the war in Iraq*. New York: Riverhead Trade.

De George, R. T. (1997). *Academic freedom and tenure: Ethical issues.* Lanham, MD: Rowman & Littlefield.

De la Garza, S. A. (2004). *Maria speaks: Journeys into the mysteries of the mother in my life as a Chicana.* New York: Peter Lang.

Denzin, N. K. (1997). *Interpretive ethnography: Ethnographic practices for the 21st century.* Thousand Oaks, CA: Sage.

Denzin, N. K. (2001). The reflexive interview and a performative social science. *Qualitative Research,* 1, 23–46.

Denzin, N. K. (2002). Cowboys and Indians. *Symbolic Interaction,* 25, 251–261.

Denzin, N. K. (2006). Pedagogy, performance, and autoethnography. *Text and Performance Quarterly,* 26, 333–338.

Denzin, N. K. (2007a). *Flags in the window: Dispatches from an American war zone.* New York: Peter Lang.

Denzin, N. K. (2007b). Report. 3rd Congress on Qualitative Inquiry, Champaign-Urbana, IL, May 2.

Denzin, N. K., & and Lincoln, Y. (Eds.). (2001). *The qualitative inquiry reader.* Thousand Oaks, CA: Sage.

Donovan, S. K. (2004). Writing successful covering letters for unsolicited submissions to academic journals—comment. *Journal of Scholarly Publishing,* 35, 221–222.

Eggers, D. (2000). *A heartbreaking work of staggering genius.* New York: Simon & Shuster.

Eisenberg, E. M., Baglia, J. & and Pynes, J. E. (2006). Transforming emergency medicine through narrative: Qualitative action research at a community hospital. *Health Communication,* 19, 197–208.

Ellis, C. (1995). The other side of the fence: Seeing black and white in a small southern town. *Qualitative Inquiry,* 1, 147–167.

Ellis, C. (2002). Take no chances. *Qualitative Inquiry,* 8, 170–175.

Ellis, C. (2006). *The ethnographic I: A methodological novel about autoethnography.* Walnut Creek, CA: AltaMira Press.

Ellis, C. (2007). Relational ethics in research with intimate others. *Qualitative Inquiry,* 13, 3–29.

Ellis, C., & Berger, L. (2002). Their story/my story/our story: Including the researcher's experience in interview research. In J. Gubrium & J. Holstein (Eds.), *Handbook of interview research: Context and method* (pp. 849–875). Thousand Oaks, CA: Sage.

Ellis, C., & Bochner, A. P. (2000). Autoethnography, personal narrative, reflexivity: Researcher as subject. In N. K. Denzin & Y. Lincoln (Eds.), *The handbook of qualitative research,* 2nd ed. (pp. 733–768). Thousand Oaks, CA: Sage.

Ellis, C., Kiesinger, C., & Tillmann-Healy, L. (1997). Interactive interviewing: Talking about emotional experience. In R. Hertz (Ed.), *Reflexivity and voice* (pp. 119–149). Thousand Oaks, CA: Sage.

Evans, K. D. (2007). Welcome to Ruth's world: An autoethnography concerning the interview of an elderly woman. *Qualitative Inquiry,* 13, 282–292.

Fagan, B. (2006). *Writing archaeology: Telling stories about the past.* Walnut Creek, CA: Left Coast Press.

Felman, D. (2006). What are book editors looking for? *The Chronicle of Higher Education.* Retrieved November 6, 2007 from http://chronicle.com/jobs/news/2006/07/2006072101c/careers.html

Fine, G. A. (1994). Ten lies of ethnography: Moral dilemmas of field research. *Journal of Contemporary Ethnography,* 22, 267–294.

Fisher, W. R. (1984). Narration as a human communication paradigm: The case for public moral argument. *Communication Monographs,* 51, 1–22.

Fisher, W. R. (1987). *Human communication as narration: Toward a philosophy of reason, value, and action.* Columbia: University of South Carolina Press.

Flewelling, L. (2005). The complete nobody's guide to query letters. Retrieved November 6, 2007 from http://www.sfwa.org/writing/query.htm

Flyvbjerg, B. (2001). *Making social science matter: Why social inquiry fails and how it can succeed again*. Cambridge: Cambridge University Press.

Fogg, P. (2003). The gap that won't go away. *The Chronicle of Higher Education*, N.P. Retrieved November 6, 2007 from http://chronicle.com/weekly/v49/i32/32a01201.htm

Fogg, P. (2005). Presidents favor scrapping tenure. *The Chronicle of Higher Education*, November 4, A31.

Fox, R. (2007). Skinny bones #126-774-835-29; Thin gay bodies signifying a modern plague. *Text & Performance Quarterly*, 27, 3–19.

Frank, A. W. (2004). Asking the right question about pain: Narrative and phronesis. *Literature and Medicine*, 23, 209–225.

Furman, R. (2006). Poetic forms and structures in qualitative health research. *Qualitative Health Research*, 16, 560–566.

Gates, Jr., H. L. (1992). *Loose canons: Notes on the culture wars*. New York: Oxford University Press.

Geertz, C. (1973). *The interpretation of cultures*. New York: Basic Books.

Gilgun, J. F. (2004). Fictionalizing life stories: Yukee the wine thief. *Qualitative Inquiry*, 10, 691–705.

Glesne, C. (1997). That rare feeling: Re-presenting research through poetic transcription. *Qualitative Inquiry*, 3, 202–221.

Goltz, D. B. (2007a). Artist's statement: Forgive me, audience, for I know not what I do. *Text and Performance Quarterly*, 27, 231–235.

Goltz, D. B. (2007b). Banging the bishop: Ladder day prophecy. *Text and Performance Quarterly*, 27, 236–265.

Goodall, Jr., H. L. (1989a). *Casing a promised land: The autobiography of an organizational detective as cultural ethnographer*. Carbondale: Southern Illinois University Press.

Goodall, Jr., H. L. (1989b). On becoming an organizational detective: The role of intuitive logics and context sensitivity for communication consultants. *The Southern Communication Journal*, 55, 42–54.

Goodall, Jr., H. L. (1991). *Living in the rock n roll mystery: Reading context, self, and others as clues.* Carbondale: Southern Illinois University Press.

Goodall, Jr., H. L. (1996). *Divine signs: Connecting spirit to community.* Carbondale: Southern Illinois University Press.

Goodall, Jr., H. L. (Bud) (1998). *Food talk: A man's guide to cooking and conversation with women.* Greensboro, NC: Snowgoose Cove Press.

Goodall, Jr., H. L. (2000). *Writing the new ethnography.* Walnut Creek, CA: AltaMira Press.

Goodall, Jr., H. L. (2002a). Fieldnotes from our war zone: Living in America during the aftermath of September eleventh. *Qualitative Inquiry, 8,* 74-89.

Goodall, Jr., H. L. (2002b). Voice, originality, and scholarship: The lasting influence of Gerald M. Phillips on my life and work. In M. C. McGee (Ed.), Meet your footnotes. *American Communication Journal,* 5, N.P. Retrieved November 5, 2007 from http://acjournal.org/holdings/vol5/iss2/phillips.htm

Goodall, Jr., H. L. (2004). Deep play in a poker rally: A Sunday among the *Ferraristi* of Long Island. *Qualitative Inquiry,* 10, 731–766.

Goodall, Jr., H. L. (2005). Narrative inheritance: A nuclear family with toxic secrets. *Qualitative Inquiry,* 11, 492–513.

Goodall, Jr., H. L. (2006a). *A need to know: The clandestine history of a CIA family.* Walnut Creek, CA: Left Coast Press.

Goodall, Jr., H. L. (2006b). Why we must win the war on terror: Communication, narrative, and the future of national security. *Qualitative Inquiry,* 12, 30–59.

Goodall, Jr., H. L., & Phillips, G. M. (1984). *Making it in any organization.* Englewood Cliffs, NJ: Prentice-Hall/Spectrum.

Goodall, Jr., H. L., Wilson, G. L., & Waagen, C. L. (1986). The performance appraisal interview: An interpretive reassessment. *The Quarterly Journal of Speech,* 72, 74–87.

Goode, J. (2006). Women's Studies: 1959–2005. *Qualitative Inquiry,* 12, 769–796.

Gregg, R. B. (1984). *Symbolic inducement and knowing: A study in the foundations of rhetoric*. Columbia: University of South Carolina Press.

Guba, E., & Lincoln, Y. (1989). *Fourth generation evaluation*. Thousand Oaks, CA: Sage.

Gump, S. E. (2004). Writing successful covering letters for unsolicited submissions to academic journals. *Journal of Scholarly Publishing*, 35, 92–102.

Gust, S. (2007). Champaign and mouthwash, at last: A performance of mourning and cyber-identity. Performance presented at the 3rd annual International Congress on Qualitative Inquiry, Champaign-Urbana, IL, May 2.

Hall, R. (2006). Patty and me: Performative encounters between an historical body and the history of images. *Text and Performance Quarterly*, 26, 347–370.

Hamerow, T. S. (1989). The bureaucratization of history. *The American Historical Review*, 94, 654–660.

Hartnett, S. J. (2002). 9/11 and the poetics of complicity: A love poem for a hurt nation. *Cultural Studies-Critical Methodologies*, 2, 315–326.

Hartnett, S. J., & Stengrim, L. A. (2006). *Globalization and empire: The U.S. invasion of Iraq, free markets, and the twilight of democracy*. Tuscaloosa: University of Alabama Press.

Haworth, K. (1996). Florida Regents approve post-tenure reviews for all professors. *The Chronicle of Higher Education*, October 11, A15.

Heaton, D. D. (1998). Twenty fragments: The "other" gazing back or touring Juanita. *Text and Performance Quarterly*, 18, 248–261.

Heaton, D. D. (2002). Creativity: Between chaos and order or my life as a messy text—A case study and a challenge. *American Journal of Communication*, 6, N.P. Retrieved November 5, 2007 from http://www.acjournal.org/holdings/vol6/iss1/special/heaton.htm

Hemingway, E. (1937). The bombing of Madrid. *New York Times*. Retrieved November 5, 2007 from http://www.nytimes.com/books/99/07/04/specials/hemingway-madrid.html

Holman Jones, S. (2007). *Torch singing: Performing resistance and desire from Billie Holiday to Edith Piaf.* Walnut Creek, CA: AltaMira Press.

Holstein, J. A., & and Gubrium, J. F. (2004). *Inside interviewing: New lenses, new concerns.* Thousand Oaks, CA: Sage.

Howard, J. (2007). Universities should support a broader concept of publishing in the digital age, report says. Retrieved on November 14, 2007 from http://chronicle.com/daily/2007/07/2007072601n.htm

Hynes, J. (2002). *The lecturer's tale.* New York: Picador.

Jackson, A. Y. (2004). Performativity identified. *Qualitative Inquiry, 10,* 673–690.

Jago, B. (2006). A primary act of imagination: An autoethnography of father-absence. *Qualitative Inquiry, 12,* 398–426.

Kaplan, A. (1994). *French lessons: A memoir.* Chicago: University of Chicago Press.

Karr, M. (2001). *Cherry.* New York: Penguin.

Karr, M. (2005). *The liars club.* New York: Penguin.

Kaysen, S. (1993). *Girl, interrupted.* New York: Vintage.

Kiesinger, C. E. (1998). From interview to story: Writing Abbie's life. *Qualitative Inquiry, 4,* 71–96.

Kiesinger, C. E. (2002). My father's shoes: The therapeutic value of narrative reframing. In A. P. Bochner & C. Ellis (Eds.), *Ethnographically speaking: Autoethnography, literature, and aesthetics* (pp. 95–114). Walnut Creek, CA: AltaMira Press.

Kiesinger, C. E. (2003). He touched, he took. In R. C. Clair (Ed.), *Expressions of ethnography: Novel approaches to qualitative methods* (pp. 177–184). Albany: State University of New York Press.

Kingston, M. H. (1989). *The woman warrior: Memoirs of a girlhood among ghosts.* New York: Vintage Reissue Edition.

Krug, S. (2005). *Don't make me think: A common sense approach to web usability,* 2nd ed. Berkeley, CA: New Riders Press.

Kulick, D., & Willson, M. (1995). *Taboo: Sex, identity, and erotic subjectivity in anthropological fieldwork*. London: Routledge.

Lamott, A. (1995). *Bird by bird: Some instructions on writing and life*. New York: Pantheon Books.

Langellier, K. M. (1989). Personal narratives: Perspectives on theory and research. *Text and Performance Quarterly, 9*, 243–276.

Larson, E. (2003). *The devil in the white city: Murder, magic, and madness at the fair that changed America*. New York: Vintage.

Lemelin, H. (2006). Running to stand still: The story of a victim, a survivor, a wounded healer—A narrative of male sexual abuse from the inside. *Journal of Loss & Trauma, 11*, 337–350.

Levitt, S. D., & Dubner, S. J. (2007). Let's just get rid of tenure (including mine). *The New York Times*, N.P. Retrieved November 6, 2007 from http://www.freakonomics.com/blog/2007/03/03/lets-just-get-rid-of-tenure/

Lewis, L. (2007). *The blind side: Evolution of a game*. New York: W. W. Norton.

Lincoln, Y., & & Guba E. (1985). *Naturalistic inquiry*. Thousand Oaks, CA: Sage.

Lindemann, K. (2005). *Living out of bounds, pushing toward normalcy: (Auto)ethnographic performances of disability and masculinity in wheelchair rugby*. Ph.D. dissertation, Arizona State University.

Lockford, L. (2004). *Performing femininity: Rewriting gender identity*. Walnut Creek, CA: AltaMira Press.

London, J. (1906). The story of an eyewitness. Retrieved November 5, 2007 from http://www.sfmuseum.net/hist5/jlondon.html

Madison, S. (2005). *Critical ethnography: Method, ethics, and performance*. Thousand Oaks, CA: Sage.

Madison, S. (2007). Keynote address. 3rd International Congress on Qualitative Inquiry, Champaign-Urbana, IL, May 2.

Malagreca, M. A. (2005). I want justice: A performance about impunity in Argentina. *Qualitative Inquiry*, 11, 570–575.

Malinowski, B. (1989). *A diary in the strict sense of the term.* Reissued with an introduction by Raymond Firth. Stanford, CA: Stanford University Press.

Malinowski, B. (1961). *Argonauts of the western Pacific.* New York: Dutton Press.

Maraniss. D. (2004). *They marched into sunlight: War and peace in Vietnam and America in October 1967.* New York: Simon & Shuster.

Marcus, G. E. (1994). What comes (just) after "Post"? The case of ethnography. In N. K. Denzin & Y. S. Lincoln (Eds.), *The handbook of qualitative research* (pp. 563–574). Thousand Oaks, CA: Sage.

Markowitz, F. & Ashkenazi, M. (Eds). (1999). *Sex, sexuality, and the anthropologist.* Urbana: University of Illinois Press.

McCormack, C. (2004). Storying stories: A narrative approach to in-depth interview conversations. *International Journal of Social Research Methodology*, 7, 219–236.

Miller, K. (2002). The experience of emotion in the workplace: Professing in the midst of tragedy. *Management Communication Quarterly*, 15, 571–600.

Minge, J. M. (2007). The stained body: A fusion of embodied art on rape and love. *Journal of Contemporary Ethnography*, 36, 252–280.

Murrell, D. (2007). In the year of the storm: The topography of resurrection in New Orleans. *Harper's Magazine*, 315, 35–52.

Myers, W. B. (2007). Straight and white: Talking with my mouth full. Performance presented at the 3rd International Congress of Qualitative Inquiry, Champaign-Urbana, IL, May 3.

Nafisi, A. (2003). *Reading Lolita in Tehran: A memoir in books.* New York: Random House.

Newton, E. (1996). My best informant's dress: The erotic equation in fieldwork. In E. L. Leap & W. L. Leap (Eds.), *Out in the field: Reflections of lesbian and gay anthropologists* (pp. 212–235). Urbana: University of Illinois Press.

Nightingale, D. J. & Cromby, J. (Eds.). (1999). *Social constructionist psychology*. Buckingham, UK: Open University Press.

Nilan, P. M. (2002). Dangerous fieldwork re-examined: The question of researcher subject position. *Qualitative Research*, 2, 363–386.

Oakley. A. (1981). Interviewing women: A contradiction in terms. In H. Roberts (Ed.), *Doing feminist research* (pp. 30–61). London: Routledge & Kegan Paul.

Ohlen, J. (2003). Evocation of meaning through poetic condensation of narratives in empirical phenomenological inquiry into human suffering. *Qualitative Health Research*, 13, 557–566.

Orwell, G. (1946). Why I write. *Gangrel*. Retrieved November 5, 2007 from http://www.orwell.ru/library/essays/wiw/english/e_wiw

Ott, J., & Geist Martin, P. (2003). Narratives of healing: Exploring one family's stories of cancer survivorship. *Health Communication*, 15, 133–143.

Owen, J. A. T., Mcrae, C., Adams, T. E., & Vitale, A. (forthcoming). truth troubles . *Qualitative Inquiry*, 15.

Pacanowsky, M. E. (1988). Slouching towards Chicago. *The Quarterly Journal of Speech*, 74, 453–468.

Parker, M. (2004). Becoming manager: Or, the werewolf looks anxiously in the mirror, checking for unusual facial hair. *Management Learning*, 35, 45–59.

Parry, D. (2006). Women's lived experiences with pregnancy and midwifery in a medicalized and fetocentric context. *Qualitative Inquiry*, 12, 459–471

Payne, D. (1996). Autobiology. In C. Ellis & A. P. Bochner (Eds.), *Composing ethnography: Alternative forms of qualitative writing* (pp. 49–75). Walnut Creek, CA: AltaMira Press.

Pelias, R. J. (1997). Confessions of an apprehensive performer. *Text and Performance Quarterly*, 17, 25–32.

Pelias, R. J. (1999). Writing performance: *Poeticizing the researcher's body*. Carbondale: Southern Illinois University Press.

Pelias, R. J. (2004). Mirror, mirror. In R. J. Pelias (Ed.), *A methodology of the heart: Evoking academic and daily life* (pp. 39–45). Walnut Creek, CA: AltaMira Press.

Pessl, M. (2007). *Special topics in calamity physics*. New York: Penguin.

Petersen, E. B. (2007). A day at the office at the University of Borderville: An ethnographic short story. *International Journal of Qualitative Studies in Education*, 20, 173–189.

Phillips, G. M., & Goodall, Jr., H. L. (1983). *Loving & living: Improve your friendships and marriage*. Englewood Cliffs, NJ: Prentice-Hall/Spectrum Books.

Pierce, T. (2007). Nine tips for finding a literary agent. Retrieved on November 14, 2007 from http://www.alanjacobson.com/nine_tips_for_finding_an_agent.htm

Pinney, A. (2005). Ethics, agency, and desire in two strip clubs: A view from both sides of the gaze. *Qualitative Inquiry,* 11, 716–723.

Polkinghorne, D. (2007). Validity issues in narrative research. *Qualitative Inquiry*, 13, 471–486.

Pollock, D. (1999). *Telling bodies; performing birth*. New York: Columbia University Press.

Pollock, D. (2007). The performative I. *Cultural Studies/Critical Methodologies*, 7, 239–255.

Poulos, C. N. (2006). The ties that bind us, the shadows that separate us: Life and death, shadow and (dream) story. *Qualitative Inquiry,* 12, 96–117.

Poulos, C. N. (2007). My story. 3rd International Congress on Qualitative Inquiry, Champaigne-Urbana, IL, May 3.

Powdermaker, H. (1967). An agreeable man. *New York Review of Books*, 9, N.P. Retrieved November 5, 2007 from http://www.nybooks.com/articles/11916

Puller, L. B. (1991). *Fortunate son: An autobiography*. New York: Grove Press.

Rahdert, M. C. (2007). The Roberts court and academic freedom. *The Chronicle of Higher Education,* N.P. Retrieved November 5, 2007 from http://chronicle.com/weekly/v53/i47/47b01601.htm?=attw

Rambo, C. (2005). Impressions of grandmother: An autoethnographic portrait. *Journal of Contemporary Ethnography,* 34, 560–585.

Reissman, D., with Glazer, N. & Denney, R (1950). *The lonely crowd: A study of the changing American character.* New Haven, CT: Yale University Press.

Richardson, L. (2000a). Evaluating ethnography. *Qualitative Inquiry,* 6, 253–256.

Richardson, L. (2000b). Writing: A method of inquiry. In N. K. Denzin & Y. S. Lincoln (Eds.), *The handbook of qualitative research second edition* (pp. 923–948). Thousand Oaks, CA: Sage.

Richardson, L. (2005). Sticks and stones: An exploration of the embodiment of social classism. *Qualitative Inquiry,* 11, 485–491.

Ronai, C. R. (1995). Multiple reflections of child sex abuse: An argument for a layered account. *Journal of Contemporary Ethnography,* 23, 395–426.

Rorty, R. (1979). *Philosophy and the mirror of nature.* Princeton, NJ: Princeton University Press.

Rubin, H. J., & Rubin, I. S. (2005). *Qualitative interviewing: The art of hearing data.* Thousand Oaks, CA: Sage.

Russo, R. (1999). *Straight man.* New York: Random House.

Ryan, M. (1998). Review of *Academic capitalism: Politics, policies, and the entrepreneurial university. College & Research Libraries,* 59, 293–294.

Ryle, G. (1968). The thinking of thoughts: What is *'Le Penseur'* doing? Lecture, University of Saskatchewan. Retrieved November 5, 2007 from http://lucy.ukc.ac.uk/CSACSIA/Vol14/Papers/ryle_1.html

Safire, W. (2007). Hotting up. *The New York Times Magazine Section,* June 6, p. 18.

Saldana, J. (Ed.). (2005). *Ethnodrama: An anthology of reality theatre.* Walnut Creek, CA: AltaMira/Rowman & Littlefield.

Scheeres, J. (2005). *Jesus land.* New York: Counterpoint/Perseus Books.

Scott, J. W. (1991). The evidence of experience. *Critical Inquiry,* 17, 773–797.

Scott, R. L. (1967). On viewing rhetoric as epistemic. *Central States Speech Journal,* 18, 9–16.

Scott, R. L. (1976). On viewing rhetoric as epistemic: Ten years later. *Central States Speech Journal,* 27, 258–266.

Sennett, R. (1982). *Authority.* New York: Vintage.

Shields, J. (2000). Symbolic convergence and special communication theories: Sensing and examining dis/enchantment with the theoretical robustness of critical autoethnography. *Communication Monographs,* 67, 392–421.

Shope, J. H. (2006). You can't cross a river without getting wet: A feminist standpoint on the dilemmas of cross-cultural research. *Qualitative Inquiry,* 12, 163–184.

Shorris, E. (1984). *Scenes from corporate life: The politics of middle management.* New York: Penguin.

Shostak, J. (2005). *Interviewing and representation in qualitative research.* Berkshire, UK: Open University Press/McGraw-Hill.

Sims, N. (1984). (Ed.). *The literary journalists: The new art of personal reportage.* New York: Ballantine.

Slaughter, S., & Leslie, L. (1999). *Academic capitalism: Politics, policies, and the entrepreneurial university.* Baltimore: The Johns Hopkins University Press.

Smiley, J. (1996). *Moo.* New York: Flamingo.

Smith, Z. (2007). Fail better. *The Guardian,* N.P., January 13.

Sparkes, A. C., & Douglas, K. (2007). Making the case for poetic representations: An example in action. *The Sport Psychologist,* 21, 170–190.

Spry, T. (2006). A "performative-I" copresence: Embodying the ethnographic turn in performance and the performative turn in ethnography. *Text and Performance Quarterly*, 26, 339–346.

Stone, J. (2006). The price of loyalty. *The Chronicle of Higher Education*, N.P. Retrieved November 5, 2007 from http://chronicle.com/jobs/news/2006/04/2006042001c/careers.html

Talese, G., & Lounsberry, B. (1995). *Creative nonfiction: The literature of reality*. Lakewood, NJ: Watson-Guptill.

Talese, G., & Lounsberry, B. (Eds.) (2003). *The Gay Talese Reader: Portraits and Encounters*. New York: Walker & Company.

Taylor, B. C., & Trujillo, N. (2001). Qualitative research methods. In F. Jablin & L. Putnam (Eds.), *The new handbook of organizational communication* (pp. 161–194). Newbury Park, CA: Sage.

Taylor, B. C., Kinsella, W. J., DePoe, S., & Metzler, M. S. (Eds.) (2007). *Nuclear legacies: Communication, controversy, and the U.S. nuclear weapons complex*. Lanham, MD: Lexington Books.

Thyer, B. A. (1994). *Successful publishing in scholarly journals*. Thousand Oaks, CA: Sage.

Tillman, L. (2005). The state of unions: Activism (and in-activism) in Decision 2004. Performance given at the 2nd International Congress of Qualitative Inquiry, Champaign-Urbana, IL, May 6.

Tillmann-Healy, L. (1996). A secret life in a culture of thinness. In C. Ellis & A. Bochner (Eds.), *Composing ethnography: Alternative forms of qualitative writing* (pp. 76–108). Walnut Creek, CA: AltaMira Press.

Tillman-Healy, L. (2001). *Between gay and straight: Understanding friendship across sexual orientation*. Walnut Creek, CA: AltaMira Press.

Tompkins, P. K. (1996). In cold fact. *Esquire*, June, 65, pp. 125 et passim.

Tompkins, P. K. (2007). Public scholarship revisited. CRTNET Archive. Available to members of the National Communication Association online via their website at http://natcom.org

Toor, R. (2007). The care and feeding of the reader. Retrieved September 10, 2007 from http://chronicle.com/jobs/news/2007/09/2007091001c/careers.html

Tracy, S. J. (2004). The construction of correctional officers: Layers of emotionality behind bars. *Qualitative Inquiry*, 10, 509–533.

Trethewey, A., & Goodall, H. L., Jr. (2007). Leadership reconsidered as a historical subject: Sketches from the Cold War to post-9/11. *Leadership*, 3, 457–477.

Trujillo, N. (1994). Interpreting November 22: A critical ethnography of an assassination site. *Quarterly Journal of Speech*, 79, 447–466.

Trujillo, N. (2004). *In search of Naunny's grave: Age, class, gender, and ethnicity in an American family*. Walnut Creek, CA: AltaMira Press.

Trujillo, N., & and Trujillo, L. (2008). *Cancer and death: A love story in two voices*. Cresskill, NJ: Hampton Press.

Trujillo N., & Vande Berg, L. (2008). *'Wuv 'Ou: A love story in two voices*. Cresskill, NJ: Hampton Press.

Tumminello, W. (2005). *Exploring storyboarding*. Clifton Park, NY: Thomson/Delmar.

Turner, P. K. (2004). Mainstreaming alternative medicine: Doing midwifery at the intersection. *Qualitative Health Research*, 14, 644–662.

Turner, V. (1988). *The anthropology of performance*. New York: PAJ Publications.

Van Alstyne, W. W. (1993). *Freedom and tenure in the academy*. Durham, NC: Duke University Press.

Van Maanen, J. (1988). *Tales of the field: On writing ethnography*. Chicago: University of Chicago Press.

Verela, F., Thompson, E., & Rosch, E. (1991). *The embodied mind*. Cambridge, MA: MIT Press.

Vidal, G. (1996). *Palimpsest: A memoir*. New York: Penguin.

Wais, E. (2005). "Trained incapacity": Thorstein Veblen and Kenneth Burke. *KB Journal*, 2. Retrieved November 5, 2007 from http://kbjournal.org/node/103

Wallace, D. F. (1997). Tennis player Michael Joyce's professional artistry as a paradigm for certain stuff about choice, freedom, discipline, joy, grotes-querie, and human completeness. In D. F. Wallace (Ed.), *A supposedly fun thing I'll never do again* (pp. 213–255). Philadelphia: Little, Brown.

Wallace, D. F. (2006). Federer as a religious experience. *The New York Times Play Magazine*. Retrieved November 5, 2007 from http://www.ny-times.com/2006/08/20/sports/playmagazine/20federer.html?ex=1183780800&en=ff0775f0518ee1da&ei=5087

Weaver, R. M. (1984). *Ideas have consequences*. Chicago: University of Chicago Press.

Wengraf, T. (2001). *Qualitative research interviewing: Biographic narrative and semi-structured methods*. London: Sage.

Whitman, W. (1855). Song of myself, part I. *Leaves of Grass*. New York: Library of American Poets/Collectors Reprints, 1992.

Williams, K. (2005). *Love my rifle more than you: Young and female in the U. S. Army*. New York: W. W. Norton & Company.

Wolcott, H. (1990). *Writing up qualitative research*. Newbury Park, CA: Sage.

Wolcott, H. (2002). S*neaky kid and its aftermath: Ethics and intimacy in fieldwork*. Walnut Creek, CA: AltaMira Press.

Wolfe, T. (1998). *The new journalism*. New York: Macmillan/Picador.

Wolff, T. (2000). *This boy's life: A memoir*. New York: Grove Press.

Worth, S. E. (2004). Narrative understanding and understanding narrative. *Contemporary Aesthetics*, 2, N.P. Retrieved November 7, 2007 from http://www.contempaesthetics.org/newvolume/pages/article.php?articleID=237

Worth, S. E. (2005). Narrative knowledge: Knowing through storytelling. MIT 4: Fourth Media in Transition Conference, Cambridge, MA, May 6–8.

Retrieved November 7, 2007 from http://web.mit.edu/comm-forum/mit4/subs/mit4_agenda.html

Wright, D. (2004). Creative nonfiction and the academy: A cautionary tale. *Qualitative Inquiry*, 10, 202–206.

Zack, A. (n.d.). The makings of a perfect pitch. Retrieved November 5, 2007 from http://www.zackcompany.com/submissions/perfectpitch.pdf

Index

247

About the Author

H. L. (Bud) Goodall, Jr. is professor of communication and director of the Hugh Downs School of Human Communication at Arizona State University. He is the author or coauthor of twenty books, including *A Need to Know: The Clandestine History of a CIA Family* (Left Coast Press, 2006), which won the "Best Book of 2007" award from the Ethnography Division of the National Communication Association, as well as over 150 articles, chapters, and papers.

A pioneer in the field of narrative ethnography, he introduced the "detective" metaphor to study high technology organizations and cultures in *Casing a Promised Land: The Autobiography of an Organizational Detective as Cultural Ethnographer* (Southern Illinois University Press, 1989); toured and played rhythm guitar in the Whitedog band to investigate rock and roll as a social theory of everyday working life in *Living in the Rock'n Roll Mystery: Reading Context, Self, and Others as Clues* (Southern Illinois University Press, 1991); and went "undercover" to explore alternative forms of religion and spirituality in the southern region of the United States in *Divine Signs: Connecting Spirit to Community* (Southern Illinois University Press, 1996). With Eric Eisenberg and Angela Trethewey, he is the coauthor of the award-winning best textbook, *Organizational Communication: Balancing Creativity and Constraint* (Bedford/St. Martin's, 2007), now in its fifth edition, and he authored the highly acclaimed *Writing the New Ethnography* (AltaMira Press, 2000). In 2003, he was awarded the Gerald M. Phillips Award for Distinguished Applied Communication Scholarship, an honor bestowed to scholars for their work over a 20-year span of time.

His most recent public scholarship applies theories of communication and narratives to the challenge of countering ideological support for terrorism. In that role, he has served as a U.S. Department of State international speaker.

He is married to the historian Sandra Goodall and together they have one child, Nicolas.